The Moral Vision
of Jacobean Tragedy

The
Moral Vision
of Jacobean Tragedy

ROBERT ORNSTEIN

GREENWOOD PRESS, PUBLISHERS
WESTPORT, CONNECTICUT

Library of Congress Cataloging in Publication Data

Ornstein, Robert.
    The moral vision of Jacobean tragedy.

    Reprint of the ed. published by the University of
Wisconsin Press, Madison.
    Bibliography: p.
    Includes index.
    1. English drama (Tragedy)--History and criticism.
2. English drama--Early modern and Elizabethan, 1500-
1600--History and criticism. 3. English drama--17th
century--History and criticism. I. Title.
[PR658.T707 1975]   822'.051   74-25893
ISBN 0-8371-7864-9

Reprinted with the permission of University of Wisconsin
Press

Reprinted in 1975 by Greenwood Press,
a division of Williamhouse-Regency Inc.

Library of Congress Catalog Card Number 74-25893

ISBN 0-8371-7864-9

Printed in the United States of America

TO MADELEINE DORAN

Acknowledgments

My dearest obligation is expressed in the dedication of this book to Professor Madeleine Doran. Always generous with her learning, encouragement, and criticism, she was and remains still my teacher. Great too is my debt to the late Una Ellis-Fermor, with whom I had the privilege of working as a Fulbright scholar. Those who are familiar with her books will recognize their influence on all that I have written.

It would be impossible to name all the others who in various ways helped me to define my view of the Jacobean tragedians, but I have attempted, in my text and notes, to acknowledge my very considerable debt to earlier scholarship and criticism. The award of a Fulbright scholarship in 1951, which enabled me to study at the British Museum and the University of London, made possible my initial research. A later grant from the Penrose fund of the American Philosophical Society helped me to complete the research and the manuscript. Parts of Chapter I, Chapter IV, and Chapter IX appeared first as articles in *Studies in Philology*, the *Journal of English Literary History*, the *Journal of English and Germanic Philology*, the *Univer-*

sity of Kansas City Review, and the *Shakespeare Quarterly*. I am grateful to the editors of these journals for permission to reprint this material. And lastly I am grateful to my wife, who had more confidence than I that someday this book would be finished.

Robert Ornstein

Urbana, Illinois
September, 1959

Contents

The Moral Vision
of Jacobean Tragedy

Tragedy and the Age

The Problem of Interpretation

WE APPLAUD the Jacobean tragedians but we do not always approve of them. Their poetry seems at times superior to their principles and their sense of the theater more highly developed than their sense of values. Because we do not find in other Jacobean literature a cynicism comparable to theirs or detect in Jacobean culture the wormwood ingredients which might explain their distaste for society, we wonder what reality if any lay behind their hectic portraits of vice and depravity. We do not assume that scholarly research can ever explain the flowering of tragic drama in the first decade of the seventeenth century, but we do expect that a study of the cultural background will help us to understand the dramatists' preoccupation with evil and their heightened awareness of the tragic anguish and disorder of experience.

Because we cannot find in Elizabethan literature the seeds of Jacobean pessimism, we assume that some fairly sudden shock of disillusion darkened the literary imagination at the turn of the century.

And because we realize that a tragic sense of life is alien to our conception of the Elizabethan humanistic temper,[1] we look for ideological conflicts which might have shattered the once traditional confidence in rational order and cosmic harmony. We look for the challenge of antihumanistic philosophies which might have created Jacobean skepticism or uncertainty about the nature of man and the universe. The late Theodore Spencer advanced the brilliant hypothesis that such a challenge to humanistic ideals was focused in the works of Machiavelli, Montaigne, and Copernicus.[2] More recently Paul N. Siegel has extended this hypothesis by emphasizing the social, economic, and political tensions of late Elizabethan society and by labeling Donne and Marston spokesmen for new antihumanistic attitudes.[3] We must be careful, however, not to exaggerate the subversive influence of ideas which the Jacobeans themselves did not find greatly disturbing. One doubts, for instance, that other Jacobeans took Marston more seriously than Jonson did. And there is no evidence that the many Jacobean readers of Montaigne recognized that his skepticism was shaking the Elizabethan world view "to its foundations."[4]

It would be a mistake to assume that belief in rational order was challenged in the early seventeenth century as fundamentalist belief in the Bible was challenged by Darwinian theory in the Victorian age. What we call "the Elizabethan World Picture" died quietly of old age, cherished by the metaphysical poets and by Milton long after it had ceased to interest seventeenth-century philosophers. The encyclopedias of Du Bartas and La Primaudaye continued to be printed and to be popular well into the century. Nature moralized remained a profound inspiration to the literary mind even while a mathematical conception of the physical universe opened new horizons for scientific investigation. Even Bacon admitted, nay insisted, that through a study of the universe man discovers the regularity of natural causes which bears witness to a divine plan. In the seventeenth century the Elizabethan world view slowly defaulted to the scientific because of its seeming sterility, because it offered ancient moral and metaphysical formulas to an age eager for empirical and utilitarian knowledge.[5] Moreover the transfer of authority from the humanistic to the scientific epistemology went peacefully unnoticed because in England, unlike in Italy, there had never been a conflict between humanistic and scientific interests.

Modern scholars, who see with centuries of hindsight the essential myopia of Bacon's prophetic vision, may be forgiven their dislike of Verulam. But a nostalgia for the medieval synthesis of knowledge and faith does not justify the accusation that Bacon inaugurated the seventeenth-century divorce of science from moral or religious ideals. We can scarcely attribute to Bacon's influence a habit of thought which had been developing since the height of Scholastic philosophy. The disintegration of the medieval synthesis began, as Wilhelm Windelband remarks, with Duns Scotus' separation of philosophy and theology. "The more philosophy established itself by the side of theology as an independent secular science, the more its peculiar task was held to be the *knowledge of Nature*. In this result all lines of the philosophy of the Renaissance meet. Philosophy shall be natural science,—this is the watchword of the time."[6] Bacon is a child—perhaps a thankless child—of his time. His critical spirit and his plans for the investigation of nature are at once a culmination and an annihilation of the humanistic intellectual adventure. While he eloquently defends scientific research against obscurantist opposition, he presupposes, without lengthy argument, that natural philosophy will be completely dissociated from religious dogma. He assumed quite correctly that his contemporaries were prepared to accept the philosophical authority of a completely unmoral, unreligious concept of physical nature, which testifies only indirectly to the existence of a providential order.[7]

When we read Bacon in the quiet of our studies we can hear in the background the melancholy, long, withdrawing roar of the medieval sea of faith. If Bacon's contemporaries did not hear it, it was because there were a hundred more immediate and strident alarums. The gradual encroachment of secular interests on ecclesiastical authority had been so long a part of Renaissance life that Bacon's inversion of the medieval hierarchy of studies and his contemptuous references to the barren inquisition of final causes did not seem very shocking. His defense of socially useful scientific research, confined to its proper sphere of inquiry and circumscribed by religious and moral doctrine, was eminently successful. Indeed, the separation of science and religion seemed to guarantee the sanctity of religious belief by eliminating possible conflicts between empirical reason and faith.

So long as we continue to portray Elizabethan thought as a set of fixed postulates which have no relation to Bacon's new epistemology, so long will we have difficulty connecting Elizabethan and Jacobean literary attitudes. For it is the evolving form of Elizabethan speculations—the changing humanistic approach to politics, to moral philosophy, and to nature—which explains the "un-Elizabethan" character of Jacobean tragic thought. Instead of hunting subversives and antihumanists, our goal in succeeding pages will be to discover how humanistic interests in the world of man led to the search for intrinsic values in experience which we find in Jacobean tragedy. Then it will become clear that the "crisis" which Jacobean tragedy reflects is epistemological, not moral or ideological. The dramatists are not torn between humanistic and antihumanistic views of man. They are caught between old and new ways of determining the realities upon which moral values rest. In an age of rapid intellectual and cultural change, they—and not they alone—confound knowledge with knowledge.

Tragedy and the Jacobean Audiences

To be sure, the frontiers of Renaissance thought did not lie on the Bankside. Of all the Jacobean tragedians only Chapman can be tentatively identified with an *avant-garde* school of thought and he was hardly a Sartre or Camus. Although his place in literary history is unquestioned, he does not deserve an obscure footnote in the history of Renaissance philosophy. Other dramatists—Shakespeare and Jonson—had, one suspects, finer minds than Chapman, but they were not concerned with metaphysical speculations or at least did not impose them on their listeners. The "popular" dramatists played to large, predominantly bourgeois audiences, whose intellectual interests are revealed in Louis B. Wright's *Middle-Class Culture in Elizabethan England*. The private audiences may have been more intellectually inclined, but one doubts that they came to Marston's plays to improve their minds or wished that *Byron's Tragedy* had been longer. Some Jacobean tragedies are more philosophical than others; none contain thought too abtruse for a reasonably intelligent listener to follow, though Chapman's verse and syntax required, no doubt, more attention than Jonson's or Webster's. The dramatists communicated with their audiences in terms that their audiences could understand, and we can suppose that they shared the taste for sententious platitudes which they satisfied; like most of their contemporaries they did not flinch from the commonplace.

Still we must remember that the ethical and intellectual substance of a Jacobean tragedy includes more than the sum of ideas expounded or referred to in its pages. The dramatist's vision is also, and more importantly, expressed in character, in plot, and in the total poetic impression of life which his play creates. If we are not sensitive to poetic and ironic nuance—if we do not see that the informing vision of a play transcends its explicit statements—we will make a naïve equation not only between the thought of a dramatist and the ideas of his characters but also between the thought of a dramatist and the commonplace assumptions of his audience. And applying that equation we will seek the solution to all that seems ambiguous in Jacobean tragedy in the books which the Jacobean audiences read.

We would not dare apply this method of interpretation to modern drama lest we conclude that the key to the plays of Tennessee Williams and Arthur Miller lies in the works of Norman Vincent Peale, an ethical psychologist more widely read, more widely imitated, and, we must assume, more influential than were Charron, Coeffeteau or La Primaudaye. To be sure, Dr. Peale sheds some light on the fates of Willy Loman and Blanche DuBois. They have no mustard seeds, no "Attitude of Gratitude"; they might both have been saved had they been more positive thinkers. We would not be surprised, moreover, to find startling resemblances between Dr. Peale's ideas and those expressed by Williams' and Miller's characters. Yet we must all agree that Williams' view of life and Miller's view of life are not Dr. Peale's. One can argue perhaps that Williams and Miller are not popular dramatists in the sense that Shakespeare was and therefore cannot be expected to mirror popular beliefs as Shakespeare did. But if we say that *Hamlet* was a popular drama because it played to many thousands of Elizabethans, then must we not also say that *A Streetcar Named Desire* and *Death of a Salesman* are popular dramas, because they played for many months to thousands of bourgeois theatergoers and then, in faithful screen adaptations, were admired by millions of fairly average Americans? The truth of course is that neither *Hamlet* nor *A Streetcar* is popular literary fare. Although Elizabethans loved *Hamlet* on the stage, they preferred by far to read the somewhat banal *Mucedorus*, which, by the standard of printed editions, was the most popular dramatic literature of its period. Similarly today, the American public may thrill to Tennessee Williams on the stage or screen, but they do not read his plays and they satisfy their literary appetites with more pedestrian and less challenging "art."

The mystique of Shakespeare's "popularity" has grown up because though we talk constantly of the need to read Elizabethan plays as works of the theater, we constantly ignore the unique magic of the stage. To be popular a novelist must pitch his art to the level of popular understanding and taste. A dramatist, however, need not rely on the untutored literary abilities of the "average man," for his intention will be realized on the stage by skilled professionals; his art will be interpreted for a popular audience in a way that that audience could not interpret it for itself. We may reasonably assume that for every hundred Elizabethans who could appreciate *Hamlet* in the theater, there were only a few who, without seeing a performance, could have grasped Shakespeare's intention from the printed page. Similarly today the theater is the one common meeting ground of literary genius and the mass audience.

I do not mean to sneer at the literary capabilities of the "average" Elizabethan or the "average" American. On the contrary, I prefer to believe that Elizabethans were capable in the theater of responding sympathetically to a vision of evil completely alien to their mundane view of life than to believe that they could admire only plays which confirmed a rotarian optimism and scale of values. And it is far more accurate to say that the Jacobean tragedians accepted the challenge of the stage, that they sought always to elevate their audiences to their own level of poetic apprehension, than to say that they pitched their art to the level of popular literary taste indicated by *Mucedorus*. Although some of the Jacobeans complain that the vulgarity of the multitude prevented them from writing "true" tragedies, none of them confess to have written down to their audiences. And even those who so complain would have their plays judged by the highest standards of critical excellence.

Like Hollywood before World War II, the Elizabethan popular

stage was a commercial enterprise which provided inexpensive entertainment for a national audience. Inevitably, therefore, the great mass of Elizabethan plays, like the great mass of Hollywood movies, was pedestrian diversion created by hacks of little talent and mean ambition, who satisfied popular tastes for low comedy, pious sentiment, escapist romance, patriotic spectacles, and melodramatic tales of crime and passion. Out of these masses of uninspired entertainment, however, we can pick a handful of great plays and movies, which prove that in the theater excellence can be commercially feasible if not always highly profitable. The fact that these works of genius resemble in genre a hundred indifferent plays or movies does not mean that they too were written to formula and that they too employ stereotypes of character and plot. Alfred Harbage has suggested that we require one set of generalizations for the popular stage and another for the private theaters. Equally if not more important is the need to distinguish between Jacobean drama as popular entertainment and as serious and inspired art. Otherwise we will continue to interpret the inspired fraction of seventeenth-century plays by reference to a grossly inapplicable "norm" of pedestrian thought and stagecraft.

We can agree with Mr. Harbage that however debased the popular drama was in the early Elizabethan period, it possessed a vitality, variousness, and freedom lacking in the courtly and academic stages and it offered to men of genius a challenge and opportunity they did not find elsewhere. But Mr. Harbage's attempt to attribute the greatness of Elizabethan and Jacobean drama to its broadly popular base and to the nobility of popular humanistic ideals leads to an opposite conclusion about tragedy. According to Mr. Harbage, Chapman, Jonson, Middleton, Beaumont, and Marston were coterie dramatists, and the masterpieces of Tourneur and Webster, though performed in the popular theater, were not of the popular tradition.[8] Ford's tragedies were, of course, a product of the private theaters. Marlowe and Kyd may have been, as Mr. Harbage suggests, influenced or "restrained" by the popular tradition, but *Tamburlaine, The Jew of Malta, Edward II, The Massacre at Paris*, and *The Spanish Tragedy* are hardly emblems of "Christian humanist" beliefs. If we agree with Mr. Harbage that Shakespeare's tragedies were inspired by popular humanistic ideals, then we must decide whether Shakespeare was outside the main tragic tradition represented by the other dramatists or whether they were outside the main tradition represented only by Shakespeare. Or perhaps we cannot define the main tradition of tragedy by reference to the theaters or popular ideals.

The thesis of the rival traditions is extremely valuable in defining the general characteristics of the public and private theaters, but since it does not distinguish the inspired fraction from the pedestrian "norm" of dramatic entertainment it is most accurate in its description of pedestrian playwrights and most dubious when it attempts to force the greater playwrights into Procrustean categories.[9] There is an interesting parallel between Mr. Harbage's dichotomy of the dramatic tradition and Hiram Haydn's dichotomy of the Renaissance intellectual tradition. Indeed, Mr. Harbage attributes to the coterie dramatists skeptical and antihumanistic attitudes remarkably similar to those which Mr. Haydn attributes to the "naturalists" of the "Counter-Renaissance."[10] Ordinarily we assume that the most gifted and original thinkers and artists create the central intellectual and artistic traditions of any age. But Mr. Harbage and Mr. Haydn suggest that most of the original thinkers and almost all of the gifted playwrights of the late Renaissance were actually outside the main humanistic tradition and indeed united intellectually in their assaults on "Christian humanism," an abstraction created by modern scholarship.

Of course the main stream of Renaissance thought was humanistic; and philosophical humanism, particularly in the early sixteenth century, was deeply influenced by religious ideals. But the humanistic approach to the classics, religion, art, and morality was not fixed in the early sixteenth century. There is as much difference between the humanism of Chapman and of More as there is between the humanism of More and the Scholasticism of Duns Scotus. When we abstract Elizabethan ideas from books of different decades without assessing the intellectual quality or nature of those books and without defining the function of the ideas in the writers' total thought, we achieve an intellectual montage that is perfectly accurate in every detail and perfectly misleading in its impression of static homogeneity. Moreover, when we define Renaissance humanism as a doctrine rather than an approach to literature and to life, we reach the incredible conclusion that Montaigne, who was steeped in the humane wisdom of antiquity, was not really a humanist. We cannot correctly interpret the great Elizabethan artists if, like unimaginative Elizabethan thinkers, we believe that ideas are authoritative because they are repeated endlessly by writers incapable of an original thought. We must temper our admiration for the community of Elizabethan beliefs by an awareness that the most vital and stimulating ideas of any age are often the uncommon ones, those which are fresh and original and not yet grown commonplace.

We cannot chart the intellectual topography of the sixteenth century as a broad plateau of humanistic beliefs through which currents of heterodoxy flow from obscure origins to still more obscure destinations. Like all periods of intellectual ferment and change, the Renaissance was slowly, often imperceptibly, but continually reshaping its traditions so that what was inconceivable to the fifteenth-century English mind (e.g., a national Church whose articles of faith were politically determined) was traditional if not universally accepted in the Jacobean era. We must view freethinkers like Machiavelli and Montaigne as the intellectual offspring as well as the intellectual rebels of their age—as men who found in humanistic learning (in Titus Livius and Sextus Empiricus) the stimuli and the materials for new interpretations of contemporary life. If they led the thought of their age, they led it necessarily in the direction it was already heading and thus, in one sense at least, epitomized it. They were the intellectual pioneers who gave theoretical sanction to the ever-increasing desire to study the purely human world even as Bacon in *The Advancement of Learning* gave theoretical sanction to the ever-growing desire to study the purely physical world of nature.

In the late Renaissance the gap between inherited concepts encapsuled in popular treatises and the vanguard of original speculation was constantly increasing. This original speculation in art as well as in philosophy *was* subversive in that directly or obliquely it examined unexamined postulates. Yet to say that the free-inquiring spirit of late Renaissance thought was unhumanistic or antihumanistic is to suggest wrongly that the humanist tradition was intellectually moribund and incapable of stimulating the curiosity of men like Ralegh or Donne. In defense of humanistic ideals we should not be quick to condemn Renaissance dissent or to assume that Renaissance humanists, like some modern humanists, hoped to convince the world of the value of clichés simply by repeating them.

Mr. Haydn does not convince us that there was a "Counter-

Renaissance." He convinces us rather that despite the circumstances which separated them, the most creative minds of the Renaissance were closer to each other in spirit than they were to unimaginative and uncreative minds. Similarly the common bond of their genius transcended and annihilated the supposed divisions between the great dramatists. Although we may attempt to make sharp ideological distinctions between the plays of the public and private theaters, we cannot say that the dramatists were very conscious of belonging to alien traditions. Chapman, Jonson, Webster, and Dekker wrote for both stages; all the Jacobeans found inspiration in each other's work. Tourneur imitates both Marston and Shakespeare; Shakespeare is influenced by Jonson's "coterie" satire and in turn probably inspired Jonson's attempt at Roman tragedy. All in all there is a greater kinship between Shakespeare's tragedies and Middleton's than between *King Lear* and *A Woman Killed with Kindness*. There is a more significant relationship between the art of Shakespeare, Chapman, Jonson, and Webster than between the art of Shakespeare, Heywood, and Munday.

Thus in studying the major Jacobean tragedies as a group apart from the great mass of uninspired drama in both theaters, we are not isolating them from the context which explains them but instead are placing them in the context in which they are best understood. We are simply recognizing that in their own age the genius of the major tragedians separated them from mediocre talents and united them in common pursuits and interests. We do not know all the circumstances which determined Jonson's shifting "allegiance" to the public and private stages, but we do know that genius in the arts seeks and establishes its own small but pre-eminent community.

Tragedy and Religious Belief

Just as studies of Elizabethan culture have emphasized the uniformity of belief in rational order, so too they have emphasized the deep and abiding faith of Elizabethans, their unquenchable thirst for religious and moral exhortations, their consuming interest in religious issues, and their customary habit of relating all events to providential design. Is it possible, some ask, that the dramatists were untouched by the religious fervor of the age? Is it possible that they did not view the momentous issues of tragedy in essentially religious terms? Certainly Jacobean tragedy is Christian in the sense that its moral values derive primarily from a Christian ethical tradition or from classical ethics made compatible with Christianity. But that tragedy is Christian in the more significant sense that it is concerned with man's salvation or with his obedience to divine law is far more dubious. Like Elizabethan sonneteers, who often use religious terms to heighten the expression of feeling in their love poems, Jacobean tragedians frequently use religious ideas and images to heighten the emotional, moral, and spiritual drama of their plays. They will also on occasion pay rare artistic tribute to the beauty and dignity of religious faith. If we assume, however, that the characters who represent religious belief in Jacobean tragedy necessarily speak for the dramatists, we will misinterpret the plays of Chapman, Webster, and Ford, whose friars and cardinals are somewhat doubtful spiritual guides.

Just as all poetry (witness Ovid) can be moralized, so all tragedy can be seen under the aspect of eternity. Just as the apologist for the stage can find a moral in the most prurient play, so too the pious can interpret the moral resolution of any dramatic fable as a demonstration of Providence. No doubt there were some Elizabethans, as there are some modern critics, who liked to believe that Shakespeare's virtuous characters will be rewarded after death and his villains eternally punished. Yet to say that Jacobean tragedy was religious because it had to be or that it was religious even though we, who are not used to viewing life under the aspect of eternity, do not see it as such is simply to beg the question we are trying to answer. And even if we could be certain that the Jacobean dramatists were as pious as we think they should have been, such a priori reasoning makes a mockery of the scholarly goal of basing interpretation on objective fact.

To the naïve question, "Could Elizabethan artists and intellectuals view life in other than religious terms?" the answer must be that they could and did, increasingly so. The total evolution of Elizabethan culture (of the stage, of literature, music, politics, moral and natural philosophy) was a slow but steady progress towards the secular. To be sure, the growth of secularism in England was quite different from that in Italy or France. Between Ockham and Bacon England made practically no contribution to philosophical ideas. Indeed sixteenth-century England had no indigenous philosophical tradition worthy of the name; it produced no thought comparable in significance or originality to the speculations of Machiavelli, Pomponazzi, Telesio, or Bruno. The glory of Elizabethan England was artistic not philosophical, and it is not surprising, therefore, that the most original and emancipated Elizabethan thinkers we know of were poets and dramatists, not compilers of household philosophy. To find Elizabethan political theorizing akin to Machiavelli's we must turn to Ralegh; to find a critical analysis of moral assumptions comparable to Montaigne's, we must turn to Donne; to find an approach to history comparable to Bacon's we must turn to Marlowe, Shakespeare, and the Jacobean dramatists. On the other hand, secularism gained a far more significant triumph in the practical life of Protestant England than it did in Catholic Italy and France because of the destruction of papal authority. The result of this "practical" triumph was that the intellectual climate of Jacobean England was more liberal and receptive to Bacon's secular ideas than the intellectual climate of Italy was to Galileo's scientific theories.

To say that in England as on the Continent men learned during the Renaissance to think in divided and distinguished worlds is not to question the sincerity of Elizabethan piety. There is, after all, no necessary connection between the depth of personal piety in an age and the scope of religion's influence over thought and art. Personal piety may increase even while the total cultural influence of religion decreases, particularly when religious doctrine emphasizes the individual conscience and quest for salvation rather than the all-embracing sovereignty of the Church. Thus it is not extraordinary that Jacobeans should argue passionately over religious doctrine and yet accept Bacon's idea that science is in itself totally independent from religion. Although left-wing Puritanism cherished theocratic ambitions, no less a Protestant authority than Luther recognized a separation between man's inner spiritual life—his Christian freedom—and his participation in temporal society that would have shocked St. Thomas.

We no longer live in divided and distinguished worlds because our religious belief and our passion for life have become equally attenuated and institutionalized. We refer so mindlessly to the abiding spiritual values which underlie the enormous materialism of American society that we see no conflict between the two. We will not find our accommodation of worldliness and piety among the Elizabethans, who considered pride a deadly sin and yet admired the extravagant splendor of the Court—and found sanction for that splendor in the Aristotelian ideal of magnificence. According to our logic Shakespeare's Henry V must be a hypocrite because he takes God as his copilot on a ruthless military adventure; however, our logic is not based on a firsthand acquaintance with the Elizabethan character.

To determine the relation of Jacobean tragedy to contemporary religious belief we must indeed use our historical imagination. We must read not only the character of the Jacobeans revealed in their religious treatises but also the character revealed in their daily lives, in their worldly values and aspirations. Remembering Wolsey's palaces as well as More's devotions, we must bring to the study of English Renaissance culture some of the breadth of Burckhardt's investigation of sixteenth-century Italy. It is unfortunate but unavoidable that our knowledge of Jacobean culture is based primarily on the books of the period which have survived. It is disastrous, however, to assume that the Jacobean dramatists, who were superb observers of contemporary life, derived all their ideas, values, and knowledge of men from the books which their audiences read. We do not have to make "moderns" of the Jacobean dramatists to recognize that their psychological insights were more profound and permanently significant than were the crude psychological theories of their time. For quite often in the past the artistic perception of human behavior has been more scientific than the prevailing theories of psychology. We must remember too that every age has its official and semi-official pieties, which form the stock in trade of popular writers, and which determine how much of the total character of a civilization will be recorded in the books most widely read. (Today we write about our religious revival and live our gross materialism. And, as is only fitting, the evidence of our search for ephemeral pleasure is ephemeral itself: our cars end in junk heaps but our piety will be recorded for all time.) We must suppose that in the Renaissance as today creative writers were more candid and critical in their confrontation of living issues than were manufacturers of popular treatises of inspiration and self-help. Perhaps instead of trying to interpret Jacobean tragedy by reference to Elizabethan commonplace thought, we would be wiser to use, let us say, the political plays of Marlowe, Shakespeare, Chapman, and Jonson to help us interpret Elizabethan platitudes of government which seem to have little connection with Elizabethan political realities.

Every age has its taste in ideas as well as in literature. The violence of Elizabethan tragedy, we say, does not reflect the violence of the Elizabethan character but the contemporary love of melodrama. What then shall we say of the platitudes endlessly repeated in popular treatises of the age? Are these the ideas in which Elizabethans believed wholeheartedly, or are these the ideas which for various reasons they liked to see in print? Consider the enormous popularity in recent years of the doctrines of Dr. Peale and his many imitators. Do Americans read these books because they share Dr. Peale's faith in the power of positive thinking or because in an age of stress and anxiety they would like to believe that they can will themselves to happiness and security? The late sixteenth century was no less an age of anxiety and insecurity. Power was shifting rapidly from one class to another; social unrest accompanied rising prices and the destruction of feudal agrarianism. The plague was a yearly visitation and a daily *memento mori*. Fear of the unsettled succession reinforced fear of foreign intervention and of internal dissension between religious and political factions. It is perfectly understandable that in such an age men emphasized not only the need for stable order but also the inherent natural order of the universe.

I do not suggest that the idea of cosmic decorum was the Elizabethan equivalent of the power of positive thinking. I would suggest, however, that Elizabethan uniformity of belief was frequently as mindless as modern conformity of belief and no doubt inspired by similar motives. I would suggest also that the idea of universal rational order had different values for different thinkers—for the popular reader, the intellectual, the poet, and the theologian. The Thomistic idea of universal law is the axiom upon which all of Hooker's thought rests. A scheme of cosmic decorum also provides an intellectual frontispiece to Ralegh's *History of the World;* but it is not the basic premise or starting point of Ralegh's most interesting and original political and philosophical speculations; it has little or no relevance to the empirical and pragmatic political observations of his *Cabinet-Council*. Like Elizabethan political theory, our modern democratic principles rest upon metaphysical postulates, such as those recorded in *The Declaration of Independence*. Like the Elizabethans we hold these truths to be self-evident. We expect our statesmen to remind us of them even as Ulysses reminds the Greek leaders of the hierarchical cosmic order which their authority reflects. But we no more expect a real connection between these metaphysical postulates and the practical conduct of political affairs than the Greeks expect that Ulysses will adhere to high principles in his manipulation of Achilles. In short we must distinguish between ideas which are at the vital center of late Renaissance creative thought and those which are cherished as intellectual pieties.

Hardin Craig remarks that "the uncertainties and misfortunes of their lives may be said to have thrown the Elizabethans into the lap of religion."[11] They found security in religion, not only in the Puritan faith in Providence but also in the determinism of the Calvinist creed which, like the fatalism of Stoic philosophy, negates the significance of earthly accidents. They found solace in the pious moralism of Thomas Beard, who demonstrates that if one chooses one's illustrations carefully enough one can view the world as the theater of God's judgments. Undoubtedly the tragedians were influenced by the religious spirit of the age, particularly by Calvinist disgust with the flesh and with fallen man's depravity. One feels, for example, that Tourneur and Marston were at times no less Augustinian than the Precisians they satirized. Still the tragic poets were not theologians. The piety and moralism of Elizabethan popular culture is one response to anxiety. The tragic vision, as we see in our own time, is a quite separate and quite different response.

Scholars of the twenty-fourth century may see little connection between the optimism of Dr. Peale and the pessimism of *Death of a Salesman*. We can see, however, that they are parallel responses to one of the deepest anxieties of American life—the fear of failure in a society that worships success. Dr. Peale tells us that we need not feel inadequate; Miller suggests that all men cannot succeed. Dr. Peale believes that one need not be intimidated or corrupted by social pressures; Miller suggests that the very nature of our society intimidates and corrupts. Similarly in the Jacobean age the tragedian confronts the anxiety which the popular moralist would exorcise: the cynicism of Italianate tragedies and the pious faith of the *Theatre of Gods Judgements* are, as Tourneur's drama indicates, opposite sides of a single coin. The lurid melodrama of *The Revenger's Tragedy* incarnates a disillusioned protest against the decay of agrarian society. *The Atheist's Tragedy* marks Tourneur's retreat from disillusion into a literalistic piety that is exactly parallel to Beard's. The Renaissance preachers assure us that the guilty will get what they deserve in life. The tragedians reply, "Perhaps so, but will the innocent?" The preachers excuse God from any responsibility for the anguish of human experience. The tragedians see that all suffering is not merited or explicable. The preachers predict that all tears will be dried in heaven. For the tragedians the rest is silence.

Tragedy and the Dramatic Tradition

When we consider the secular character of the Elizabethan stage and of much of Elizabethan literature, the influence of Seneca and of classical thought, and the mundane emphasis of humanistic morality, it seems perfectly logical that tragedy was, to borrow Miss Ellis-Fermor's phrase, "an interim reading of life."[12] But if later dramatists had chosen to imitate *Doctor Faustus* rather than *The Spanish Tragedy* or *Edward II*, we could find equally cogent reasons for their choice and their religious interests. Since Elizabethan culture was diverse enough to admit many and, indeed, diametrically opposed literary currents, we cannot say that the nature of tragedy was determined by contemporary moral or religious viewpoints. All that we can say is that many cultural forces shaped the tenor of tragedy and are reflected in its substance.

It is possible therefore that Willard Farnham draws too neat a parallel between the evolution of tragedy and the development of humanistic morality in fifteenth and sixteenth-century England.[13] If we look only at what medieval writers called "tragedy," we may well conclude that the medieval mind had too naïve and irrational a view of man's fate to have felt genuinely tragic emotion. But if we look at the concluding pages of medieval epics, we may decide that medieval

writers had as haunting a sense of the tears in things as did the Elizabethans, that they too understood the irony and pathos of heroic
defeat, and the tragedy of noble ideals and aspirations betrayed. Since
even in the seventeenth century formulations of the idea of tragedy
were hopelessly inadequate to the tragic intuitions expressed in dramatic art, it is perhaps misleading to compare the Elizabethan *art* of
tragedy with the medieval *idea* of tragedy. And it may not be completely accidental that *Tamburlaine* and *The Spanish Tragedy* are
more akin in spirit to the romanticism and heroism of medieval epic
than to the moralism of *The Mirror for Magistrates*.

Compared to other genres of medieval literature and compared
to medieval philosophy, *De casibus* tragedy is quite naïve in its view of
human destiny; it does not represent the highest reach of contemporary speculation about the human condition. There is no absolute evidence, moreover, that Elizabethan tragedy actually evolved out of the
crude *De casibus* concept. We can find quite a few dull Elizabethan
plays which dramatize with a simple moral or Senecan emphasis the
fall of a prince. We can even say it was inevitable that the *De casibus*
idea of tragedy should have received dramatic expression on the Elizabethan stage. But when we say that Elizabethan tragedy grew out of
De casibus tragedy, we make anomalies of *Tamburlaine* and *The
Spanish Tragedy*, the very plays which created the vogue and the art
of Elizabethan tragedy. These early masterpieces do not embody
humanistic belief in rational order or cosmic justice. On the contrary,
Tamburlaine openly challenges the idea of fixed hierarchical order
and mocks the moralistic view that the world is a theater of God's
judgments; Hieronimo's tragedy lies in his discovery that justice
is *not* the governing principle of the universe. Only in a contingent
sense are Tamburlaine and Hieronimo responsible for their fates.
Although passion makes them both hysterical murderers, they are
driven beyond reason by the indifference of the universe to heroic
achievement and to man's yearning for justice. They are, we are supposed to feel, doomed by circumstances they cannot alter—by flaws
in the nature of the universe, not by flaws in their own character.
Tamburlaine and *The Spanish Tragedy*, then, are not links in an inevitable evolutionary chain which led from Lydgate to *Lear*. For the genius of Marlowe and Kyd brought to the drama a tragic emphasis

which was not foreshadowed in earlier plays or in the metrical tragedies. They were the first dramatists to question artistically the optimistic rationalism of humanistic assumptions, and it is quite probable that
if they had not written, Jacobean tragedy, as we know it, would not
exist.

If studies of dramatic tradition make the development of tragedy
seem more logical and inevitable than it actually was, it is because they
minimize the accidental and unpredictable nature of literary genius.
They create the impression that literary ideas and forms have a life of
their own, that they evolve and grow more sophisticated through some
inner dialectical necessity or necessarily change as the climate of opinion in an age changes. Similarly studies of convention seem to rob the
dramatists of their individuality and their artistic freedom by creating
the impression that even the greatest playwrights were enslaved by
the memories and expectations of their audiences. We study convention in an attempt to view Elizabethan drama through "Elizabethan"
eyes, but our conscious scholarly attempt to categorize characters and
define formulas of plot is not equivalent to an Elizabethan audience's
unconscious acceptance of contemporary dramatic practice. Even as
we know the Elizabethan "world picture" more completely and scientifically than did most of Shakespeare's audience, so too we know the
dramatic tradition more completely and scientifically than any Jacobean could have. Thus it is possible that we can discover conventions
of plot and character which even the dramatists did not know existed.
With our long view of the dramatic tradition we may describe Ford's
Orgilus as a final development of the malcontented revenger origi-
nated by Kyd. But we would thoroughly misinterpret Ford's intention if we attempted to explain Orgilus by reference to a conventional
character type that held the stage thirty years before, even though
Ford, who studied the earlier dramatists, probably based his characterization to an extent on that type. Moreover we cannot assume that
the Caroline theatergoers recognized the "conventionality" of Orgilus
unless we credit them with an archetypal memory of characters they
probably never saw.

Seated in our studies, surrounded by the texts of Elizabethan and
Jacobean plays, we may be far more burdened by the weight of dramatic tradition than were the Jacobean playwrights or their audiences,

whose memories of performances were no doubt dimmed by time. We perhaps assume that Middleton and Ford, writing after a long and rich period of drama, were driven to sensationalism by the need to be different from their predecessors or by the need to stimulate jaded tastes. We should not forget, however, that relatively few good tragedies were written between 1611 and 1621 and that by the death of James most Elizabethan plays were unknown to those who did not collect quartos. Actually, as Ford's overt plagiarism of *Othello* indicates, the late Jacobean and Caroline playwrights were freer to imitate and to borrow from Shakespeare than were Tourneur and Webster.

Wading through the gross implausibilities of a hundred dull Elizabethan and Jacobean plays, we may conclude that such implausibilities must have been conventional and uncriticized by contemporary audiences. It is quite possible, however, that a Jacobean playgoer who chose his authors intelligently was far more critical of slipshod plotting in bad plays than we imagine and far more appreciative than we of the dramatic genius that can make the "implausible" convincing in the context of a great play. It is curious that we credit Jacobean audiences with a remarkable knowledge of the dramatic tradition and of quaint and curious lore, and with an ability to discern obscure allegories and allusions, and yet we do not assume that they could respond differently to plays of widely differing quality. I suspect that sophisticated Jacobeans accepted implausibility in bad plays much as we today accept it in bad movies—not because it is "conventional" but because one does not demand from casual entertainment the kind of truth which one expects from great art. In the interpretation of pedestrian plays convention may explain all. In the interpretation of great dramatic art the appeal to convention can become like the Renaissance appeal to authority—merely a substitute for critical thinking.

Until the millennium, when Jacobean tragedy regains the stage, we must be skeptical of our "knowledge" of Renaissance dramatic conventions. For we find in the drama what we look for; our method of investigation biases our conclusions. When we study the character of the revenger in Jacobean plays, we may legitimately ask: "How does each dramatist vary the character created by his predecessor?"

But it is not legitimate to assume that the primary problem in each dramatist's mind was: "How shall I vary the conventional type?" It is fairly evident, for example, that Webster is not very interested in the motives or the moral nature of his revenger (Lodovico) in *The White Devil*. Like Middleton and Ford he uses the revenge motive simply to obtain the obligatory tragic catastrophe. And although *Women Beware Women*, as we shall see, is one of the most unconventional of all Jacobean tragedies, it closes with the hackneyed device of a murderous masque because Middleton, unlike more pedestrian talents, does not devote his energy to achieving an original twist on a conventional formula.

A literary art can become highly conventional only if writers are willing to work within the boundaries set by their predecessors' achievements and if they are willing to respect and preserve the "rules" of artistic practice which custom has formulated. We find no such willingness to respect convention among the Jacobean tragedians. Nothing could be more cavalier than their treatment of Kyd's revenge formula; in short space they discard the ghost, the chorus, the madness and the hesitation of the revenger. After *Hamlet* only fragments of the original formula can be found in the great tragedies and they are either vestigial or are given completely new meaning.

One expects to find a highly or clearly developed form in conventional art, yet one is struck by the constant and usually unsuccessful struggle for form in Jacobean tragedy from Chapman to Ford.[14] The reason is not that the greater dramatists lack the ability to construct a neat conventional five-act structure. (Their comedies are often superbly organized and unified.) It is rather that the tragedians are constantly attempting to make the conventional materials of the stage serve new and unconventional purposes. Compared to modern drama Jacobean tragedy is highly conventional; but compared to Jacobean comedy it is remarkably experimental.

We do not have to refer to the "power" of convention to explain the vogue of revenge tragedy on the English stage. We need only admire the vitality and originality of *The Spanish Tragedy*. We need only appreciate with the Jacobean dramatists how the revenge motive focuses diverse passions of love, hatred, and ambition, how it lends itself to mordant ironies of disguised intention, hidden intrigue and counterintrigue. It may also be, as F. T. Bowers suggests, that revenge tragedy was popular because Elizabethans were preoccupied with the subject of private revenge.[15] Yet there is not one great tragedy of the period in which the ethical attitude towards blood revenge is a central moral issue. In *Hamlet,* the greatest revenge play of the age, the question is quite simply ignored, although Shakespeare has many opportunities to raise it and does explicitly focus attention on a dozen other moral and philosophical questions. We "accept" the ethic of revenge unquestioningly because Hamlet the noble idealist does so, and nothing that we can learn about Elizabethan opinions of revenge can alter that acceptance. Only very briefly and in only three plays (*Antonio's Revenge, The Revenge of Bussy D'Ambois,* and *The Atheist's Tragedy*) do major playwrights question the rightness of revenge. Marston's concern with the problem is, as we shall see, specious. Chapman resolves the question ambiguously because it is not essential to the philosophical meaning of his play. Tourneur alone unequivocally "rejects" revenge so as to clear the stage for the central dramatic conflict of his play, which is between the atheist and God. But one would hesitate to say that he is therefore more enlightened in his moral attitudes than is Shakespeare, who "accepts" revenge.

It is significant that the revenging hero almost invariably has no way of bringing his criminal opponent to justice, either because no proof of the crime exists, or because the criminal is placed beyond the reach of justice, or because justice itself is a mockery in the hero's society. Thus the crucial issue in revenge tragedy is not, "Shall there be private vengeance or recourse to law?" but "Shall one take action in an evil world or retreat into Stoic resignation?" Unlike Aeschylus the Jacobean tragedians are not concerned with the ethic of blood vengeance; through the vehicle of revenge tragedy they grapple with the question of how virtuous action can be taken in an evil world when that action itself must be devious, politic, or tainted with evil.

A knowledge of convention reminds us—if we need reminding—that the Jacobeans do not attempt to hold a mirror directly up to nature—that their tragic visions must be interpreted poetically, not literally. We can assume, for example, that the portrait of depravity in *The Revenger's Tragedy* would have been quite different if the myth of Italianate decadence had not been a common property of the stage. Indeed we feel that convention provided Tourneur not only with a vehicle for personal inspiration but with the inspiration itself. Still we cannot explain by reference to convention the sardonic bitterness of his tragedy, or of Webster's Italianate plays, or of Chapman's furious attack on policy in *Bussy D'Ambois*. I spoke earlier of Jacobean tragedy as a response to anxieties. Some of the anxieties were newly created by contemporary circumstances, for instance, by disillusion with the reign of the new King. Others were long-standing but newly focused in the literary consciousness. The optimistic temper of Elizabethan humanism reflected the excitement of an age discovering new cultural, intellectual, and artistic horizons. The Jacobean tragedians do not so much lament the end of the Renaissance adventure of discovery as reckon its costs and darker consequences. Embodied in their plays is an awareness that familiar ways of life are vanishing and that traditional political and social ideals are losing their relevance to the contemporary scene. Against the pessimism and disillusion of Jacobean tragedy we must place the constant refrain of contemporary evil and misery that runs through late Renaissance treatises of religion and moral philosophy. Against the Jacobeans' envisioned savageries we must place the actual horror of internecine religious and political warfare on the Continent, which made Stoicism a living rather than academic philosophy for the late Renaissance mind. Particularly in the first Jacobean decade the drama was keenly sensitive to contemporary issues. On platform stages where fact and fantasy intermingled, the spiritual and moral dramas of the age found oblique artistic expression. For a few brief hours in the theater the demons that haunted the Jacobean artistic mind assumed a flesh and blood as well as poetic reality.

Tragedy and Politics

Chief among these demons, if ubiquity is our criterion, was the satanic figure of the Machiavel. There is scarcely a Jacobean tragedy in which a Machiavel does not play a significant, or in the plays of Chapman and Jonson, a dominant role. But the very ubiquity and diversity of the politicians in Jacobean drama confuse our attempts to analyze them. We know, of course, that the conventional Elizabethan stage portrait of the Machiavel has little direct connection with

Machiavelli's thought. The inhumanly cunning Elizabethan intriguer is, as Mario Praz has explained, an artificial "literary" construct—part Senecan tyrant, part pseudo-Machiavel.[16] Outside of Shakespeare's and possibly Marlowe's plays, the Elizabethan Machiavel has little political significance. His *raison d'être* is a primitive cynicism and aesthetic appreciation of his own villainies. He has an instinctive appetite for horrendous crimes but only the vaguest interest in holding a scepter. He is, in short, not a political subversive but an archenemy of the moral order, a "modern" representative of ancient evils, a diabolical incarnation of at least six of the Deady Sins.

If the Jew of Malta were the most convincing spokesman for Machiavelli's ideas on the Elizabethan stage, we might then conclude that Machiavelli was not an appreciable influence on English drama. There are, however, far more credible politicians and political opportunists in Elizabethan and Jacobean plays, whose genealogies are by no means obvious. They may be sophistications of the crude pseudo-Machiavels; they may derive from an actual knowledge of Machiavelli's thought; or they may be realistic studies that are totally independent of any Machiavellian influence. For the Elizabethan dramatists did not require Machiavelli's aid to gloss the sordid facts of English history—the incredible savagery and treachery recorded in contemporary accounts of the War of the Roses. We have grown so used to contrasting Elizabethan idealism and Machiavellian realism that we have almost convinced ourselves that sixteenth-century Englishmen derived all their knowledge of politics from Starkey and Elyot. But surely the political realities which Machiavelli discussed were not unknown to men who lived under the Tudors and their ministers of state, who witnessed the daily struggle for position that surrounded the throne and the recurrent processions to the Tower scaffold. We should remember that the Tudor writers who described the true, well-governed commonwealth were not naïve recluses creating theoretical ideals in ignorance or denial of worldly fact. They were knowledgeable, hardheaded reformers who candidly faced and bitterly protested the economic opportunism that was destroying a feudal, agrarian way of life.[17]

We cannot assume that Elizabethans were so naïve and frail in their convictions that they were demoralized by reading what oft was thought (and acted on) though ne'er so candidly expressed. But neither can we assume that the Elizabethan stage Machiavel was a theatrical fantasy which had no meaning outside the playhouse. The dramatists, after all, did not invent the Machiavel. They popularized and exploited, at first for sensational purposes, an already existing political bogyman—a myth which grew and spread with baroque elaborations throughout sixteenth-century Europe. Like most political myths, the myth of the Machiavel did not arise spontaneously. The initial vilification of Machiavelli by the Church was a counterattack on the Italian antipapal sentiment which Machiavelli exemplified. The thorough distortion of Machiavelli's thought in Gentillet's *Contre-Machiavel* was, in effect, a Protestant polemic against the Italian influence at the French court. But how shall we explain the flowering of the pseudo-Machiavel on Elizabethan soil? No specific faction exploited it for political advantage; indeed, no fear of Italian political influence existed to be exploited. Undoubtedly the robust Elizabethan fascination with Italianate decadence enhanced the lurid attraction of the Machiavel.[18] Still it is hard to believe that a myth of purely alien or abstract evil could have exercised such a hold over pragmatic Elizabethans. I would suggest that the myth flourished because it came to have a very immediate, native significance for the English mind—because it epitomized, in grotesque caricature, the ruthless economic and political opportunism of the time. Evidence in the drama and the use of the terms *politician* and *Machiavel* outside the drama suggest that the myth of the Machiavel provided artists and moralists with a malevolent prototype of the New Man, the devil at loose in the well-ordered commonweal, intriguing for wealth and power, for royal license and monopoly, and for the landed estates that could now be exploited for commercial profit. In this regard Leicester's infamy is highly instructive. He was not hated and feared because there was genuine evidence of his alleged Machiavellian practices; rather he was accused of committing fiendish murders because he was considered a caterpillar of the commonwealth, an upstart with a "twice-attainted" name who had risen to dizzy heights through the Queen's favor.[19] That is to say, the myth of the Machiavel expressed and intensified popular anxieties and hatreds, it did not create them.

The political bogyman—well-poisoning Machiavel or bomb-throwing anarchist—is always "unreal" because the minds that create and accept it wish it to be so. By making the politician the incarnation of every imaginable depravity, the Elizabethan casts the political opportunist outside the pale of ordinary humanity; he turns the all too human hunger for personal aggrandizement into a monstrous aberration. Similarly the caricaturing of the Machiavel is an act of exorcism, a sticking of magical pins of art into a grotesque wax figure. The hated politician becomes an entertaining, faintly ridiculous, bombastic villain, or, like Satan on the medieval stage, is reduced to ranting ludicrousness. Thus the melodramatic portrait of the Machiavel is, in a sense, the obverse of the Tudor portrait of the ideal commonwealth. Both are, to the modern mind, "unreal," and yet both embody very real protests against the breaking down of ancient, communal, moral norms.

The crudest Machiavels of Elizabethan drama are, to be sure, melodramatic clichés. One sees quite clearly in Marston's tragedies the grafting of pseudo-Machiavellian rant on the conventional Senecan tyrant. In later Jacobean plays, however, the relation between Machiavel and New Man becomes more and more overt. Tourneur's D'Amville, who worships gold and murders to found a dynasty; Jonson's Sejanus, who intrigues for power against a decaying ancient nobility; Shakespeare's Edmund, the bastard nobleman made legitimate by "loyal" service and royal favor[20]—these and all the politicians in Chapman's tragedies are literally New Men, who subvert traditional aristocratic hierarchies. Even in Webster's tragedies, where the Machiavels maneuver for courtly favor rather than power, there is a constant undercurrent of economic discontent and sardonic commentary on the amoral relationship between servant and lord.

For the Jacobean dramatists, who seem to possess an accurate knowledge of Machiavelli's thought, the moralistic formulas of Tudor political interludes do not adequately account for the facts of political experience. In their tragedies the Machiavels are not isolated villains or seeds of ungodly infection in a Christian society. In their tragedies the politicians "belong," at least in the sense that they dominate the political scene and are the prime movers of political action. The norm of politics is no longer conceived in medieval terms as the well-governed state; it is the Machiavellian jungle in which the fittest survive. Like Bacon and Ralegh, contemporaries who were familiar with Machiavelli's writings, the Jacobean dramatists are ambivalent in their response to the Machiavellian view of politics.[21] They seem to accept and assimilate Machiavelli's realistic appraisal of the mechanics of political behavior, but they violently reject the completely relativistic political ethic which they assumed was Machiavelli's moral philosophy.

To accept Machiavelli's realism and protest his ethical conclusions was not, however, an adequate solution to the challenge of Machiavelli's thought. For Machiavelli's conclusions are implicit in his observations: Machiavellian "fact" is the premise of Machiavellian *Realpolitik*. And though some modern readers find nothing abhorrent in Machiavelli's writings, we can assume that the instinctive reaction of most Elizabethan and Jacobean readers was to recoil from Machiavelli's cynicism about human nature, from his views of religion and morality, and from his insistence on the necessity and legitimacy of fraud or treachery in political life. As the drama reveals, even those Jacobeans who seem to share Machiavelli's cynical premises are finally appalled by the blindness of clear-sighted policy. They sense that the power of Machiavelli's thought derives as much from what he ignores as from what he perceives—that like all cynical "realists" he sees life steadily but not whole.

Machiavelli's abhorred theories would undoubtedly have had little influence on humanists like Chapman and Jonson if contemporary events had not given a startling immediacy and prophetic quality to Machiavelli's commentaries on fifteenth-century Italy. On the most crucial political issues of Chapman's age—the limitations of royal authority and the relation between church and state—Machiavelli had little directly to say. But the misery of his enslaved Italy led him to formulate what was to become a basic political postulate of sixteenth-century Europe: the necessity for strong, centralized national authority embodied in an absolute Prince. In his more academic theorizing, Machiavelli conjectures that a mixed form of republican government will provide the greatest measure of stability in necessarily unstable political states. He assumes, however, that popular government can be neither achieved nor maintained in a decadent society. If Italy is to be freed, a political savior, a ruthless, ambitious, powerful

Prince, must seize and maintain power through his own strength and cunning. In other words, to Machiavelli the realist, despotism is the only practicable solution to contemporary crisis.

Sixteenth-century French and English statists, faced with similar problems of national unity and security, echoed Machiavelli's insistence on the supreme authority of a Prince. The horror of civil and religious warfare in late sixteenth-century France led to the formulation of the absolutist and divine right theories which place monarchic prerogative above the authority of traditional laws. In early Tudor political tracts, the medieval idea of the Prince as a living law was still prominent. But as the Tudor monarchy consolidated its power, emphasis grew on the need for centralized royal authority to preserve order and secure the national weal against foreign encroachments. As J. N. Figgis points out, the Tudor theory of divine right was fundamentally designed to safeguard the new national sovereignty against the Church's claim to supremacy over temporal rulers.[22] By the Elizabethan age it was no longer wise to advance the medieval idea that the king is the chief guarantor of the laws of nature and God, which are the supreme authority in the commonwealth. The politic writer preferred to interpret literally the traditional correspondences of divine and royal authorities. As the Homilies testify, the religious duty of unquestioned obedience to the throne became the official dogma of the Elizabethan regime. Finally James I, caught in the vise of Puritan and Catholic opposition, promulgated an absolutist theory based on Roman concepts of law and political authority. For James divine right entailed (in theory) a literal possession of the realm, an absolute power over the lives and properties of his subjects, and a right to amend or cancel the statutes of the realm.[23] Where the medieval king was, in theory, absolute under law, the Stuart king was, in theory, absolute through and above law. He was not God's deputy; he was God's heir, who received at birth an unquestionable claim to the succession.

The Jacobean dramatists do not attempt naïve and dangerous equations between contemporary despotic theories and Machiavellian policy. They do recognize, however, essential links and parallels between the two. Chapman, in particular, sees that both the absolutist and Machiavellian view of political power negate the natural rights and liberties guaranteed, in medieval theory, by the rule of law. And to Chapman, Jonson, and Shakespeare, despotism is the breeding ground of Machiavellian ambition. The concentration of power at the throne leads to rule by favorites and to unholy alliances between autocratic vanity and sycophantic opportunism.

The Jacobeans are not concerned merely with delineating the intrigues of Machiavels. Their primary interest is in the relation between political opportunism and the total moral well-being of the state. To some extent their view of politics is like that of Sir Thomas More, who dealt with political issues in their larger social context. But it is only in Machiavelli that we find a conviction, comparable to Chapman's and Jonson's, that the root of political corruption is social decadence. Looming behind Jonson's *Sejanus* and *Cataline* and Chapman's Bussy plays is a Jacobean awareness of the decay of the ancient aristocracy (of the Great Houses and their immemorial feudal traditions) given intense political meaning by Machiavelli's attribution of Italian slavery to the ignobility of the ruling classes.[24]

Yet the light which Machiavelli sheds on contemporary political issues is for the Jacobean mind a darkness visible. His thought defines the crucial problems but offers no solutions—or no acceptable solutions. Although Machiavelli brushes aside as useless speculation the medieval theological ideal of the state, his discussion of political realities does not offer a substitute ideal. And although he insists that political realism will lead to utilitarian conclusions, his discussion of what is does not lead clearly and conclusively to what should be. Of course a detached modern reader can abstract from various parts of *The Discourses* and *The Prince* a half-articulated or implied Averroistic concept that the end of political action is to preserve the internal peace and external security of the state. But the Renaissance reader was more likely to see in Machiavelli a thinker who could give advice to ruthless opportunists as well as to selfless patriots, to usurpers as well as saviors, and who could admire the tyrant who had the boldness and determination to commit terrible but successful crimes. One doubts, in fact, that the Jacobean impression of Machiavelli could have been more impartial than that of Harald Höffding:

> He [Machiavelli] was possessed to such a degree by the thought that it was of no use to have an end, however noble, without the means

necessary to attain it, that he finally forgot the end in the means, or
omitted to inquire whether the means which he admired were calculated, in the long run, to promote the great ends which, there can be
no doubt, he always regarded as the highest. He was so disheartened
by the power of the means that he ended by attributing value to
them, in and for themselves, and apart from the end which was to
consecrate them.[25]

Despite Machiavelli's optimism about the value of political action,
he seemed to the Jacobean dramatists a guide to political ruins. For the
opportunism and despotism which he considered a practical cure for
political malaise was to the Jacobeans the very root of contemporary
evils. They believed that they saw the failure, or rather the catastrophic success, of Machiavelli's doctrine in every facet of political
life. To be sure, the Jacobean attack on Machiavellianism is often
hopelessly naïve in its portrayal of politicians and in its confusion of
Machiavellianism and Machiavelli. But if Chapman's response to politic evil seems hopelessly in excess of its historical object, we must remember the moral tradition which he and the other Jacobeans inherited. We must remember also that their ideal of truth in art is not
a literal description of historical realities but a heightened depiction of
the essential moral realities of human experience. Caught between a
dying feudal order and a modern society struggling to be born, per-
plexed by conflicting interpretations of political fact which they can
neither reject nor wholly accept, the Jacobeans seek to moralize about
the very political realities which, if admitted, vitiate moral conclusions.
They cling to a traditional moral view of politics even though they
sense that medieval ideals are no longer meaningful to their society.
Thus the constant choric attack on policy in Jonson's drama is under-
cut by an ironic awareness that words alone will not alter the shape of
things. And thus there develops, particularly in Chapman's tragedies,
a certain detachment at last from who's in, who's out, a pervasive sense
of the futility of contention with political evil. To the challenge of
policy the Jacobean dramatists offer, finally, only private philosophical
solutions.

Tragedy and Moral Philosophy

Because the Elizabethan artist and political controversialist nat-
uralized the myth of the politician, it is pointless to seek the influence

of Machiavelli each time the explicit or implicit thought of a tragedy resembles the ideas of *The Prince* or *The Discourses*. It is possible that the Machiavellian ideas in Jacobean tragedy are a symptom rather than cause of uncertainty—that Webster, for example, is fascinated with the Machiavel's cynical realism because it seems to reduce otherwise contradictory aspects of experience to a logical and apprehendable unity. Instead of ascribing too much to the influence of Machiavelli, we should instead ask why, apart from political conditions, did Machiavelli's thought seem more challenging to Jacobean than to Elizabethan intellectuals, many of whom must have had direct contact with the ideas of *The Prince* and *The Discourses*.

The emotionalism of Chapman's attack on policy is, I have suggested, different from the emotionalism of Elizabethan attacks. It is also different from Hooker's assured rejection of Machiavelli's *Realpolitik*. In *The Discourses* Machiavelli announces that "whoever desires to found a state and give it laws, must start with assuming that all men are bad and ever ready to display their vicious nature, whenever they may find occasion for it."[26] Hooker seems to quote this passage almost verbatim in the *Ecclesiastical Polity*:

> Laws politic, ordained for external order and regiment amongst men, are never framed as they should be, unless presuming the will of man to be inwardly obstinate, rebellious, and averse from all obedience unto the sacred laws of his nature; in a word, unless presuming man to be in regard of his depraved mind little better than a wild beast, they do accordingly provide notwithstanding so to frame his outward actions, that they be no hindrance unto the common good for which societies are instituted: unless they do this, they are not perfect. It resteth therefore that we consider how nature findeth out such laws of government as serve to direct even nature depraved to a right end.[27]

The apparent moral anarchy which leads Machiavelli to desperate conclusions does not shatter Hooker's faith, for he is confident that the light of nature, however dimmed by man's depravity, cannot be extinguished in men's minds and that fallen nature will not only be redeemed at last but will always be subject to the ordering laws of the cosmos. He sees no tragic disparity between political "ideal" and political reality. The former comprehends and explains the latter. The idea of rational order in the cosmos is not a possible theoretical hypothesis; it is a statement of the ultimate, immutable metaphysical reality of the universe.

Why did not the Jacobean playwrights view political issues in Hooker's way? The obvious answer is that they were not theologians any more than were Bodin and other political theorists of the late Renaissance. Also they were looking for more immediate answers to Machiavelli's arguments than would issue from a discussion of the natural laws of government which "serve to direct even nature depraved to a right end." Although Bacon sneered at the inquisition of final causes that "like a virgin dedicated to God produces nothing," he and his contemporaries acknowledged that theology should be concerned with Scholastic pursuits. But as seventeenth-century attacks on "vain speculations" indicate, Jacobeans doubted that scientific knowledge of history, or of nature, or of man, could be obtained by deductive reasoning from a priori postulates.

It is not only Machiavelli and Bacon who insist that knowledge must be useful and must enable man to cope with the realities of the world in which he lives. The same thought is expressed again and again by the humanistic moralists of the late Renaissance. Let the Scholastics quarrel about the nature of metaphysical realities. The humanistic moralist is concerned with the practical knowledge that will enable man to lead a reasonable, virtuous life. Medieval Catholicism placed the burden of ethical discipline upon the institution of the Church, which interpreted God's law, commanded obedience to it, and punished the recalcitrant sinner through its juridical authorities. The Reformation shifted the burden of moral discipline to the individual conscience. The Protestant spirit is manifest in the extraordinary Elizabethan taste for sermons and hortatory literature, for books of devotion and guides to moral conduct and godliness. The desire for practical ethical disciplines was satisfied more intellectually in treatises of ethical psychology and moral philosophy, which set forth the nature of man, and defined his familial, social, and political roles, duties and obligations. Even if the Scholastic mind had been interested in such mundane "science" it could not have conceived of moral philosophy as a body of knowledge separate from theology, for it could not conceive of virtue as having meaning except in relation to divine law or as possible without the attainment of grace.[28]

The humanistic scholarship of the Renaissance, however, loosened and, in some instances, severed the intrinsic medieval knot of morality and theology. The sixteenth-century moral philosopher inherited the Scholastic concept of natural law; but he also discovered in the newly reprinted works of Cicero, Seneca, and Epictetus a classical ideal of right reason which was outside of and independent of the previously all-embracing theological framework—an ethical ideal which proclaimed the self-sufficiency, or rather the all-sufficiency, of reason in determining moral behavior. The Renaissance didacticist humbled himself before the eloquence, the wisdom, and the sententiousness of the Greek and Roman philosophers. He marveled (somewhat naïvely) at the identity of Christian and classical ethics. But he was most profoundly impressed by the fact that the great pagan systems of morality had been established *without* the aid of revelation.

An actual return to the classical ideal of virtue was, of course, rare in the sixteenth century. Only in such works as Pomponazzi's *De Immortalitate Animae* was a humanistic ethic consciously divorced from its customary supernatural sanction. Much more common was the unconscious rationalism of the moral philosopher who insisted that natural laws are innate ideas implanted by God in the human breast, but whose concept of right reason was essentially more Stoic than Christian. Where the medieval theologian, intent on assimilating pagan truths, stressed the contingency of human reason on the divine, the moral philosopher stressed the independence of natural reason and revelation. He customarily defined natural law as that light of reason which governs purely "humane" affairs, not as that which leads men to a knowledge of God. In theory the moral philosopher recognized the "incompleteness" of an ethical system based only on reason; he announced in his prefaces that revelation and grace are necessary to lead men to their eternal good. But in practice he severed this theoretical link between natural law and theology by reducing morality to a purely humane discipline based on the ideas of antiquity. Pedagogical treatises designed to instill virtue in Christian youths and Princes read more and more like commonplace books of pagan wisdom, which in fact they often were. In *The Governour*, written by the very Christian gentleman Sir Thomas Elyot, we find a statement that would have confounded Aquinas: namely, that for pedagogical purposes the first two books of the *Nicomachean Ethics* contain "the definitions and propre significations of every vertue."[29] In short, the sixteenth-century moral philosophers established an ideal of right reason that was, in relation to medieval thought, more secular than religious, and more classical than Christian, because (as Léontine Zanta remarks) they were "incapables d'aller au bout d'une doctrine et de voir les dangers qui la guettent; ils sont encore chrétiens, mais pensent en païens."[30]

How pagan we consider the moral philosophers depends upon how strictly we define the "Christian." Certainly we should not misinterpret Elyot's humanistic enthusiasms or think that reliance on classical doctrine weakened religious faith. Yet it is true that while the moral philosophers sought a discipline which would help men attain a Christian virtue, they did not define virtue in Christian terms: for them immoral desire was a breach in sovereign reason, not a destruction of the eternal order, which grace alone can recreate. They may refer often to God and to the efficacy of prayer, but they nevertheless view the struggle for "humane probity" as having its intrinsic value and meaning apart from the ultimate question of man's eternal destiny. And when warring religious factions drove many to the refuge of fideism, it is not remarkable that a humanist like Chapman found his moral security in philosophical reason, not in the dogmas of any particular creed. If Elizabethan moral philosophers had pursued a purely philosophical definition of virtue they might have arrived at Montaigne's conclusion that a virtue based solely on rational discipline is more ideal than a religious virtue enforced by dread of eternal damnation or hope of eternal rewards. They might even have come to Charron's conclusion that Christian doctrine is not a fountainhead of universal moral truth but merely one particular kind of moral truth, so that it is possible to be moral and not religious, and religious but not moral.[31] But one does not find such heresies in other moral philosophers, who believe with Erasmus that the only difference between a Christian and a philosopher is one of nomenclature. Though by Thomistic standards humanistic moral philosophy was often shockingly secular, it was based upon medieval assumptions and intellectual methods. Its interest in the mundane details of human experience foreshadowed by centuries the researches of modern psychologists and sociologists, but its deductive generalizations and its reliance upon authorities wed it firmly to a medieval past.

In glorifying reason, the sixteenth-century moral philosopher did not divorce natural law from the divinely established universe of the medieval theologian. He merely focused his attention on the world of man and allowed that world to fill his horizon. In fact, his exposition of natural laws was usually based upon the explicit premise of a cosmos governed by ascending hierarchies of law. Disdainful, however, of Scholastic superstitions and speculations, he ascertained the universal laws of nature by supposedly objective, rational criteria. In practice, though, he was not far removed from the medieval didacticist. The ancient custom of obedience to authority was too deeply engrained to change; what changed were the authorities themselves. Instead of appealing to the Church Fathers, the moral philosopher quoted the *sententiae* of antiquity; or, more usually, he combined his Christian and classical learning with no awareness of incongruity. He did not find philosophical method and discipline in antiquity; he found instead a great body of accumulated wisdom which seemed to him authoritative precept. He systematized "natural laws" by turning the classical ethical theories into a body of absolute imperatives.[32]

Not all sixteenth-century "natural laws" derived from classical Greece and Rome. As in preceding centuries, men in the Renaissance attempted to validate their particular beliefs by asserting their naturalness or universality. And with the humanistic emphasis on the achievements of reason, natural law was enthroned as the arbiter of even minute details of social, political, economic, moral, and familial life. Inevitably many of the natural laws supposedly universal among men were simply rationalizations of the existing political and social hierarchies (or of the desire to overthrow them). Through the centuries the Stoic concept of right reason had been transformed from an ethic based on individual conscience to one of inflexible dogma variously and confusedly expounded;[33] the final result in the Renaissance was a vast and uncritical accumulation of natural rights, laws, prerogatives, and prohibitions in multivolumed encyclopedias.

Unreason masquerading as universal law could not forever remain unchallenged, especially when the very forces of intellectual change which enthroned natural law (the increasing secular and naturalistic interest in man and society) made it vulnerable to skeptical analysis. Even while the moral philosophers elaborated their ideal of reason, more empirical observers of human nature were announcing that passion, appetite, and desire are as natural to man as reason and moral prohibition. Exploration and scholarly research brought to the relatively unified society of western Europe knowledge of the diversity of moral laws throughout the world and throughout the centuries. What did this diversity suggest? Not that moral law is universal and natural, but that it is the variable product of custom. By the close of the sixteenth century, the time was growing ripe for the critical re-examination of traditional assumptions. All that was needed were minds as independent as Donne's and Montaigne's—minds schooled in dialectical argument or the methodology of ancient skepticism; and the results were *Biathanatos* and such essays as "An Apologie of *Raymond Sebond*."

Although it is possible, as Louis I. Bredvold has suggested, that the libertine ideas of Donne's early poems derived in part from Montaigne's *Essays*,[34] it does not seem that *Biathanatos* was influenced by the *Essays* or is indebted to them. We are not dealing here with libertine denials of the laws of reason, but with quite independent and discrete criticisms of the unphilosophical methods of Renaissance moral philosophy. Liberal, skeptical humanists, Donne and Montaigne anatomize the moral idols of the tribe and marketplace even as Bacon dissects contemporary intellectual fallacies. They recognize that the encyclopedic moral speculation of the sixteenth century was, on the whole, uncritical, unrigorous, and unsystematic, and that it was based on oversimplified formulas and overhasty generalizations. Though noble in its assumptions, the moral philosophy of the Renaissance lacked the intellectuality of classical thought even as it rejected the logical discipline of Scholasticism. It accepted the security of centuries of Christian belief in universal law without also accepting the dogmas which had safeguarded that belief. More than that, it pretended to a rationality in moral values which it never actually possessed.

The compilers of sixteenth-century moral treatises find it easy to ignore intellectual contradictions and inconsistencies. Donne and Montaigne, however, perceive the magnificent irony of centuries of disagreement over the nature of natural law. They wonder how moralists can confidently enumerate its precepts when they cannot agree on its fundamental definition.[35] Accepting universality as the mark of natural law, Donne concludes that by that criterion we must number among the natural customs of men idolatry, "which like a deluge overflowed the whole world, and only *Canaan*, was a little Ark swimming upon it," and "immolation of men," which was so ordinary that "almost every nation, though not barbarous, had received it" (*Biathanatos*, p. 40). Like Donne, Montaigne agrees that "generalitie of approbation" is "the onely likely ensigne, by which they may argue some lawes to [be] naturall." But he finds no moral laws universally accepted. Instead change, diversity, and contradiction are so characteristic of the various moral codes of the world that no action is "so extreame and horrible, but is found to be received and allowed by the custome of some nation" (*Essays*, II. xii. 297–98).

A Renaissance theologian would explain that the precepts of Christian morality are natural and would be universally observed by all civilizations, Christian or pagan, were it not that original sin has darkened the light of natural understanding. Donne and Montaigne do not reject this thesis, but they are not interested in making the world of fact conform to an a priori metaphysical postulate. They seek instead to understand the cultural and psychological forces which create the diversity of moral codes. Foreshadowing modern psychological hypotheses, Donne suggests that the horror with which a certain act is regarded and the severity of the laws which forbid it do not necessarily argue its intrinsic "unnaturalness," but rather "a propensnesse of that people, at that time, to that fault" (*Biathanatos*, p. 93).

More than once Donne approaches the conclusion which Montaigne makes explicit: that moral codes are usually the product of custom and are obeyed because they are customary, not because they are rational. Whatever *is* in our morality, Montaigne suggests, seems right and natural to us however artificial it would seem to another civilization. This does not mean, however, that Donne and Montaigne are relativists who deny the existence of objective moral standards. Although Donne with superb irony makes the appeal to a hundred contradictory authorities an irrefutable appeal against authority, he insists that the fundamental law of man's nature is to obey discursive "primary reason," which has a "soveraigne, and masculine force" in human nature and "against which none can plead lycense, law, custome, or pardon" (*Biathanatos*, p. 76). The essential point of *Biathanatos* is that dogmatists speak of reason but do not use it. They escape from the problem of judgment by applying formulas. Instead of studying life, they study authorities; instead of defining the quality of individual human acts—instead of recognizing that circumstances "condition" acts and "give them their nature"—they attempt to specify the rules of conduct which should govern all men regardless of circumstances. Their approach to ethical problems is legalistic and not humane.

Montaigne's skepticism is more radical, for he is not convinced that it is natural for men to be rational, even though the possession of reason makes man unique among the animals and determines his nature. For Montaigne reason is the source of man's tragedy as well as his greatness. Because it sophisticates his appetites, he cannot live instinctively as do the animals: custom is for him a second nature. Yet he is too much an animal still to find rational behavior a simple accomplishment. And because his powers of reasoning are imperfect, he must struggle not only to use his reason but also to use it well—as an instrument of truth not of self-delusion. Perhaps though he lived in a nation torn by religious fanaticism and civil butchery, Montaigne should have been more confident of human rationality; but no man who loved antiquity as Montaigne did can be said to have denied the true greatness of human reason or the true dignity of man.

Though modern scholars attempt to place Montaigne in the libertine tradition, a Jacobean reader of the *Essays* could not have failed to discover in them a humanistic ideal of virtue, which affords tranquility and happiness in this life. Convinced of the limitations and fallaciousness of reason, Montaigne nevertheless believes that through reason man can learn about himself and his society and order his life accordingly. Candidly endorsing sensual pleasures, he would not have man ruled by instinctive (or sophisticated) appetites: ". . . we ought somewhat," he writes, "to yeeld unto the simple auctoritie of Nature: but not suffer her tyrannically to carry us away: only reason ought to have the conduct of our inclinations" (*Essays*, II. viii. 68). He attacks metaphysical concepts of the universe which exalt man's cosmological place because he considers them intellectually absurd. And he would not have men diverted from the real and useful knowledge which experience offers by a search for the ultimate realities which lie beyond human comprehension.

Biathanatos was not published in Donne's lifetime. The *Essays* were immensely popular, but few if any of Montaigne's contemporaries recognized them as sources of subversive doctrine.[36] Of the many Jacobeans who plagiarized the *Essays* only Shakespeare seems to have understood the implications of the "Apologie." Montaigne's subjective and rambling style, his irony, his conservatism, and his use of orthodox fideistic arguments prevented all but the most discerning from penetrating to the heart of his thought. He won few disciples, and the chief, Pierre Charron, had as serene a faith in the idea of natural law as had Aquinas. Indeed, despite Montaigne's skepticism, the idea of natural law flourished in the seventeenth century as a fundamental principle of jurisprudence. Actually the significance of Donne and Montaigne is not that their conclusions were widely paralleled in contemporary thought but that their approach to moral problems characterizes the empirical tendencies of late Renaissance humanism. Their substitution of pragmatic, humane judgment for moral legalism helps us to understand the ethical issues of *King Lear* and *The Broken Heart*. Their attempt to explain the diversity of moral codes in societal and psychological terms is a radical application of the humanistic thesis that man's unaided powers of reasoning can comprehend the nature of the world in which he lives.

The empirical tendencies of late Renaissance moral thought are perhaps most clearly etched in its theories of ethical psychology. Still swayed by medieval asceticism and conceptual idealism, sixteenth-century moralists were deeply attracted to Stoic rationalism. At the same time, however, they were, for quite opposite reasons, drawn to the pragmatic Aristotelian ideal of the mean, which varies with the individual differences between human temperaments. On the whole the Aristotelian ideal prevailed in Renaissance morality because it was more congenial to humanistic aspirations: it sanctioned in moderation those worldly ambitions and values which Stoicism rejected as irrational entanglements. Although humanists relished the sententiousness of the Stoics, they doubted that true Stoic apathy, utter indifference to all worldly accidents, was either practicable or desirable. They had too real an appreciation of the power of human affections to believe that man could extirpate his passions; as early as Erasmus, they suspected that the Stoic ideal of rationality is not only an unrealistic denial of man's emotional nature but a denial also of his essential humanity.[37]

This suspicion did not, however, prevent humanists from adopting a fundamentally Stoic theory of the passions. Whereas St. Thomas agreed with Aristotle that the passions are in themselves morally neutral, the Renaissance moral philosophers agree with the Stoics that the passions are infirmities or perturbations of the soul. Thus Coeffeteau, for example, sneers at the Stoics and yet offers a characteristically Stoic definition of a passion as a "change, which is made in man, contrary to his naturall constitution and disposition, from the which hee is as it were wrested by this change."[38]

As we read Coeffeteau, Wright, and other ethical psychologists, however, we realize that they are seldom true to their Stoic definition of the passions. According to their theory, all passions are by definition "unnatural," and yet they speak again and again of passions which are so instinctive and universal that even in excess they are natural to man. For example, the ethical psychologists warn that ambition is one of the most dangerous passions because man *naturally* covets glory and power; and they cannot condemn outright a worldly aspiration so near allied to greatness and so frequent a spur to noble action. Thus we gain from Renaissance moral philosophy the ideal concept that man obeys nature when he leads a life of rational moderation. But we also gain the empirical observation that man is by nature a passionate rather than a rational animal.

Because they are students of experience, humanistic moralists find it difficult to be Stoic even in their Stoic treatises. Consider Cardan's *Comforte*, one of the most popular Elizabethan translations, that depresses the reader with a recital of worldly evils and cheers him with the Stoic platitude that life is opinion. If he were faithful to his Stoic principles, Cardan should announce that man lives naturally by obeying reason. Instead he anticipates Montaigne's conclusion that reason actually prevents man from living "naturally" because it sophisticates his appetites. According to Cardan one decides whether a certain

human behavior is natural, not by speculative reasoning, but by studying "other lyving thinges" to see whether they naturally behave in a
similar way.[39]

Even more remarkable is the passage in Du Vair's *Treatise of
Constancie* which describes Nature as "the lawfull Mistrisse of our
passions," whose "garrison of . . . affections . . . narrowly observe and
watch us, and upon all occasions that are offered, exact from us the
tribute that we owe her."[40] In "fits" of adversity, Du Vair announces,
Nature and Stoicism "cannot agree together" because man at such
times is naturally passionate. Du Vair is not confused about Stoic
doctrine; he shows in his various works a clear understanding of its
precepts. But like other late Renaissance thinkers he finds it impossible
to adhere to an a priori concept of human nature that denies the truths
of actual experience, and he does not believe that through rational
discipline man can always control his emotions. A comparable pragma-
tism underlies Coeffeteau's remark (*Table of Humane Passions*, pp.
71–72) that when certain passions "prevent the *reason* and anticipate
all the resolutions of man, wee cannot hold them bad, seeing they are
meere motions of nature without any shew of liberty." According to
Coeffeteau (p. 72), no man, however wise, is always free from passions
"seeing that vertue how eminent soever, cannot so subiect the *sensitive
appetite*, (over which she doth not command as a slave, but as a Citti-
zen) but it will anticipate the Empire of reason." Coeffeteau is no
more a psychological determinist than is Du Vair or Montaigne or
any of the Jacobean dramatists. Nevertheless he believes that at times
nature "will out," that despite metaphysical ideals, it is not always
natural for man to act rationally. Indeed, rational moral behavior is so
difficult to achieve precisely because it opposes man's instinctive and
natural emotional drives.

Quite unconsciously the moral philosophers of the late Renaissance adjust inherited precepts to a more empirical view of the nature
of man. In their theoretical postulates nature and reason are identified.
In their discussions of particular ethical problems, however, they
recognize that reason and nature may divide and even conflict. They
would have men follow nature—except when nature opposes reason.
They would have men follow reason—insofar as nature will allow.
They do not develop a new concept of nature, but they give the

empirical facts of nature a significance which the medieval mind would not have allowed. They shape moral doctrine according to the observed data of experience in contradiction to the Scholastic dogma that speculative reason alone determines moral truth. Because the moral philosophers are not systematic thinkers, they can shift back and forth between a priori and experiential views of human nature without recognizing any inconsistency. And though they are inconsistent in their definitions, their awareness of the naturalness of the passions leads to more critical attempts to discriminate the sanctions for moral doctrine. The Friar's position in *'Tis Pity* becomes more comprehensible, as we shall see, when it is related to Charron's opinion that incestuous desire is natural though immoral.

The tragedians do not debate the questions which the moral philosophers ignore. Theirs is an independent and at times more philosophical inquiry into the "table of Nature" which experience or the history of experience reveals. They are more aware of the divergence of conceptual and empirical truths, more aware of the ambiguities and complexities of human nature. Steeped in humanistic traditions they look to philosophy for a guide and often turn wearily away from its "idle questions" and its "painted words." They would follow nature if they could be sure that nature spoke with a single tongue. But as the "Chorus Sacerdotum" of Greville's *Mustapha* announces, the indivisible truths of reason and nature have divided "more wider than the sky and earth":

"O wearisome Condition of Humanity!
"Borne under one Law, to another bound:
"Vainely begot, and yet forbidden vanity,
"Created sicke, commanded to be sound:
What meaneth Nature by these diverse Lawes?
Passion and Reason, selfe-division cause:
Is it the marke, or Maiesty of Power
To make offences that it may forgive?
Nature herselfe, doth her owne selfe defloure,
To hate those errors she her selfe doth give.
For how should man thinke that he may not doe
If Nature did not faile, and punish too? [41]

Occasionally we find passages in the professional drama similar in spirit and in substance to Greville's, but never so clear and explicit a statement of the contradictory truths inscribed in the "table of Nature." Shakespeare far more greatly confronts the epistemological question of the nature of nature in *King Lear*, but he is concerned with the drama of man's attempt to relate himself to the universe, not with the validity of philosophical assumptions. Whether the passions are natural or unnatural does not interest the tragedians. They would know, however, whether the heroic fury of human desire deserves only condemnation—whether there is not more nobility in consuming passion than in timid, irresolute virtue. They leave us with a terrifying sense of the fragility of the moral order which the moral philosopher finds everywhere in the cosmos. For though good usually triumphs and evil is destroyed at the close of Jacobean tragedy, we are made to feel how vulnerable are the walls—the political, religious, legal, and familial institutions—which seek to check or contain the uncivilized fury of civilized man.

Different as the tragedians are in other respects, they are one in their scorn for the sham and the pretended, and in their search for the realities that lie hidden behind deceptive appearances or comforting platitudes. Chapman's search for essential moral realities has, one feels, a very personal, philosophical importance. Ford is far more objective in his attempt to recapture the meaning of ideals of love and marriage to which society pays only lip service. But both would discover what connection exists between the truth of an ideal and the truth of experience. They would know the reality upon which ideal values can securely rest. Like the other Jacobeans, they would find out what in the nature of man or the universe man can finally depend upon.

We can, of course, find more immediate and specific links between the drama and contemporary thought. Marston, Tourneur, Shakespeare, Fletcher, and Ford, for example, bring to the stage the shocking heresies of libertine and atheistic naturalism. Yet we should not exaggerate the importance of topical themes which are obviously employed or exploited for sensational purposes. There is no evidence that amoral philosophies of nature constituted a genuine challenge to religion or morality in the Jacobean era, and there is, significantly enough, no Jacobean equivalent of François Garasse's attack on the French *libertins* of the early seventeenth century.[42] (It would seem that Englishmen, who were accustomed to a frank sensuality in amatory verse, did not take Jack Donne's witty naturalism any more seriously than he did himself.) Even though the late Renaissance admission of the naturalness of the passions seemed to give new sanction to libertine ideas, libertinism remained a purely "literary" creed and it apparently won few English converts even among the poets.

The atheistic naturalism which Tourneur refutes in *The Atheist's Tragedy* is another matter, for though he is the only Jacobean to take up the subject, his ideas derive from the prose confutations of the age, which give the impression that atheism was a serious problem. No doubt there were Jacobean "naturalists," somewhat less melodramatic than D'Amville, who denied the existence of any power over nature. But because fear of the stake prevented the publication of atheistic doctrine, and because the term "atheism" was so widely and loosely applied, it is difficult to assess the actual scope of Jacobean disbelief. The academic and derivative nature of the arguments in the confutations would suggest that the apologies for Christianity were exercises of faith rather than responses to present dangers.[43] And though the apologists were probably not fighting against a purely mythical enemy, they seem to have been battling the ghosts of Lucretius, Lucian, and Seneca, not clearly defined "modern" ideologies.

By comparing Marston's, Tourneur's, and Ford's treatment of libertine and atheistic naturalism, we can reach some tentative conclusions about the reconciliation of nature and moral law in the Jacobean and Caroline periods. Within the drama, however, there is no pattern of intellectual resolution, nor a continuing interest in specific ethical questions. After the first Jacobean decade the character of the drama changes radically as Chapman, Jonson, Tourneur, Webster, Marston, and Shakespeare desert the stage or complete their tragic masterpieces. Even before tragedy loses its cosmological proportions, its focus shifts from the heroic to the romantic and from the political to the psychological in plays like *The Maid's Tragedy* and *The Duchess of Malfi*. When, after the hiatus of the second decade, great tragedy returns to the stage in the art of Middleton and Ford, it is detached and analytical, completely untouched by the anger or the disillusion of the first decade. Neither in *The Changeling* nor in *'Tis Pity* shall we find the answers to the questions raised in *King Lear* or *The White Devil*.

If we could assume that the temper of tragedy was at all times an accurate reflection of the temper of Jacobean thought, we might read the progress of tragedy as the spiritual biography of the age. But the tragic vision did not belong to the age; it belonged to the small handful of great dramatists who weighted the conventional form of tragedy with the splendor of their personal intuition. Moreover as tragicomedy became the dominant dramatic genre, great tragedy became less and less characteristic of the temper of the stage, even as the stage itself became less and less attuned to the national mood and feeling. It is aesthetically satisfying that great tragedy begins with the sound and fury of *Tamburlaine* and *The Spanish Tragedy* and ends with the relative stillness of *The Broken Heart*. Yet Ford does not write the inevitable conclusion to tragedy, as some critics would argue. If the drama evolved in a perfectly logical and linear progression, then we might say that Ford's psychological interests came near to extinguishing the dramatic impulse. There is no reason, however, why a playwright of genius after Ford could not have turned to earlier tragedies for his inspiration, even as Middleton, writing during the vogue of Fletcherian romance, turned to the dramatic techniques of an earlier decade in *The Changeling*. Although we may expect an individual play to have unity and form, we can hardly expect that Jacobean tragedy, like all good Aristotelian tragedies, will have a logical beginning, middle, and end.

Despite their imperfect and ambiguous ethical sympathies, the Jacobeans cherished those virtues which literature has immemorially enshrined: courage, fealty, resolution, the strength to accept and endure, and the capacity to love and to sacrifice. They define these virtues so variously, however (and sometimes redefine them in play after play as their dramatic viewpoints change), that we cannot generalize about the "moral vision" of Jacobean tragedy. Abstracted from the plays and studied in the light of daily experience, the values of the Jacobeans may seem jejune or fantastic. Only if we surrender ourselves to the moods of the individual plays—only if we enter as it were, the tragic universes in which the actions unfold—can we "know" the ethics of the tragedies. If we cannot become Jacobeans by reading the books which they read or the books which we write about them, still we can appreciate, with the aid of historical research, the vitality and immediacy of the Jacobean inquiry into man's tragic fate. But for that we must turn to the dramatists themselves.

CHAPTER II

George Chapman

CHAPMAN came to tragedy twenty years too late, after the Spenserian dream of chivalry had become something of a joke to skeptical Jacobean minds. By training and inclination he was a humanistic scholar, steeped in classical philosophy, and dedicated to the pursuit of the heroic in literature if not in life. As the great translations of Homer testify, he could so immerse himself in the grandeur of antiquity as to appear immune to contemporary anxieties. But his drama, which is more closely attuned to the temper of the age, reveals the vulnerability of his humanistic idealism. His comedy descends rapidly from the superficial satire of *An Humorous Day's Mirth* to the cynical depths of *The Widow's Tears*. His tragedies span the poles of Jacobean disillusion from the bitter scorn of *Bussy D'Ambois* (1604) to the meditative Stoic resignation of *Caesar and Pompey* (1612–13).[1] There are, of course, many echoes of Marlowe and of Elizabethan melodrama in his earliest tragedies, yet even in *Bussy* we can trace a confused attempt to unite Elizabethan convention and Jacobean vision, to dramatize through hackneyed theatrical devices the essential political and moral issues of the time. Only late in his career as a tragedian did Chapman free himself completely from the heritage of Elizabethan revenge melodrama and then the price of victory was dullness. His last plays are upright Moralities, noble in thought and sentiment, but only incidentally or coincidentally dramatic in conception.

It is possible to explain the evolution of Chapman's drama from melodrama to Morality wholly by reference to his subject matter. We can say that he turned away from the Marlovian titan presented in *Bussy D'Ambois* and the Byron tragedies (1607–8) to affairs of state and Stoic philosophy. But it seems to me that Chapman's artistic concerns never changed, that from first tragedy to last he dramatized a personal quest for values in an age when it no longer seemed possible to assent to established political, religious, and moral dogmas. The quest began, to be sure, in confusion, but in play after play he criticized and revised his intellectual position until he arrived at what seemed to him an eternally valid, philosophical solution to the problem of evil. Thus the Stoicism of Chapman's last tragedies, far from being a conventional exposition of Epictetian precepts, is (as we shall see) the journey's end of a long intellectual and artistic pilgrimage.

Scholars have often left the impression that there is little if any serious moral thought in Chapman's early tragedies. Some are content to describe *Bussy D'Ambois* and the Byron plays as Marlovian spectacles or to ascribe the ethics of the tragedies to Chapman's supposed belief in psychological determinism.[2] A counteremphasis long overdue has arrived with Ennis Rees's recent study of the tragedies. Mr. Rees has performed a valuable service by emphasizing the ethical bias of Chapman's art and by demonstrating the parallels of thought in his dramatic and nondramatic works. But Mr. Rees's conception of Chapman as a clear-sighted Christian humanist who confidently lectured to his audiences on the need for learning and the dangers of an active life seems oversimplified if not insensitive to the moods of *Bussy* and the Stoic plays.[3] Indeed Mr. Rees's thesis that the core of Chapman's ethical thought is a traditional Christian doctrine proves embarrassing in the discussion of the *Revenge* and *Caesar and Pompey*; it seems to this reader to obscure rather than to elucidate Chapman's attitudes towards his Stoic heroes.[4]

I think we misinterpret the Stoicism of the tragedies if we assume that the sincere piety expressed in Chapman's poetry is the sunlit reality of his ethical doctrine and his Stoicism the artistic shadows on the wall of the cave. Even if we grant that Chapman's poetry is more personal than his drama, we cannot ignore its public and conventional aspect. And we cannot assume that the essence of his thought lies in any single work or segment of his work, when he seems to use all of his art (his plays as well as his poems) to develop his ideas. Actually we need not oversimplify Chapman's ethical ideas to make them consistent, because there is no contradiction between the sincere piety of "A Hymne to Our Saviour on the Crosse" and the Stoicism of the *Revenge* and *Caesar and Pompey*. On the contrary, these are the characteristic dualities of Renaissance humanistic thought; they represent the divided and distinguished worlds native to the humanistic moral speculation of the late sixteenth century.

We find much in the "Hymne" that reminds us of the tragedies. It expresses the same skepticism about established religions, the same disgust for the corruption of Churches that one finds in *Bussy*. Like other contemporaries Chapman is driven by the diversity of religious factions to a Protestant faith that is deeply fideistic and, as we might expect, individualistic. He is intellectual in his ethics but anti-intellectual in his religion; like Webster and Marston he is uninterested in and disdainful of theological controversies. In the "Hymne" he insists that the Bible reveals with great simplicity the sum of religious truth.[5] He seeks salvation through virtue and simple faith in Christ's redemptive love.

In the "Hymne" Chapman sets forth the ultimate goal of a virtuous life, which is to bring man to God and enable him to fulfill his divinely appointed destiny. In "The Teares of Peace," his most important philosophical poem, he treats quite separately the *practical* humane problem of achieving virtue—a problem which is to be solved by learning rather than piety. In "The Teares of Peace" as in Chapman's tragedies moral issues are viewed philosophically; victory over the passions is to be gained by obedience to reason, not by an act of faith.[6] To be sure, as Chapman moves from the public issues of the Byron tragedies to the more personal concerns of the Stoic plays, his moral philosophy becomes increasingly theological in nature. The Stoicism that was in early plays an instrument of philosophical reason becomes at last profoundly religious in itself. But even when Chapman's divided and distinguished worlds melt into one, we cannot square his ethical position with any particular orthodoxy.

Because Chapman attempted an intellectual drama, we face the continuing problem of distinguishing between his philosophical and his artistic failings. The problem is acute in the interpretation of *Bussy D'Ambois*, a play that seems at first too naïvely moralistic in characterization and design. A keynote of moral fervor is struck in its opening lines as Bussy castigates an effete nobility and sings the praises of virtue. Before long he sets off on a chivalric adventure to reform his society, his lance securely aimed at the dragon of policy. Exactly what policy stands for in *Bussy* is not easy to say, but the term recurs with almost hysterical emphasis, especially in Bussy's diatribes against Monsieur:

> He'll put his plow into me, plow me up;
> But his unsweating thrift is policy,
> And learning-hating policy is ignorant
> To fit his seed-land soil; a smooth plain ground
> Will never nourish any politic seed; . . . (I. i. 123–27)

The meaning of policy would be clearer if the portrait of Monsieur, the arch-Machiavel, were more sharply defined. In some respects he anticipates such later Machiavels as Baligny in the *Revenge*, but he does not have their totally unscrupulous ideology. Ambitious for a throne and armed with the cold, cynical intellect of Kyd's Lorenzo, he nevertheless has firm scruples against killing a king, and so far as we can tell, he is not engaged in illicit intrigue for power. Apart from his attempt to seduce Tamyra and his later machinations against Bussy (which are defensive in intention) he does not show a devil's hand. Still he is accused by Bussy of every diabolical crime popularly attributed to the pseudo-Machiavel. Asked for a candid opinion, Bussy answers Monsieur:

> . . . your political head is the curs'd fount
> Of all the violence, rapine, cruelty,
> Tyranny, and atheism flowing through the realm:
> .   .   .   .
>   you will jest
> With God, and your soul to the Devil tender;
> For lust kiss horror, and with death engender:
> That your foul body is a Lernean fen
> Of all the maladies breeding in all men;
> That you are utterly without a soul; . . . (III. ii. 479–89)

In these lines the thought is conventional but the feeling intense. As in *The Revenger's Tragedy*, the reality of moral passion jars against the unreality—the almost perverse hyperbole—of the portrait of evil. Chapman, it would seem, does not exploit Machiavel for Machiavel's sake. If anything he seems to take the Jew of Malta too seriously and engages the full range of his artistic powers in attacking a monster fabricated of literary clichés.

Taking a larger view, however, we see that Chapman's conception of policy is by no means commonplace. The term is not a collective noun for every imaginable depravity; it stands rather for the decay of social and political order. Far from constructing his play out of anti-Machiavellian clichés, Chapman actually dramatizes the harsh realities of Renaissance society which Machiavelli described. Bussy wars against a society fallen from its "original" noblesse, devoid of honor or loyalty. True worth is neglected while unscrupulous courtiers, the hollow colossi of power, grow rich exploiting the poor. The good King Henry is powerless except to complain that his court is a stable. The aristocratic dames disguise their politic whoredoms under pseudo-platonic ideals; the "perfum'd muskcats" waste their time in frivolities and intrigue. Even the bulwarks of morality, law and religion, have been subverted by politicians.

For Chapman, then, *policy* stands for a failure *in the present* of ancient moral values; it represents the triumph of lawless appetite over traditional norms of social and ethical behavior. Where the hyperbole of Elizabethan anti-Machiavellianism was an attempt to exorcise the opportunistic demon from the commonweal, the hyperbole of Chapman's diatribes seems an anguished admission that the medieval communal ideal is no longer cogent—that the Machiavellian assessment of society is, within its limitations, all too accurate. The New Man has arrived in Chapman's tragedy and recreated society in his image. It is Bussy who is an aberration and exception, an isolated virtuous man without a place in the society which destroys him. An ideal protagonist, he embodies man's natural aristocratic virtues in an unnatural world. In contrast to the Guise, who is "great only in faction and in peoples' opinion," Bussy is great in spirit, valor, intellect, and learning. He is also great in aspiration; he knows his own powers and believes he holds the fates fast bound. He is, in a sense, the Marlovian superman moralized and turned anti-Machiavel. Or more correctly, he is an "anti-Prince," a would-be savior of a decadent society who combats the political opportunism which Machiavelli recommended as the way to moral reformation.

Bussy is doomed, Monsieur explains, because nature itself is devoid of rational purpose:

> Now shall we see that Nature hath no end
> In her great works responsive to their worths;
> That she, that makes so many eyes and souls
> To see and forsee, is stark blind herself;
> And as illiterate men say Latin prayers
> By rote of heart and daily iteration,
> Not knowing what they say, so Nature lays
> A deal of stuff together, and by use,
> Or by the mere necessity of matter,
> Ends such a work, fills it, or leaves it empty
> Of strength or virtue, error or clear truth,
> Not knowing what she does; but usually
> Gives that which we call merit to a man,
> And believe should arrive him on huge riches,
> Honour, and happiness, that effects his ruin. (V. ii. 1–15)

But for a brief time Bussy recalls within himself an unfallen world of natural goodness, in which virtue and valor were the rule, not the exception. King Henry, who serves consistently as Chapman's moral chorus, describes Bussy as

> A man so good, that only would uphold
> Man in his native noblesse, from whose fall
> All our dissensions rise; that in himself
> (Without the outward patches of our frailty,
> Riches and honour) knows he comprehends
> Worth with the greatest: kings had never borne
> Such boundless empires over other men,
> Had all maintain'd the spirit and state of D'Ambois;
> Nor had the full impartial hand of Nature
> That all things gave in her original,
> Without these definite terms of Mine and Thine,
> Been turn'd unjustly to the hand of Fortune,
> Had all preserv'd her in her prime, like D'Ambois;
> No envy, no disjunction had dissolv'd,

Or pluck'd one stick out of the golden faggot
In which the world of Saturn bound our lives,
Had all been held together with the nerves,
The genius, and th' ingenuous soul of D'Ambois. (III. ii. 90–107)

Because there are so many casual poetic allusions to the golden age in Renaissance literature, we may easily overlook the reference in Henry's speech to the centuries-old concept of man's natural freedom and equality. Considering the political climate of Stuart England, it is not surprising that Chapman's reference is couched in classical myth and given to a stage monarch. In an age when the crown claimed absolute and divine authority, the traditional idea of natural equality had become a subversive doctrine.[7] In context, however, Henry's speech is not political. Although Bussy demonstrates his "naturalness" by allegiance to the king, his nobility is intrinsic, it is not measured by the sum of his loyalty. He represents the natural freedom of man in an enslaved world because he is completely and fiercely self-sufficient. An ideal Renaissance courtier, he is also a Stoic, noble in mind and body, who, in theory at least, governs himself by the law of his own reason. There is, in fact, a remarkable parallel between the portrait of Bussy and Seneca's portrait of the "entire" man:

> A man that is entyre ought not to be surmounted with exterior things, he must admire nothing but himselfe, he ought to be confident, disposed against all casualties, a composer of his own life, & see that his resolution be accompanied with science & constancie, that that which he once hath conceived, remayne unaltered, & that no exception accompany his resolution. It is understood likewise although I adde it not, that such a man should be addressed and ordered as hee ought, gracious & magnificent in all his entertaynments, that true reason shall be ingraffed in his senses, and that from thence hee take his principles.[8]

Perhaps only Chapman would have imagined the Marlovian titan and the Senecan "whole man" as a single figure, yet the types are in some ways congruous. Both have heroic proportions; both are laws unto themselves. Moreover the Stoicism of *Bussy* is not a counsel of resignation or a buckler against adversity, it is an intellectual sword aimed against the relativism of policy. Not yet aware of the futility of aspiration, and too much an Elizabethan still to retreat from life's struggle,

Chapman seeks to resurrect an aristocratic ideal of active, self-sufficient virtue: his hero must prove his mettle by taking arms against his decadent society. Though scorning to play the sycophant, Bussy must accept Monsieur's aid so that he can rise and set a new fashion of virtue at court.

As soon as Bussy springs into action, however, the moral design of Chapman's play begins to disintegrate. By the last scene, the ideal protagonist has revealed himself to be a headstrong individualist, a killer, and an adulterer. And yet somehow we are to believe that he has never lost his pristine innocence or his exalted motive. He dies as he lives, locked in mortal combat with policy, wreathed in ecstatic poetry, and eulogized by vicious and virtuous alike for his incomparable nobility.[9] We cannot pinpoint the place at which Chapman's moral intention goes awry, because from the beginning there is a contradiction between Bussy's moral character (as expressed in the dialogue) and the actions in which he engages. From the outset, moral design and dramatic fable conflict with one another.

How can we explain Chapman's choice of a fable that brings his play as well as his hero to disaster? An obvious answer would be that in this instance he allowed his melodramatic imagination to overwhelm his moral intent. But if we take a broad enough view of Chapman's tragedies, we may arrive at a quite different explanation: namely, that he consistently lacked the ability to construct plots which would translate his vision of life into vital dramatic terms. All the feverish incidents of *Bussy* do not successfully dramatize the rhetorically announced conflict of Machiavel and anti-Machiavel, because the arch-politician of the play has no policy which Bussy can combat. In other words, there is, in an Aristotelian sense, too little action in *Bussy*, not too much. Moreover, while Chapman brings to the stage a new tragic idea, he depends upon hackneyed devices—incantations, letters written in blood, torture scenes, and ambushes—to provide dramatic excitement. With the exception of Bussy, he peoples his tragedy with stock figures: the satanic Machiavel, the helpful Friar, and the "weak" woman. Other dramatists breathe new life into the stale conventions of revenge tragedy, but when Chapman uses a cliché it remains a cliché still. Because his Jacobean hero wanders through Elizabethan mazes, it is not surprising that both hero and play stumble into confusion.

Of course Chapman attempts to integrate melodrama and moral intention. The different, loosely connected incidents of the plot are designed to illumine Bussy's native virtue as courtier, liege man to the King, duelist, and lover. Restored to rightful elegance by Monsieur, Bussy immediately demonstrates his "noblesse" by courting the Guise's wife in her husband's presence. His deliberate grossness exposes the sham delicacy of the court even as his sophisticated arguments mock platonism. He begins his career as reformer in full stride, more intent on irritating the Guise than in cuckolding him. Before long his daring provokes three courtiers to engage him in a duel. Lest we misinterpret this turn of events, King Henry explains:

> This desperate quarrel sprung out of their envies
> To D'Ambois' sudden bravery, and great spirit. (II. i. 1–2)

But when Bussy returns triumphant, having killed two opponents, the King regretfully announces that "these wilful murthers/ Are ever past our pardon." Here would seem to be a hopeless impasse! Chapman cannot justify Bussy's actions, nor can he condemn his hero without destroying the moral intention of his play. We discover, however, that the purpose of the duel and of the debate that follows is to clarify the contrast between Bussy and his politic antagonists. Bussy's advocate, Monsieur, argues the way of the world; he justifies revenge when the offense to honor cannot be rectified by law. Henry is not impressed by a code that gives each man the right to kill. Monsieur attempts with even less success to draw a casuistic distinction between murderous minds and just revengers. At last Henry reluctantly pardons Bussy with a warning that he never presume "to be again so daring." At this ticklish moment Bussy defends himself by explaining his own credo. He announces that he too hates murder, and he asks only the chance to

> make good what God and Nature
> Have given me for my good; since I am free,
> (Offending no just law), let no law make
> By any wrong it does, my life her slave:
> When I am wrong'd, and that law fails to right me,
> Let me be king myself (as man was made),
> And do a justice that exceeds the law;
> If my wrong pass the power of single valour
> To right and expiate; then be you my king,
> And do a right, exceeding law and nature:

Who to himself is law, no law doth need,
Offends no law, and is a king indeed. (II. i. 194–204)

Here Chapman moves from the immediate issue of revenge to the larger and more significant problem of action in an evil world. Bussy does not sacrifice virtue to honor, and although he assumes that he is a rational law unto himself, he does not exempt himself from conventional codes. He admits that he is naturally free only if he does not offend any just laws. But there do not seem to be any just laws in Bussy's society. Every reference to positive law in the play is pejorative. Sacred law, which should be the "scourge of rapine and exortion," is the protean instrument of policy which makes "poor men offend." Since law is venal, then it follows that the incorruptible rational law of the Stoic takes precedence. Exactly what that Stoic law is, however, Bussy does not make clear. The Stoic concept of right reason, which supposedly objectifies and universalizes moral precept, becomes for Bussy purely subjective and individualistic. Ironically enough Bussy's ethic, though presumably superior to the empty forms of conventional law, is itself mere form without substance.

We can easily believe that Bussy's casuistical speeches in the latter half of the play are, at least in part, improvisations, attempts to retain a moral thread in a fable that is hopelessly ensnared in melodrama. And yet Bussy's moral philosophy (if we may so grace it) is strangely consistent even in its obliquities and even when it provides a rationalization of illicit love. The affair with Tamyra, which is by far the most ambiguous part of the play, introduces Chapman's most bewildering character, the Friar, a politic bawd dedicated to Bussy's cause, who views lust as an appetite that must be satisfied. He is "in voice/ A lark of heaven, in heart a mole of earth." By depicting the Friar as a politic bawd, Chapman gives a curious flavor to the Christian sentiments which close the play. Indeed all standards of judgment collapse when the Friar and Montsurrey confront each other over Tamyra's tortured body. Montsurrey defends unmanly cruelty in the name of honor; the Friar drapes the cloak of religion over the filthiness of adultery.

The Friar's deterministic credo serves to extenuate Tamyra's sin. She is one of the "weak dames" who cannot keep a "constant course in virtue," who want desperately to be good but who lack courage and determination. Bussy cannot plead such weakness, nor can he admit sin. Thus he chides Tamyra's troubled conscience after the consummation of their love:

> Sin is a coward, madam, and insults
> But on our weakness, in his truest valour:
> And so our ignorance tames us, that we let
> His shadows fright us: and like empty clouds,
> In which our faulty apprehensions forge
> The forms of dragons, lions, elephants,
> When they hold no proportion, the sly charms
> Of the witch Policy makes him like a monster
> Kept only to show men for servile money:
> That false hag often paints him in her cloth
> Ten times more monstrous than he is in troth:
> In three of us the secret of our meeting
> Is only guarded,
>
> . . . .
> Why should we fear then? (III. i. 20–35)

Bussy seems to denigrate conscience in the same way that Monsieur argues against Tamyra's honor:

> Honour, what's that? Your second maidenhead:
> And what is that? A word: the word is gone,
> The thing remains: . . . (II. ii. 10–12)

But as in the debate over revenge, Monsieur's casuistry is foil to Bussy's "sincerity." The politician does not believe that virtue, honor, or sin exist; the terms merely serve his vicious purposes. Bussy, in contrast, stoically distinguishes between true moral judgments and vulgar opinions. He shares Hamlet's knowledge that there is nothing good and evil in the world but thinking makes it so. He knows that politic religionists terrify the ignorant with superstitious fears of crimes and punishments. His inner law of reason tells him that Tamyra is still "chaste," and he is therefore anxious for secrecy only to preserve her good name against vulgar calumnies.

Together with Bussy's earlier manifesto this speech provides a key to the moral confusion which eventually blankets Chapman's drama. Through his hero's Stoic ethic, Chapman seeks to reaffirm the validity of rational moral absolutes against the slippery, relativistic code of the Machiavel. Yet the Stoic ideal of right reason, so frequently "adapted" in the Renaissance, is here distorted by a skepticism about traditional values which is in itself Machiavellian.[10] Intended as an anti-Prince, Bussy eventually becomes a Stoic version of the Prince, who must transcend conventional law to reform his society.

One cannot imagine that Chapman was oblivious to the moral ambiguities which surround Bussy, Tamyra, and the Friar. For in the last act, he trembles on the edge of condemning all three and of turning his play into a moralistic exemplum of the wages of sin. Early in *Bussy* Chapman does in fact suggest a moralistic interpretation of his hero's fall. After Bussy announces that he will rise by virtue alone, he admits that in politic surroundings "no man riseth by his real merit." He speaks of blind fortune ("time's restless wheel") and hints of the fatality of infinite aspirations. Thus it might seem that the self-sufficient hero loses his freedom of action and betrays his Stoic code by accepting Monsieur's aid. And, to be sure, before he sets out for his fatal appointment, Bussy gloats that he will flank policy with policy. He relishes adopting the stealthy craft of the Machiavel in his campaign against Montsurry. We can see, though, why Chapman did not —in a sense could not—develop this tragic idea to its logical conclusion. If Bussy is to be condemned, who will condemn him? King Henry, the detached moral chorus, has no place in the Tamyra incident. Monsieur exclaims at Tamyra's looseness, but he is himself a disappointed lecher. Montsurry condemns the Friar's hypocrisy but he is a politic cuckold and cowardly assassin. Moreover if Bussy is condemned for his actions, no moral note can sound in the final chaos; Bussy's fall from virtue will merely confirm and exalt the politician's cynicism about human nature. Bussy's tragedy does not prove that the active life is dangerous to villains like Monsieur and the Guise. It does not convince us that policy is futile because Monsieur exists triumphant. Indeed, an ironic interpretation of Chapman's tragedy reduces it to a confused comedy of vice in which Bussy's pretension to virtue is mocked but Monsieur's outright villainy is unsatirized—in which false virtue is punished but true viciousness is unreproved. Thus the attempt to read *Bussy* as a deliberately ironic, cautionary exemplum makes it seem morally absurd.

Instead of seeking to erase any taint of obliquity from *Bussy*, I think we must assume that Chapman did not successfully achieve his dramatic purpose. And though he muddled his high design, he finally had no alternative than to endow Bussy's death with heroic significance. Unable to end his play on a positive moral note, he had to be content with a negative standard of values by which all actions that conflict with policy assume the name of virtue. The reader is to believe that Bussy maintains his integrity by trading insults with Monsieur (Bussy is a master of invective) in a purely verbal war on policy. And lest the reader think that Bussy dies trapped by adulterous lust, Chapman uses Monsieur and the Guise to impart the "correct" moral interpretation. We learn from them that Bussy falls because he is "young, learned, valiant, virtuous, and full-mann'd." Monsieur explains:

> Yet as the winds sing through a hollow tree
> And (since it lets them pass through) let it stand;
> But a tree solid (since it gives no way
> To their wild rage) they rend up by the root:
> So this whole man
> (That will not wind with every crooked way,
> Trod by the servile world) shall reel and fall
> Before the frantic puffs of blind-born chance,
> That pipes through empty men, and makes them dance.[11]
>   (V. ii. 37–45)

The shock of discovering his mortality at first shakes Bussy's self-confidence. His mood of disillusion soon passes, however, and he dies triumphant, certain that he has achieved immortal fame in his fight against evil.

Tamyra shares Bussy's tragedy because she too cannot wind with the crooked way of the world. Unable to reconcile her love for Bussy with the demands of conscience, she is trapped in a hopeless (and hopelessly rhetorical) dilemma:

> O had I never married but for form,
> Never vow'd faith but purpos'd to deceive,
> Never made conscience of any sin,
> But cloak'd it privately and made it common;
> Nor never honour'd been in blood or mind;
> Happy had I been then, as others are
> Of the like licence; I had then been honour'd;
> Liv'd without envy; custom had benumb'd

All sense of scruple and all note of frailty;
My fame had been untouch'd, my heart unbroken:
But (shunning all) I strike on all offence,
O husband! Dear friend! O my conscience! (V. iv. 174–85)

In any other context this lament would seem remarkably obtuse. The pathos of Tamyra's fate is not that she has fallen victim to unlawful desires but that she has too much integrity to assume a hypocritical pose. Like some of Hemingway's heroes she remains "moral" despite her sins simply because she is not totally hardened to them.

Byron's Conspiracy

After the extravagant emotionalism of *Bussy D'Ambois*, the clarity and rationality of Chapman's next tragedy, *Byron's Conspiracy*, seems almost an act of penance, a demonstration that he could study the Marlovian individualist and the Machiavel with some measure of artistic decorum. Although Chapman again creates a titanic hero, the *Conspiracy* is, in almost all respects, a much smaller play than *Bussy*. The context of action and of philosophical reflection is almost exclusively political. The verse is more subdued and utilitarian; the isolated passages which glow with Promethean fire seem recollections of an emotion to which Chapman can no longer uncritically assent. The long, even-tempered, sententious passages already signal a pyrrhic victory of moralizing intellect over dramatic instinct. Eliminating the clichés of Senecan melodrama Chapman creates in the *Conspiracy* a static political Morality whose titanic hero plays an incongruously passive role.

Perhaps we would not notice Byron's passivity if the "inward" drama of his temptation and redemption were an adequate substitute for suspenseful external action. But he is too naïve morally and intellectually to be the hero of a sophisticated psychomachia. Instead of being a tragic protagonist he is, I suspect, Chapman's personal scapegoat, a hero sacrificed to expiate the obliquity of *Bussy D'Ambois*. As we shall see, the real drama of the *Conspiracy* lies not in Byron's struggle against temptation but in Chapman's retrospective analysis of Bussy's confused ethic. In the *Tragedy* Byron's doomed figure does stir the depths of Chapman's imaginative sympathies. In the *Conspir-*

acy Byron's majestic aspirations are surrounded by an almost constant mockery that brings the play closer to farce than to tragedy.

In his finer moments Byron, like Bussy, seems to epitomize a romantic ideal of "noblesse," which as before is clothed in magnificent poetry. "To fear a violent good abuseth goodness," Byron exclaims;

> 'Tis immortality to die aspiring,
> As if a man were taken quick to heaven;
> What will not hold perfection, let it burst;
> What force hath any cannon, not being charg'd,
> Or being not discharg'd? To have stuff and form,
> And to lie idle, fearful, and unus'd,
> Nor form nor stuff shows; happy Semele,
> That died compress'd with glory! Happiness
> Denies comparison of less or more,
> And not at most, is nothing: like the shaft
> Shot at the sun by angry Hercules,
> And into shivers by the thunder broken,
> Will I be if I burst; and in my heart
> This shall be written: 'Yet 'twas high and right'. (I. ii. 30–44)

The grandeur of Byron's pronouncement, however, is threaded with ironies. Foreshadowing the fall of his titan, Chapman clearly intimates the irrationality of boundless ambition by comparing it to a futile shaft broken by thunder (a traditional symbol of retribution). Ironic too is Byron's self-pronounced epitaph, for his rise is neither high nor right. Where Bussy's sole ambition was to set a fashion of virtue, Byron has the more realistic ambition of power and an earthly crown. Where Bussy was the incorruptible opponent of policy, Byron is its dupe. And where Bussy was the "complete man" amidst the hollow nobility, Byron is described as a hollow colossus, puffed with "empty hope of much." Thus the superman springs to life from his own ashes only to face a pitiless moral judgment.

In *Bussy* the dichotomy of inner worth and outward "greatness" was blurred by an insistence that the two are compatible in an ideal aristocrat. In the *Conspiracy* the dichotomy of goodness and greatness set forth in the Prologue is unequivocal. Bryon admits that he has given hostages to policy, and that in a world ruled by Fortune ambition is inevitably tainted. Placed against the decorum of a well-ordered kingdom, the vices of the titanic spirit who "transcends" conventional limitations are clearly etched. We learn that infinite ambition, born of self-infatuation, is *in itself* a mortal flaw because it opposes the larger hierarchical order of the universe. Before his seduction Byron admits that ambition necessitates going out of one's "natural clime of truth," "out of all the bounds/ Of justice." Men who do so,

> Forsaking all the sure force in themselves
> To seek without them that which is not theirs,
> The forms of all their comforts are distracted,
> The riches of their freedoms forfeited,
> Their human noblesse sham'd, . . . (I. ii. 157–61)

At the outset Byron is a loyal subject who claims that he will support his politic flatterers in any office except treason; but he is easy prey to their sophistries because he lacks the primary attribute of the whole man, intelligence. Savoy can play upon Byron's vanity like a stringed instrument and mock him to his face when he roars out of tune:

> Nay, nay, we must have no such gall, my lord,
> O'erflow our friendly livers; my relation
> Only delivers my inflamed zeal
> To your religious merits; which, methinks,
> Should make your Highness canoniz'd a saint. (III. ii. 85–89)

As Byron continues to rage against his king, Savoy's mockery becomes bolder:

> It cannot be denied; 'tis all so true
> That what seems arrogance, is desert in you. (III. ii. 106–7)

And when Byron denounces the monstrous humours of his king, Savoy soothes his dupe:

> Well, let these contradictions pass, my lord,
> Till they be reconcil'd, or put in form,
> By power given to your will, and you present
> The fashion of a perfect government. (III. ii. 110–13)

The obvious, almost comic, irony that surrounds the portrait of Byron indicates Chapman's new awareness of the disparity between Stoic apathy and Marlovian aspiration. Because Byron has the confidence of a self-sufficient man, he scorns predictions of disaster:

> There is no danger to a man that knows
> What life and death is; there's not any law
> Exceeds his knowledge; neither is it lawful
> That he should stoop to any other law.
> He goes before them, and commands them all,
> That to himself is a law rational. (III. iii. 140–45)

But he asserts his Stoic rationality immediately after assaulting the Astrologer, who foresaw his doom. Boasting of his inner discipline, Byron is constantly at the mercy of his humours. As a "Stoic," he scorns opinion; as a soldier he feeds on the flattery of others and holds "honor" (which rests on opinion) more precious than life.

Like Bussy, Byron distorts the Stoic concept that life is opinion to rationalize his "transcendence" of moral law. Even as Bussy had claimed that "Sin is a coward," Byron asserts;

> There is no truth of any good
> To be discern'd on earth: and, by conversion,
> Nought therefore simply bad; but as the stuff
> Prepar'd for arras pictures is no picture
> Till it be form'd, and man hath cast the beams
> Of his imaginous fancy through it,
> . . . .
> so all things here
> Have all their price set down from men's conceits,
> which make all terms and actions good or bad,
> And are but pliant and well-colour'd threads
> Put into feigned images of truth;
> To which to yield and kneel as truth-pure kings,
> That pull'd us down with clear truth of their gospel,
> Were superstition to be hiss'd to hell.[12] (III. i. 47–62)

There is no question of the casuistry of Byron's moral philosophy. His skepticism is not Bussy's antidote to politic relativism; it is a product of his seduction by Machiavels, whose terminology and philosophy he has learned by rote. Byron's philosophy derives from the cynical Picoté, who trains his pupil in such weird dialectic as:

> Truth is a golden ball, cast in our way,
> To make us stript by falsehood. (II. i. 156–57)

Luckily Byron's infection is not mortal and his king is merciful. With one moving speech Henry reverses Byron's traitorous career, reclaims him as a loyal subject, and lays to rest the errant ghost of Bussy D'Ambois. This denouement is so abrupt and unexpected, however, and so completely unprepared for by dialogue or dramatic action, that it seems merely a convenient way to end a drama that is more private and intellectual than public and heroic.[13] The political decorum of the *Conspiracy* seems, in fact, more of a utilitarian *donnée* than a qualification of the world view of *Bussy*. The acceptance of legitimate royal authority provides Chapman with an artistic, not a philosophical, resolution, for the alternative to the politician's amorality becomes an act of blind submission.

Byron's Tragedy

Superficially at least, *Byron's Tragedy* is a continuation of the fable tentatively "ended" in the *Conspiracy*. On the one hand Chapman traces the disintegration of Byron's unstable greatness; on the other hand he seems to expand an ideal of royalty in the noble King Henry. But close study reveals that the *Tragedy* is independent of the *Conspiracy* in theme and characterization. In some respects it is Chapman's most successful tragedy, too sententious perhaps yet powerfully conceived and executed. It shows a far more subtle and mature grasp of political issues than either of his preceding plays. It presents his most intriguing character, a Byron whose self-delusions, no longer ludicrous, border on the edge of insanity. Byron's career, as Miss Ellis-Fermor remarks, is a "fine and discriminating study of individualism becoming egotism, egotism becoming megalomania, and megalomania breaking down into hysteria."[14] Indeed, the portrait of Byron is so absorbing that one may easily ignore the political and moral issues raised by the King's maneuvers even though his council of state is the true locus of the dramatic action.[15]

During the first half of the play, the moral issue seems all too obvious; we watch the reckless charge of one Marlovian individualist against the political order. Here is a new Byron. He is no longer the greathearted loyal soldier misled by sycophantic Machiavels. He now stands alone, a confirmed traitor who conspires with his country's enemies against his rightful king. He is not duped into believing his king a tyrant; instead he masks an insatiable lust for power under the common rebel's pretext of reforming a corrupt kingdom. Byron is not a calculating opportunist, however, who deliberately invents an excuse for usurpation. His grasp on reality is always tenuous; he believes whatever he wants to believe about himself, his king, and his country. His sudden shifts of attention and his illogical leaps from premise to conclusion suggest a mind enthralled by a powerful, warped imagination. Byron is an egoist who lies more effectively to himself than to others, who is so inured to self-deception that he can no longer distinguish illusion from reality. He moves confidently into the King's trap armed with the "headless resolution" of his invincibility. Faced with the damning evidence of his guilt, he violently protests his innocence. Retreating further into his fantasy, he recreates the trial scene as a personal triumph, convinced that he has swayed the implacable judges. And at his execution, he facilely adopts a religious martyrdom to which he clings with fanatical conviction.

Chaos is Byron's native element. He is the great professional soldier who finds the meaning of life in combat and who literally believes in the stale commonplace that peace rusts men and nations. He seems less concerned with the exercise of power than with the struggle to attain it. He dwells upon a new creation

> Of state and government, and on our Chaos
> Will I sit brooding up another world.
> I, who through all the dangers that can siege
> The life of man have forc'd my glorious way
> To the repairing of my country's ruins,
> Will ruin it again to re-advance it. (I. ii. 30–35)

Although the truth seems to be that the virtuous Henry has restored order and harmony after the ravages of civil war, Byron announces that

> The world is quite inverted, Virtue thrown
> At Vice's feet, and sensual Peace confounds
> Valour and cowardice, fame and infamy. (I. ii. 14–16)

With superb illogic Byron sees himself as both Machiavellian savior and anti-Machiavel:

> Dear friend, we must not be more true to kings
> Than kings are to their subjects; there are schools

Now broken ope in all parts of the world,
First founded in ingenious Italy,
Where some conclusions of estate are held
That for a day preserve a prince, and ever
Destroy him after; from thence men are taught
To glide into degrees of height by craft,
And then lock in themselves by villany:
But God (who knows kings are not made by art,
But right of Nature, nor by treachery propp'd,
But simple virtue) once let fall from heaven
A branch of that green tree, whose root is yet
Fast fix'd above the stars;

.   .   .   .

Religion is a branch, first set and blest
By Heaven's high finger in the hearts of kings,
Which whilom grew into a goodly tree;
Bright angels sat and sung upon the twigs,
And royal branches for the heads of kings
Were twisted of them; but since squint-eyed Envy
And pale Suspicion dash'd the heads of kingdoms
One 'gainst another, two abhorred twins,
With two foul tails, stern War and Liberty,
Enter'd the world. The tree that grew from heaven
Is overrun with moss; the cheerful music
That heretofore hath sounded out of it
Begins to cease; and as she casts her leaves,
By small degrees the kingdoms of the earth
Decline and wither; and look, whensoever
That the pure sap in her is dried-up quite,
The lamp of all authority goes out,
And all the blaze of princes is extinct.

.   .   .   .

                            so are kings' revolts
And playing both ways with religion
Fore-runners of afflictions imminent,
Which (like a Chorus) subjects must lament. (III. i. 1-48)

Note the sinuous weaving of this "idealistic" argument. First justifying the right of rebellion, Byron then associates disloyalty with Machiavellianism. Lingering on the divine origin of monarchy, he loses himself in an embroidered conceit that changes shape as he speaks. Stripped of its poetic ornaments Byron's political philosophy reduces to a simple credo: repay evil with evil, royal policy with politic rebellion; "we must not be more true to kings/ Than they are to their subjects."

By the close of *Byron's Tragedy* the aura that once surrounded worldly aspiration in Chapman's drama is considerably dimmed. Byron's hysterical inability to accept imprisonment and execution reveals that

> Strength to aspire is still accompanied
> With weakness to endure. (IV. ii. 305–6)

Even Byron must admit, in a reflective moment before his death, that

> He is at no end of his actions blest
> Whose ends will make him greatest, and not best. (V. iv. 144–45)

When he speaks of the "eternal victory of Death" it sounds like an afterthought, for he goes to execution raging, embittered, and whining, obsessed by the vanity of endeavor.

One would think that the ruin of an "atheist," an individualist who challenged the rule of law and legitimacy, would provide a very satisfactory political "lesson." Yet Byron's headlong plunge from greatness does not inspire the usual platitudes about erring or wasted genius. It leaves only uncertainty about man's fate in a world of "dark and stormy night,/ Of senseless dreams, terrors, and broken sleeps." Byron's hysterical disintegration calls forth a tragic chorus of noblemen who despairingly comment on the "wearisome Condition of Humanity." Epernon exclaims:

> Oh of what contraries consists a man!
> Of what impossible mixtures! Vice and virtue,
> Corruption, and eternnesse, at one time,
> And in one subject, let together loose!
> We have not any strength but weakens us,
> No greatness but doth crush us into air.
> Our knowledges do light us but to err,
> Our ornaments are burthens, our delights
> Are our tormenters, fiends that, rais'd in fears,
> At parting shake our roofs about our ears. (V. iii. 189–98)

Soissons similarily bewails the frailty of virtue, and Vidame calls upon "real Goodness," uncertain whether it is "a power/ And not a word alone, in human uses," to give Byron religious patience. The prayer is unanswered.

It may be simply an artistic oversight that *Byron's Tragedy* ends on this pessimistic and negative note. Perhaps Chapman, exploiting to the last the drama of Byron's degeneration, simply overlooked the need for a more positive political and moral affirmation. Or perhaps, though he condemned Byron's anarchic ambition, he could not exalt the political order which sacrificed such greatness. *Byron's Conspiracy*, we recall, presented a clear-cut moral conflict between Machiavellian intrigue and legitimate monarchical authority. In the *Tragedy* political blacks and whites merge into grey. The very term *politician* becomes ambiguous because the King's party is more Machiavellian than Byron, who falls because he lacks politic guile. He relies on personal strength and reputation rather than subterfuge. He makes an error, inexcusable in a politician, of implicitly trusting La Fin, who is the King's intelligencer; and he dies proud that D'Auvergne kept faith with him. One might almost say that compared to his opponents Byron is politically "innocent." They ensnare him with spies; they corrupt his allies. They lure him home on specious pretext and trap him where he cannot resist. When La Fin testifies at the trial, Byron exclaims:

> Is it justice
> To tempt and witch a man to break the law,
> And by that witch condemn him? (V. ii. 156–58)

The Chancellor's pious answer that "witchcraft can never taint an honest mind" does not alter the impression that Byron's trial is a calculated act of state rather than an impartial judicial proceeding.

We see in *Byron's Tragedy* that even the politically virtuous must at times use politic means and that no political motive is untainted by egoism. Henry, a compassionate sovereign, is deeply concerned with his subjects' welfare; but he is also jealous of his place and prerogative and ambitious for his dynasty. Although he would, if possible, reclaim Byron as a loyal servant, he views Byron's death as a pregnant example to other would-be usurpers, especially to Byron's peers, who boycott the trial. Henry's political philosophy, moreover, places a very dangerous emphasis upon the king's personal integrity. Insisting that Byron's execution be perfectly legal, he explains:

> . . . if, because
> We sit above the danger of the laws,
> We likewise lift our arms above their justice,
> And that our heavenly Sovereign bounds not us
> In those religious confines out of which
> Our justice and our true laws are inform'd,
> In vain have we expectance that our subjects
> Should not as well presume to offend their earthly,
> As we our heavenly Sovereign. (V. i. 49–57)

Henry's sentiment is more comforting than his theory. Placing himself outside the "religious confines" which inform the laws his subjects must obey, he frees himself from the traditional limitations which medieval theorists placed on royal authority. According to Henry a king should be just, not because he is ordained a "living law" but because it would be highly imprudent to be otherwise.

While the King's claim to a supramoral absolutism is implicitly dangerous, the political philosophy of his ministers is explicitly Machiavellian in theory and terminology. Janin, for example, advises Henry to execute Byron by royal decree:

> Princes, you know, are masters of their laws,
> And may resolve them to what forms they please,
> So all conclude in justice; in whose stroke
> There is one sort of manage for the great,
> Another for inferior: the great mother
> Of all productions, grave Necessity,
> Commands the variation; and the profit,
> So certainly foreseen, commends the example. (IV. ii. 31–38)

According to Janin, the political end justifies the means. When a duke sets himself above the law, the crime is treason. When a king sets himself above the law, the rationalization is divine right.

I do not mean to imply that either the King's party or Byron's trial is portrayed as hypocritical. It was a commonplace of Renaissance political thought (even of writers bitterly opposed to Machiavelli) that to preserve the state the king may deviate from strict morality, and in particular that he need not keep strict faith with traitors.[16] Nevertheless Chapman suggests that to Janin and his colleagues Machiavellian methods are an accepted part of political behavior, not a loathsome ultimate expedient. Whereas in the *Conspiracy* submission to royal authority was the "answer" to Machiavellian temptations, in the *Tragedy* it appears that an absolute royal prerogative is potentially as dangerous as the cynical relativism of the Machiavel.

The Revenge of Bussy D'Ambois (1610–11)

After the narrowly conceived thesis drama of the *Conspiracy*, the larger horizons of *Byron's Tragedy* prepare us for Chapman's return in the *Revenge* to the moral and philosophical themes of *Bussy D'Ambois*. Having clarified his Stoic ethic and his attitude toward Marlovian aspiration, Chapman can now lucidly dramatize the conflict between philosophical hero and corrupt society. Unfortunately, however, he also returns (by popular request, one imagines) to a melodramatic revenge fable, to the ghosts, duels, sinister ambushes, and romantic liaisons of his first tragedy. He is sufficiently in control of his materials to prevent the melodrama from submerging or warping his moral design; but he achieves this only by isolating all didactic intention in the rhetoric and by making it obvious that the moral nature of his hero is utterly opposed to the role circumstances force him to play. Even then he must resort to a crude expedient to make his Senecal man play the part of blood revenger.

In recreating the political milieu of his first tragedy, Chapman discards the somewhat naïve *donnée* of a virtuous king surrounded by an unscrupulous nobility. The inherent link between despotism and policy, faintly suggested in *Byron's Tragedy*, becomes a central theme in the *Revenge*. King and politician are now mutually dependent, fellow conspirators. The King, fearful of opposition, employs the unscrupulous Machiavel to root out seeds of "treason." The Machiavel in turn plays upon royal fears for personal gain and calls opportunism loyalty. Baligny underlines the slipperiness of Janin's political ethic when he assures his monarch:

> Your Highness knows
> I will be honest, and betray for you
> Brother and father: for, I know, my lord,
> Treachery for kings is truest loyalty;
> Nor is to bear the name of treachery,
> But grave, deep policy. All acts that seem

> Ill in particular respects are good
> As they respect your universal rule.
> As in the main sway of the universe
> The supreme Rector's general decrees,
> To guard the mighty globes of earth and heaven,
> Since they make good that guard to preservation
> Of both those in their order and first end,
> No man's particular (as he thinks) wrong
> Must hold him wrong'd; no, not though all men's reasons,
> All law, all conscience, concludes it wrong. (II. i. 29–44)

The apologist for absolutism and the Machiavellian relativist agree: the state and the king are above ordinary moral laws.

In contrast to King and Machiavel, Clermont and his friends keep alive moral ideals of political behavior. "Will kings make treason lawful?" the Countess asks,

> Is society
> (To keep which only kings were first ordain'd)
> Less broke in breaking faith 'twixt friend and friend,
> Than 'twixt king and subject? Let them fear.
> Kings' precedents in licence lack no danger. (IV. iii. 41–45)

Against policy's claim that it transcends private morality to achieve public "good," Clermont's party insists upon the oneness of communal and private morality. Clermont, they announce, "would not for his kingdom traitor be," for "who hath no faith to men, to God hath none."

It is significant that there are no diabolical bogymen in the *Revenge*. The myth of satanic evil is replaced by a more rational and penetrating analysis of Machiavellian cynicism and of its protean dialectic, which can justify killing a king as well as killing for a king. The ultimate horror of policy, Chapman suggests, is not its rationalization of inhuman acts but its destruction of the fundamental trust upon which society rests. Baligny boasts that he can ruin even the virtuous Clermont because

> 'Tis easy to make good suspected still,
> Where good and God are made but cloaks for ill. (I. i. 143–44)

Since policy triumphs by exploiting suspicion and fear, it must continually create real or imagined crises; it cannot admit the existence of the "security" which presumably is the end of its vicious acts. Clermont's sincerity, Baligny remarks,

> we politicians
> Must say, grows out of envy, since it cannot
> Aspire to policy's greatness; and the more
> We work on all respects of kind and virtue,
> The more our service to the King seems great
> In sparing no good that seems bad to him. (I. i. 134–39)

In a politic society, any faith in human nature (Clermont's trust in Maillard's word, for example) is suicidal. Having made the exercise of power his ultimate goal, the politician needs no eyes, because he "has no way," or rather his is a "way / Ventur'd in deserts, without guide or path."

In the *Revenge*, Clermont assumes Bussy's anti-Machiavellian role; however, he does not engage in a futile attempt to reform his world. His ambitions are wholly private and philosophical. Where Chapman's earlier heroes supposedly chose between greatness and goodness, now there appears no choice; the only greatness resides in virtue. Thus, in retrospect, Bussy's "noblesse" seems deeply flawed. Because he lacked learning, he was "rapt with outrage oftentimes/ Beyond decorum." Bussy, Chapman has now decided, was the Senecal man whose natural virtue was philosophically unrefined, and whom Seneca describes with mixed admiration:

> There are certain passions which never take hold-fast but on the strongest spirits: even as the most strongest and fruitfullest Coppise grow on the land which is least manured, and a Forrest flourisheth in a fruitfull soyle. Therefore the mindes that by nature are most strongest endure Anger and being fierie and hote, suffer nothing that is little and feeble; but that vigor is imperfect, as may appear in all things without Art, which grow only by the benefit of nature, which except they be quickly tamed and tempered, that which was disposed to become valour is converted into audaciousnesse and rashnesse.[17]

His spirit tamed by philosophy, Clermont personifies, for all his soldierly abilities, moderation and self-discipline. His speeches, which lack the swelling vein and self-intoxicating rapture of Bussy's, have an assurance and dignity not before granted to Chapman's tragic heroes.

Clermont is not driven to climb the Everests of power because they exist. Though hardly timid or cowardly he knows

> how dangerous it is
> For any man to press beyond the place
> To which his birth, or means, or knowledge ties him;
> For my part, though of noble birth, my birthright
> Had little left it, and I know 'tis better
> To live with little, and to keep within
> A man's own strength still, and in man's true end,
> Than run a mix'd course. Good and bad hold never
> Anything common; you can never find
> Things outward care, but you neglect your mind.
> God hath the whole world perfect made and free,
> His part to th' use of th' All; men then that be
> Parts of that All, must, as the general sway
> Of that importeth, willingly obey
> In everything without their power to change.
> He that, unpleas'd to hold his place, will range,
> Can in no other be contain'd that's fit,
> And so resisting th' All, is crush'd with it.
> But he, that knowing how divine a frame
> The whole world is; and of it all, can name
> (Without self-flattery) no part so divine
> As he himself, and therefore will confine
> Freely his whole powers in his proper part,
> Goes on most God-like. He that strives t'invert
> The Universal's course with his poor way,
> Not only dust-like shivers with the sway
> But, crossing God in his great work, all earth
> Bears not so cursed and so damn'd a birth. (III. iv. 48–75)

In this final detached comment on the careers of Bussy and Byron, Chapman's idea of natural freedom takes on new meaning. Man, Clermont implies, was created free from external tyrannies but he gains inner liberty only through self-discipline and willing obedience to universal law. In contrast to his brother, Clermont studies to be quiet.

This reaffirmation of universal harmony after the confusions of *Bussy* and the uncertainties of the Byron plays seems a significant turning point in Chapman's intellectual journey. Policy still controls society and state, but, like Hooker, Clermont looks out on a fallen world convinced that beneath its external anarchies is the working of immutable law. Men cursed with Baligny's myopia find it necessary to go with the politic sway of society. A man of Clermont's vision knows that he must join himself "with th' Universe/ In his main sway." There is almost a guarded exhilaration in Clermont's recognition of necessity—a confidence that man is capable of heroic *spiritual* aspiration if he can recognize his truly godlike potentialities.

At the same time that Clermont's Stoicism provides, within the context of the play at least, a philosophical solution to the question of evil, it creates an almost insoluble artistic problem. For Clermont's Stoicism makes him an impossible protagonist in a revenge tragedy. He is Guyon in Jacobean dress, flawless, viceless, and nearly impervious to external stimuli. He is insulted with impunity; he faces calamity with a passivity that borders on inertia. And worse still he is a perfect prig, who can do no wrong and is determined the world shall know it. How can this Senecal man undertake so irrational a project as blood revenge? And why, in fact, should he feel impelled to revenge Bussy, who shattered moral decorum and died because of his "foul adulterous guilts"? Though Clermont admits that Bussy's murder was a criminal act, he regrets having pledged vengeance; he would not be "equal" with villains or call revenge "virtuous."

Only an imperative that surmounts Clermont's Stoic rationality and that sanctifies blood revenge can spur him to action. Such an imperative is brought (oh heavy irony!) by Bussy's Ghost, returned from eternal night to demand Christian retribution. Though a blunt sword with which to cut a Gordian knot, the Ghost's speeches are interesting in that they reveal Chapman's awareness of the difference between Christian orthodoxy and Stoic idealism. At one point the Ghost admonishes Clermont:

> . . . you respect not
> (With all your holiness of life and learning)
> More than the present, like illiterate vulgars;
> Your mind (you say) kept in your flesh's bounds,
> Shows that man's will must rul'd be by his power:
> When (by true doctrine) you are taught to live
> Rather without the body than within,
> And rather to your God still than yourself;
> To live to Him, is to do all things fitting
> His image, in which, like Himself, we live;

To be His image is to do those things
That make us deathless, which by death is only
Doing those deeds that fit eternity;
And those deeds are the perfecting that justice
That makes the world last, which proportion is
Of punishment and wreak for every wrong,
As well as for right a reward as strong. (V. i. 79–95)

From this speech we surmise that Bussy remains a confused moralist even though he has found religion beyond the grave. His aspersion of Clermont's Stoicism could be taken more seriously if his Christian ideal of justice was not used to vindicate an unlawful and immoral act. But remembering the Friar's role in *Bussy*, and repeated verbal linkings of religion and policy in Chapman's drama, we need not be surprised that in this instance the Stoic, who repudiates revenge, seems morally superior to the spokesman of a literal-minded and slightly obtuse orthodoxy.

Clermont accepts this heavenly command not inwardly convinced of its validity. He kills Montsurry in a courteous, gentlemanly manner only to learn in his moment of triumph that the Guise has been murdered. Having boasted insufferably of his self-sufficiency, he suddenly decides that life is intolerable without the support and comradeship of the Guise. Complaining that he is "left negligent,/ To all the horrors of the vicious time," he exercises his Senecal option of suicide. Perhaps in the abstract Clermont's suicide squares with his Stoic code even though the Stoic sanction of self-destruction is by no means casual. But in the play Clermont's suicide is almost ludicrous. What other dramatist would allow a hero, who has escaped diabolical snares and accomplished his revenge, to kill himself because a relatively minor character has been assassinated? Can we imagine a victorious Hamlet stabbing himself because Horatio has been slain? I suspect that after satisfying the demands of plot and audience by compromising his Stoical protagonist, Chapman ended his play as expeditiously as possible. There are many indications that Chapman was not at ease with his dramatic fable. The climactic duel and the scene in which Monsieur insults Clermont approach absurdity. The verse, particularly in the scenes related to the revenge, frequently descends to a weary reminiscence of Elizabethan theatrical rant. "I savour the rank blood of foes in every corner," snarls Montsurry before he meets Clermont in mortal combat.

The Tragedy of Chabot (1612–13)

The Tragedy of Chabot marks the close of Chapman's interest in policy and political issues. Indeed, even in *Chabot* the machinations of policy though prominent are of peripheral interest; they are an efficient rather than necessary cause of the central dramatic conflict between Chabot and his king. Hardly reconciled to the goals or methods of the politician, Chapman nevertheless accepts his presence as an inevitable fact of political life under the reign of an absolute monarch. Chabot, an ideal magistrate who has risen to high office through merit, is a rare and marvelous exception in his milieu. His rival, Montmorency, who is fundamentally decent though weak, is more typical of Francis' ministers. Montmorency would prefer to satisfy his ambition honestly, but he regretfully agrees to plot Chabot's ruin because one man rises in the King's favor only as another falls.

In his study of Chapman, Mr. Rees supports Mrs. Solve's contention that *Chabot* is a topical allegory on one of the most notorious judicial proceedings of Chapman's age: the trial and imprisonment of Somerset for the murder of Sir Thomas Overbury. This topical interpretation seems reasonable enough even if it would have us believe that Chapman returned to the theater after a decade of silence to appeal somewhat obscurely to James's merciful instincts.[18] Yet we should not allow it to divert attention from the larger and far more important political issue which Chapman dramatizes: namely, the conflict between absolutist prerogative and the medieval ideal of the rule of law. While Mrs. Solve identifies Sir Edward Coke with Chapman's Proctor-General, Jacobean history suggests a more fruitful parallel between Coke and Chabot, the two high magistrates who opposed their monarchs' attempts to set themselves above customary procedures of justice.

That *Chabot* is a tract for anxious times is pointed out by Professor Parrott:

Chapman, like most thinking men of his day, believed in absolute monarchy, but he held that the monarch could be absolute without being arbitrary. . . . The lesson of the tragedy is the necessity for the free play of the individual within the limits of the state organism, or, to put it more concretely, the duty of the absolute monarch to respect the liberty of the loyal subject.[19]

But if Chapman "believed" in absolute monarchy it was with grave reservations, for he was increasingly concerned in tragedy with the license granted kings by theories of divine right. In *Chabot* he does not dramatize the possibility that an evil king may turn absolute prerogative into tyranny; he dramatizes the moral dangers *inherent* in absolute government under the best of kings—under a sincere, gracious, and virtuous ruler like Francis.

Because the throne is the direct source of all authorities in the realm, it is the center of unending struggle for royal favor. The state is fortunate when the King chooses his favorites—as he chose Chabot—according to their merits. Nevertheless the very existence of favoritism produces instability, because there are no objective or absolute standards of public service; all depends upon princely whim. Chabot is toppled from his lofty position by an insignificant quarrel which would not have arisen except for Francis' pride. Chabot has no personal interest in rejecting the unlawful bill; he is simply fulfilling the routine obligations of his office. The King is similarly detached from the question. He intervenes at the request of his new favorite, although he is ignorant of the issues involved. Worse still, he is completely unaware that his interference upsets the impartial course of judgment. While he talks a great deal of justice, Francis (like Chapman's monarch, James I) cannot conceive of justice as an ideal above and beyond kingly prerogatives.[20] He is astonished that Chabot should for so petty a cause spurn his gentle request. He does not see that Chabot adheres to a conviction stronger than any personal feeling of gratitude or loyalty.

As Chabot maintains his stand, Francis becomes increasingly irritated. From a minor matter devoid of personal interest, the question inevitably becomes one of the sanctity of royal prerogative, for absolutism makes all issues political. Since the King's authority is theoretically unquestionable, then in practice it cannot be questioned, and the need to safeguard it against encroachments becomes (as it became for the Stuarts) a dominating obsession. It no longer matters why

Chabot refuses the King's request. All that matters is that he dares to refuse. Francis is wise enough to accept Chabot's display of personal integrity, but the Queen, jealous of her position (and of Chabot's wife), presses her husband to "act like a king":

> Shall the sacred name of King,
> A word to make your nation bow and tremble,
> Be thus profan'd? Are laws establish'd
> To punish the defacers of your image
> But dully set by the rude hand of others
> Upon your coin, and shall the character
> That doth include the blessing of all France,
> Your name, thus written by your royal hand,
> Design'd for justice and your kingdom's honour,
> Not call up equal anger to reward it? (II. i. 12–21)

The Queen develops an interesting variation of a familiar Stuart principle: no bill, no King.

The central issue in Chapman's drama then is not "What are Chabot's rights as a loyal subject?" but "What is the supreme authority in the state: law or princely prerogative?" Francis' position is clear. He sees himself (as did James I) as a secular god in the commonwealth, from whose divinely ordained power all lesser authorities spring. Thus, while Francis is willing to admit that perhaps in this instance Chabot's judgment is better than his own, he asks:

> Well, sir, grant
> Your force in this; my odds in benefits,
> Paid for your pains, put in the other scale,
> And any equal holder of the balance
> Will show my merits hoist up yours to air,
> In rule of any doubt or deed betwixt us.

Chabot answers:

> You merit not of me for benefits,
> More than myself of you for services. (II. iii. 88–95)

To Chabot, the king is a dispenser of justice, not a creator of authority. He believes, as did the medieval theorists, that the rule of law in the commonwealth is a *legal reality* as well as a political ideal.

Chapman allows his hero a remarkable display of integrity. Although it was a commonplace of Renaissance political theorists that no subject was forced to obey a command that broke the laws of nature or God, authorities agreed that in cases of civil law a magistrate should not oppose the king's will. And if he cannot obey, his only recourse is to resign his office.[21] Chabot, we note, refuses either to acquiesce or to resign. He upholds his rights as a magistrate against his king (or more correctly in his king's behalf). On the other hand Chapman sanctions no act of disloyalty. When Chabot's wife speaks too boldly to the Queen, his father intervenes:

> Subjects are bound to suffer, not contest
> With princes, since their will and acts must be
> Accounted one day to a Judge supreme. (III. i. 163–65)

The person and the place of royalty are sacred. The king, though not superior to the law, is not answerable to his subjects for his actions. Thus in *Chabot*, Chapman threads his way between contemporary extremes of absolutism and antimonarchism. At the same time that he criticizes the vagaries of absolutism, he suggests no way by which rule of law can be enforced against absolute prerogative except perhaps by the courage and high purpose of royal ministers. Despite the triumph of justice and Francis' repentance, *Chabot* ends on a melancholy note. Chabot dies of a broken heart and even the Chancellor's trial is tinged with irony, because it is once again apparent that "sovereign" law serves Francis' will. Though more affirmative than *Byron's Tragedy*, *Chabot* does not offer real hope of political reform, nor is Chabot's political integrity an absolute on which Chapman could rest after the Stoicism of the *Revenge*.

Caesar and Pompey

We have thus far traced the development of Chapman's thought over a period of ten years. We have seen the ambiguities and uncertainties of his earliest tragedies resolved by ethical convictions. We have seen the storm and fury of his early anti-Machiavellianism fade into Stoic resignation and acceptance of political realities. We cannot be sure that *Caesar and Pompey* is Chapman's last play, but it does seem to complete the pattern of his tragedies and to represent the end of a long artistic and intellectual pilgrimage.[22]

Having traced this pilgrimage we can understand why *Caesar and Pompey* seems, despite its turbulent action, a twilight study lost in the shadows of Aurelian meditation. Like *Antony and Cleopatra* (perhaps in imitation of it) *Caesar and Pompey* is the tragedy of an antique world well lost. But whereas Shakespeare enhances the historical drama of Plutarch's *Lives*, Chapman reduces it to an impressionistic setting for the inward spiritual drama of Pompey's self-discovery. While empires are being lost and won, while the fate of Roman civilization hangs in perilous balance, Chapman takes pains to assure us that these world-shattering events are insubstantial pageants compared to the making of a single soul. The "Argument" informs us at the very beginning that Caesar's victory is actually meaningless, that he is "(in spite of all his fortune) without his victory victor" (*The Tragedies*, p. 343). Indeed, the inner focus of Chapman's play is evidenced by his willingness to depict an ambiguous Caesar: noble in abilities and temperament, but Machiavellian in ambition; part conspirator, part savior of his country. All that matters to Chapman now is that the conquering Caesar is Fortune's favorite and therefore Fortune's fool, who labors to become the empty colossus of worldly power. Cato and Pompey, in contrast, turn military defeat into spiritual victory. Cato triumphs over adversity; Pompey triumphs over himself as well as the world. Unlike Cato, who is confirmed from the beginning in Stoic virtue, Pompey achieves greatness only by casting it away. He loses an empire to find himself.

The renunciation of power and of worldly aspiration is final in *Caesar and Pompey*. We learn now that high position is intrinsically evil and that goodness can reside only in mediocrity. In one of the most affecting scenes Chapman ever wrote, the defeated Pompey counsels his wife:

> O, my Cornelia, let us still be good
> And we shall still be great; and greater far
> In every solid grace than when the tumour
> And bile of rotten observation swell'd us.
> Griefs for wants outward are without our cure,
> Greatness, not of itself, is never sure.
> Before we went upon heaven, rather treading
> The virtues of it underfoot in making
> The vicious world our heaven, than walking there

Even here, as knowing that our home, contemning
All forg'd heavens here rais'd, setting hills on hills.

. . . .

we now are like
The two poles propping heaven, on which heaven moves,
And they are fix'd and quiet; being above
All motion far, we rest above the heavens. (V. i. 181–97)

Pathos, which must have seemed to the earlier Chapman an unfitting
sentiment in heroic tragedy, surrounds the defeated Pompey as he
announces his intention to become the complete man.

I will stand no more
On others' legs, nor build one joy without me.
If ever I be worth a house again
I'll build all inward; not a light shall ope
The common outway; no expense, no art,
No ornament, no door will I use there,
But raise all plain and rudely, like a rampier
Against the false society of men
That still batters
All reason piecemeal, and, for earthy greatness,
All heavenly comforts rarefies to air.
I'll therefore live in dark, and all my light,
Like ancient temples, let in at my top. (V. i. 203–15)

Here is Clermont's philosophy restated without priggery or self-righteousness. Through sheer simplicity of language and homeliness of
metaphor, Chapman transforms Clermont's soaring abstract lectures
on universal law into an intimate expression of religious and philosophical conviction.

The belief in universal harmony in *Caesar and Pompey* is not,
however, a Christian reconciliation with a disordered Creation, nor a
metaphysical certainty that Providence will ultimately bring good out
of evil. Those who witness Pompey's fall renounce all contention with
"this giant world," which "heaven itself/ Fails to reform":

A heap 'tis of digested villany:
Virtue in labor with eternal chaos
Press'd to a living death, and rack'd beneath it,
Her throes unpitied, every worthy man
Limb by limb sawn out of her virgin womb,
To live here piecemeal tortur'd. (V. ii. 80–85)

In "eternal chaos" liberty cannot be guaranteed by a political system; it springs only from spiritual self-sufficiency. "Only a just man is a free man"; only a Stoic rises above enslaving circumstances.

It might seem ironic that Pompey's mentor, Cato, achieves "freedom" by committing suicide, except that Cato's suicide is not, like Clermont's, an act of despair. Even as Pompey looks heavenward for inspiration, so Cato looks beyond the grave to the eternal light of the spirit. And whereas Bussy's death once proved that fallen nature works to no end, the liberation of Cato's spirit in death is seen as the triumphant end towards which all nature works. If we measure Cato's speeches against the *Manual* of Epictetus, his knowledge of things unseen—his faith in resurrection and immortality—seems incongruously Christian. If we measure them against the Stoicism of the *Revenge*, the incongruity disappears. For then it is obvious that Chapman's philosophical convictions, even at an earlier stage, bordered on religious faith. The curious scene between Fronto and Ophioneus suggests, moreover, that Chapman's skepticism about the politic aspects of religion had not completely vanished. This touch of "comic relief" reminds us that Cato's Rome has its Jacobean parallel, a disordered world "out of tune," swung this way and that by a thousand rulers and a thousand religions. There is possibly a remembrance of the Friar in *Bussy* in Ophioneus' advice that the malcontented Fronto win his fortune in the priesthood:

> And for discharge of the priesthood, what thou want'st in learning thou shalt take out in good-fellowship; thou shalt equivocate with the sophister, prate with the lawyer, scrape with the usurer, drink with the Dutchman, swear with the Frenchman, cheat with the Englishman, brag with the Scot, and turn all this to religion: *Hoc est regnum Deorum gentibus.*[23] (II. i. 111–17)

Perhaps even in his last play Chapman indirectly contrasts the protean forms of established Churches with the immutable certainties of the philosophic mind.

When we consider the extent to which Chapman used the stage for extraliterary purposes, we can understand why his drama was not a formative influence on Jacobean tragedy. Because he had more integrity and independence of purpose than creative sense of the theater,

other Jacobeans could respect and admire his plays but learn or borrow little from them. Though a Stoic fortitude in the face of death is
often characteristic of Jacobean tragic heroes, and though there are
Stoic elements in many other tragedies, no other dramatist followed
Chapman's Stoic way. All that can be said is that other Jacobeans also
found an ultimate nobility in the strength to endure and an even
greater heroism in the acceptance of circumstances than in the rebellion against them.

Dangerous as it would be to identify Chapman with his Stoic
heroes, I cannot but feel that he shared their spiritual isolation and
their sense of alienation from an unworthy society. Like Milton fallen
on evil days he despairs of worldly reformations, and yet he too discovers within himself the paradise which has been elsewhere destroyed.
He does not find security, however, through a return to Elizabethan
beliefs, nor does he burn his books and renounce his classical learning
to embrace salvation. Although in *Byron's Tragedy* knowledge illumi-
nated the way to error, in *Caesar and Pompey* Chapman with Cato
follows the light of reason beyond reason itself to the faith that looks
through death.

CHAPTER III

Ben Jonson

Time has not reversed the Jacobean verdict on Jonson's tragedies, nor is it likely that any vagary of taste will ever bring *Sejanus* and *Catiline* into general favor. They bored Jonson's audiences and they do not excite modern readers, who expect in Jacobean tragedy the vitality and variousness of Shakespeare and Webster. *Sejanus* undoubtedly deserves more readers than Jonson's reputation as a tragedian will allow, but *Catiline* remains a trial for the most sympathetic.

The truth may be that Jonson's tragedies are more interesting to discuss than to read, because artistic failure is a fascinating subject for critical analysis, more so in some respects than artistic success. If nothing else, it allows the critic a brief moment of superiority over the creative artist and affords a rare opportunity to dictate the terms of literary creation. Jonson's failure in tragedy is particularly interesting because his dramatic genius is beyond cavil and because he wrote *Sejanus* and *Catiline* at the height of his powers. To say that he could not write tragedy because his talent, like Greene's or Dekker's, lay in comedy is not even to beg the question convincingly. For Jonson was not by temperament a lighthearted satirist or a whimsical romantic. His comic muse was harsh and bitter, too bitter, in fact, for many tastes. His satire probed beneath the surface of human folly to uncover the sordid joke of inhuman vice. And in *Volpone*, we are often told, he shattered the decorums of comedy by creating a protagonist who possessed an almost tragic magnificence. We cannot say that the qualities which made Jonson triumphant in comedy were unsuited to tragedy. We can only say that these qualities (the lightning flash of wit, the pungent realism of characterization and dialogue, and the subtle understanding of the psychology of evil) are not strikingly evident in *Sejanus* or *Catiline*. If we agree with Herford and Simpson that Jonson lacked Shakespeare's depths of compassion and understanding, we merely acknowledge that he could not have written *Hamlet* or *King Lear*. If we agree that his Roman plays were the tragedies of a satirist,[1] we may still wonder why he could not have equalled, in his own fashion, the satiric tragedies of Webster and Tourneur.

Jonson was the first of many critics to explain the failure of his tragedies on the stage. The fault, he assumed, lay in the vulgarity of the unlettered, unwashed multitude, who had no appreciation of classical art. Modern critics have somewhat maliciously taken Jonson at his word. They agree that *Sejanus* and *Catiline* are too "classical" for the popular stage, but they mean by this that Jonson sacrificed his living genius at the dreary altar of neoclassical form. We should not, however, place too much significance on the failure of *Sejanus* and *Catiline* to win popular approval. It is hardly likely that Chapman's *Caesar and Pompey* was more successful (if it was ever performed), but whereas Chapman ignores his audience, Jonson's scornful attack on the common, swinish, mole-like torturers "that bring all wit to the Rack" calls vivid attention to the reception of his plays. No doubt Jonson hoped to reform the vulgar errors of the stage through the example of *Sejanus*, and no doubt his idea of tragic style derived less from popular dramatic practice than from his scholarly study of the classics and from the neoclassical literary theory of the Renaissance. Yet if we can believe the preface to *Sejanus*, he did not—or at least he thought he did not—place classical decorum above "popular delight." Nor was his view of tragedy narrowly bound by the neoclassical "laws" of tragic art. One could argue, in fact, that *Sejanus* is much more directly influenced by the popular dramatic tradition than is *Caesar and Pompey*. The portrait of Sejanus looks back to the Machiavellian hero-villains of the Elizabethan stage, and particularly to Marlowe's overreachers. The web of ironic intrigue and counter-intrigue in *Sejanus* recalls the archetypal plotting of *The Spanish Tragedy* even as the use of the revenge motive and design imitates the patterning of history in Marlowe's *Edward II*, in *Richard III*, and in *Julius Caesar*.

Unfortunately, however, Jonson's ill-success as a tragedian has made *Sejanus* and *Catiline* the classical stalking-horses of critics who defend less tutored Jacobean dramaturgy. Those who lament that "Aristotle was little thumbed on the Bankside," remarks F. L. Lucas, "might with poetic justice be condemned to read *Catiline* once a week for life."[2] At the risk of taking Mr. Lucas' casual thrust too seriously, I would point out that an attention to classical unities did not stultify Jonson's comic genius, nor is there any evidence that the demands of logic precluded the spontaneous flight of his dramatic imagination. Actually Jonson pays far more attention to conventional unities in his greatest comedies than he does in his tragedies, and yet the elaborate designs of *Volpone* and *The Alchemist* are breathless works of the imagination.

Because we are unduly impressed by, or scornful of, Jonson's "labored art," we may draw the wrong inferences from the massive structures of his tragedies. The solid characterizations, the compact verse, and the sheer weight of classical literary apparatus suggest a scholarly detachment, a firm if not throttling grasp on the subject at hand. We think of Jonson as a playwright who clearly perceived and tenaciously executed an essentially undramatic artistic intention. It is possible, however, that appearances in *Sejanus* and *Catiline* completely belie the facts. I would suggest that Jonson was unsuccessful not because his idea of tragedy was rhetorical, but because he could not come to terms with his own view of politics. Despite his careful attention to classical decorums, he could not with a divided mind achieve in tragedy the superb unity of form and vision that characterizes *Volpone* and *The Alchemist*.

To begin with, we must bury the notion, based on Jonson's

pedantic documentation of his texts, that the tragedies were antiquarian exercises, works of classical scholarship completely unrelated to the Jacobean scene or to Jacobean problems. In the more sophisticated historiography of the Renaissance (Bacon's, for example) there was no contradiction between accurate, objective recreation of the past and the use of history as a guide for the present. If *Julius Caesar* is history for art's sake, *Sejanus* and *Catiline* are not history for history's sake. Like Chapman's dramatic studies of French history, they mirror in a foreign setting political and moral issues of the time. We should not casually dismiss the fact that Jonson was called before the Star Chamber to explain the "treasonous" matter in *Sejanus*, for there are many aspects of the play that might arouse legitimate bureaucratic suspicions. He was, moreover, a friend and colleague of Chapman, who very probably was the "happy genius" mentioned by Jonson as a collaborator in the stage version of *Sejanus*.[3] The two men were kindred spirits; they shared similar humanistic interests and ideals and similarly disillusioned views of politics. Their first tragedies[4] were written within a year of each other and present comparable scenes of political decadence. The opening passages of *Sejanus* inform us that the Roman state (like Bussy's society) has fallen from its original "noblesse," that lawless ambition and intrigue have become the norms of political life. The aristocrats, once pillars of the state, have been reduced to marble-warming sycophants or ineffectual malcontents. The New Men of imperial favor grow wealthy and powerful by terrorizing Roman citizens who once enjoyed traditional privileges of law and freedom.

Although concerned with the same issues as Chapman, Jonson seems to approach the problem of political immorality from an opposite direction. Whereas Chapman's attacks on Machiavellianism presuppose specific ideals of liberty and of monarchical authority, Jonson seems to have no political theories. The only comment on forms of government in his tragedies (and in *Timber*) is the ubiquitous Renaissance commonplace that the rule of a good Prince is an ideal polity. Unlike Chapman, Jonson does not specifically challenge the absolutist claim to all-encompassing authority except in a single unimportant passage.[5] And unlike Chapman he offers no personal ideological message. If Chapman had written a play on the reign of Tiberius, his tragic hero would very likely have been, not Sejanus, but the Clermont-like Silius, who commits suicide to escape the coils of tyranny. I do not mean that Chapman admired nobility and Jonson was fascinated only with the criminal mind. (Jonson had his Cicero and Cato; Chapman, his Byron.) I mean rather that while Chapman seems a disillusioned idealist, Jonson is in tragedy as in comedy a moral realist, an ironic observer and pitiless recorder of vices and vanities.

It may not be completely accidental, therefore, that Jonson came close to tragic grandeur in comedy and achieved a primarily satiric effect in his tragedies. For the comic spirit presumes a moral security, an ineffable sense of the futility of vice, and an assurance that inhuman intent will be thwarted by human fallibility. Creating his own comic world, Jonson can delineate, through selection and emphasis, a universal moral pattern in a singular dramatic situation. Convinced of the ultimate vanity of insatiable desire, he can boldly depict the sordid comedy of greed and venality. The pattern of history, however, may not conform to ethical assumptions. Its drama may provide an apt subject for moral commentary, but its tragic events may lack moral significance or resolution.

In *Volpone* the helplessness of Celia and Bonario is inconsequential because avarice, lechery, and overreaching ambition are self-defeating. In historical drama, however, when the issues are bloody and the consequences of villainy catastrophic, the helplessness of virtue is not inconsequential. The fact that criminal ambition eventually overreaches itself does not erase the corrupting stain of tyranny. When the fate of the commonwealth hangs in the balance, the ineffectuality of decent men (the impotent gestures of the aristocracy in *Sejanus*, for example) is bitterly disillusioning. In place of the comic spirit which rules in *Volpone*, the presiding genius of *Sejanus* is the depraved Emperor Tiberius, who toys with the fates of Romans as if he were a god. Whereas *Volpone* reveals the ultimately moral pattern of psychological cause and effect, *Sejanus* implies that the ultimate reality of politics is the amoral struggle for power in which the fittest survive.

If Jonson lacked an intuition of personal tragedy—of the ruin of a noble human being—he did not lack insight into the eternal tragedy of political life. What he lacked was the nerve to present that tragedy with all the artistic powers at his command. Even more than Chapman he could accept Machiavelli's realistic appraisal of politics; but he could not share Machiavelli's appreciation of the heroic evil in politics. Although his depiction of Roman decadence makes Chapman's studies of policy seem genteel and amateurish, his Machiavellian portraits are curiously timid and unconvincing. It is almost as if he cannot admit that a politician might be heroic in stature or driven by ordinary instincts. Exaggerating the inhumanity of his villainous protagonists, he consistently denies them any redeeming traits. As Herford and Simpson point out, Tacitus' Sejanus is a credible political adventurer who stops at nothing in pursuit of his goal.⁶ Jonson's Sejanus, however, is scarcely distinguishable psychologically from the Elizabethan stage Machiavels. He has a crude appetite for villainy; his arrogant brags are grandiose but uninspired. Lacking Volpone's wit or Mosca's imagination, he carries to the summit of power the contemptible venality and vulgarity of the parvenu. His ambitions are vast but his spirit is mean; he collapses with a whimper before the Senate. All in all it is not surprising that the imitations of *Sejanus* in *The White Devil* are far more effective than the original passages, for Webster's willingness to create and admire "glorious villains" quickens the suppressed fire and brilliance of Jonson's dramatic situations.⁷

A tragedy, especially a political tragedy, can succeed even though its main figure lacks heroic stature. One thinks of Marlowe's *Edward II*, in which the weakness of the protagonist is offset by the variety and vitality of the supporting characters. But no play can succeed if the audience feels that its dramatic action centers about the wrong protagonist. And Jonson, it would seem, had a knack for creating tragedies with the wrong protagonists. The nominal hero of *Catiline* literally disappears from sight in the fourth act. Sejanus remains on stage until the final scene but as the play proceeds he is increasingly dominated by Tiberius, who even *in absentia* controls the situation. Actually Tiberius is not Sejanus' foil; he is a rival Machiavel, more psychologically convincing and more directly relevant to Machiavelli's description of the Prince. Whereas Sejanus is descended from the Elizabethan pseudo-Machiavel, Tiberius is a realistic portrait of a politician who cunningly manipulates other men's fears and desires.

Of course it is Jonson's prerogative to make Sejanus (who is a minor figure in Tacitus) his tragic hero and to relegate Tiberius (who is Tacitus' central figure) to a minor role. Unfortunately, however, Jonson leaves the impression that the inversion is arbitrary, that he has mistakenly cast a minor character in the lead while the genuine hero lurks in the wings. One could, for example, write a tragedy on the reign of Richard III in which Buckingham is the hero. But the play would be morally and aesthetically unsatisfying if when Buckingham finally ascends the scaffold, Richard continues his career of triumphant villainy. Buckingham would not seem a tragic hero to the audience; he would appear a politic dupe who failed to match wits with the more diabolical and fascinating Richard. In *Sejanus* Jonson wrote a "Roman" version of *Richard III* in which a Buckingham-like Sejanus plays the leading role even though the hero of the Machiavellian struggle for power is the more astute Tiberius.

This is not to say that Jonson deliberately avoided making Tiberius his hero. We can well believe that *Sejanus* was Jonson's attempt to rival the tremendous success of Shakespeare's drama of Roman conspiracy, *Julius Caesar*. The opening speeches of *Sejanus* indicate that Jonson, like Shakespeare, is going to present a conflict between the ancient aristocracy and the New Man of Roman politics. It is soon evident, however, that the aristocrats are no match for Sejanus' party and that the moral conflict for control of the state is an illusion nurtured in aristocratic minds. When Drusus dares to slap Sejanus' face, the Senators exclaim "A Castor, a Castor," but we already know that Sejanus has begun to seduce Drusus' wife and has plotted his murder. Arruntius, the acid-tongued moral chorus, seems, like the censors of Jonson's comedy, a spokesman for the dramatist's own sentiments and ideas. Yet his moral anger is shadowed by his wordy futility and by the fact that he is licensed by the politicians to provide a harmless source of information. Although he blusters about taking action, his gestures remain verbal. When Sabinus mentions Sejanus' imperial ambitions, Arruntius exclaims:

> By the gods,
> If I could gesse he had but such a thought,
> My sword should cleave him downe from head to heart,
> But I would finde it out: and with my hand
> I'ld hurle his panting braine about the ayre,
> In mites, as small as *atomi*, to'undoe
> The knotted bed——(I. 252–58)

Nevertheless his sword does not leave his scabbard, and he is content with a vicarious act of defiance. When Silius takes his life before the Senate, Arruntius crows that *his* thought prompted the deed.

The noble sentiments of the aristocrats provide a moral facade for the real struggle for power, which is totally amoral. Scene by scene Jonson's drama moves from moral illusion to amoral reality, gradually focusing on the deadly game of deception and pretense that absorbs Sejanus and Tiberius. At first we share Sejanus' contempt for the doting, enfeebled Emperor, who seems completely infatuated with and dependent upon his favorite. Tiberius' first address to the Senate is commonplace, couched in sententious clichés, hesitant and circuitous in movement—the expression of an apparently vapid and timorous mind. We note, however, that after acknowledging the conventional pieties, Tiberius warns his listeners not to take his professed humility too seriously:

> No man, here,
> Receive our speeches, as *hyperbole's;*
> For we are far from flattering our friend [Sejanus],
> (Let envy know) as from the need to flatter.
> Nor let them aske the causes of our praise;
> Princes have still their grounds rear'd with themselves,
> Above the poore low flats of common men,
> And, who will search the reasons of their acts,
> Must stand on equall bases. (I. 532–40)

The doting Emperor weaves his way through a maze of idealistic platitudes only to arrive at a pointed expression of absolute prerogative.

We hear of Tiberius' unnatural lusts; we witness only his political sins: his conspiracy with Sejanus to degrade and enslave the Romans. Foreshadowing the entente of Baligny and his king in Chapman's *Revenge*, Jonson dramatizes the link between tyranny and opportunism—between despotic jealousies and politic ambitions—when favorites rule. Like Baligny, Sejanus confesses that he exploits Tiberius' anxieties by exaggerating the danger of conspiracy. He gloats that he has alienated Tiberius from the Roman populace by perpetrating acts of savagery in his name:

> The way, to put
> A prince in bloud, is to present the shapes
> Of dangers, greater than they are (like late,

Or early shadowes) and, sometimes, to faine
Where there are none, onely, to make him feare;
His feare will make him cruell: And once entred,
He doth not easily learne to stop, or spare
Where he may doubt. This have I made my rule,
To thrust TIBERIUS into tyrannie,
And make him toile, to turne aside those blockes,
Which I alone, could not remoove with safetie. (II. 383-93)

On the other hand, Sejanus' ambition provides Tiberius with an un-scrupulous henchman to cut down those men who have "grown fast/ Honor'd, and lov'd":

> "Tyrannes artes
> "Are to give flatterers, grace; accusers, power;
> "That those may seeme to kill whom they devoure." (I. 70-72)

Thus fear and treachery poison the wellsprings of Roman life. No man is secure against the malice of spies or the coercions of a police state. As Chapman also suggests (in *Chabot*), the claims of absolute authority make all issues political and all dissent treasonous. Silius is accused of disloyalty because he dares to imagine that his patriotic service deserves imperial thanks. History must be revised and authors silenced to maintain the "security" of the state.

Against the grim procession of public crimes, the private drama of tyrant and favorite slowly unfolds, each interview between Sejanus and Tiberius removing another veil of ambiguity and clarifying another aspect of their relationship. In their first meeting Sejanus appears the master. His fustian soliloquy introduces the scene; his politic acumen and decisiveness contrast with the quaking fears which Tiberius admits. It is only on restudy that we realize that the interview is a Socratic dialogue on Machiavellian "necessity" conducted by a fearful Emperor, who shudders at every crime he suggests. Using Sejanus as his damned soul, Tiberius raises pious objections while Sejanus lectures by the Machiavellian card on the ends and means of policy. Tiberius makes no commitment to evil until Sejanus has pledged his villainy; then, feebly suggesting that they consult about the measures to be taken, he leaves the execution of the crimes entirely in Sejanus' hands.

Even as the aristocrats meet to voice their ineffectual sentiments, the net closes upon them. The fruits of policy begin to mature as Silius is trapped by false accusation in the Senate. Again Sejanus dominates the scene, pressing home the attack as both prosecutor and judge. Tiberius, seemingly ignorant of the proceedings, enters after Silius has been charged. He remains silent except to announce his magnanimous decision to adopt Germanicus' sons and to insist that customary legal procedure be followed in Silius' trial, which ensures his judicial murder. As in the deposition scene of *Richard II*, the henchman does the devil's work. The master politician watches silently, interrupting only with gracious gesture of justice or mercy. Bolingbroke orders the mirror and allows Richard to leave—to prison. Tiberius laments the "sad Accident" of Silius' death that "thus hath stall'd and abus'd our mercy."

Blinded by success to the ironies of his relationship with Tiberius, Sejanus pursues his career until the only let between him and imperial power is the Emperor himself. The populace is cowed; the nobility is bought or intimidated. Nothing remains for Sejanus but to ally himself with the royal family before making his final bid for supremacy. The request for Livia's hand is, of course, the fatal act of presumption, the clear warning to Tiberius that his willing cutthroat now aims too high. Tiberius refuses the request with paternal kindness. Warning Sejanus not to arouse envy by overreaching, he promises recognition of his merit at the appropriate moment. Tiberius exits and Sejanus, irritated but not enlightened, soliloquizes on the "dull, heavie CAESAR." Here is the incredible blindness of clear-sighted policy, the fundamental un-realism of Machiavellian realism, which Webster was later to drama-tize so brilliantly. Sejanus has no illusions about the ephemerality of power or the danger of rivalling princes; he knows that the passions and ambitions which he incites for politic purposes will be directed against himself when he nears the pinnacle of success. He assumes, however, that he is so much the master of the political universe that he will repeal its immutable laws of cause and effect.

Sejanus' insensitivity robs his crucial interview with Tiberius of its dramatic potentialities, but the succeeding flurry of scenes releases the suppressed tensions of the meeting. No sooner does Sejanus end his contemptuous reflection on Tiberius than the Emperor appears, his mask of indecision dropped, his mind vigorous and poised; he has already settled Sejanus' fate. The time has come not to reform the Roman polity but to change favorites, to pit the poison of ambition against itself. Summoning Macro, Tiberius assumes again his role of dotard. Again his method is an ambiguous hesitancy:

>   . . . we have thought on thee,
> (Amongst a field of *Romanes*,) worthiest MACRO,
> To be our eye, and eare, to keepe strict watch
> On AGRIPPINA, NERO, DRUSUS, I,
> And on SEIANUS: Not, that we distrust
> his loyaltie . . . (III. 679–84)

The inclusion of Sejanus' name seems almost an afterthought, until we see (with Macro) how Tiberius fastens upon it. True to his nature, Tiberius refuses to commit himself. He orders Macro to spy,

> Informe, and chastise; thinke, and use thy meanes,
> Thy ministers, what, where, on whom thou wilt;
> Explore, plot, practise . . . (III. 702–4)

with impunity. He will take no answer "but in act." Again Tiberius shrewdly chooses his tool. Drunk with the first heady wine of imperial favor, Macro is a "ready engine" to pull down Sejanus. When he learns that Sejanus has regained the Emperor's favor through the accident at Spelunca, Macro's decision is instantaneous. He cannot rise unless Sejanus falls.

While Sejanus and Macro maneuver for position, building and securing alliances, the absent Tiberius commands the political situation in Rome. Having set in motion the forces which will ruin Sejanus, he now psychologically prepares the Roman populace for their role in Sejanus' catastrophe. A series of contradictory letters perplex and divide their loyalties; Sejanus is praised and then censured; his followers rewarded and punished. Swayed by uncertainties, afraid to commit themselves one way or another, the people lose all will to action. Dependent upon imperial caprice, hypnotized by the sinuous weaving of Tiberius' favor, the Roman citizen hungers for a decision —any decision—to be made:

> Would he tell us who he loves, or hates,
> That we might follow, without feare, or doubt. (IV. 424–25)

It is not surprising that the flame of Jonson's dramatic genius burns most brightly in the last act of *Sejanus*. The moralizing choric commentators have served their function and disappear until the final scene; the stage is cleared, as it were, for the fascinating amoral maneuvers that determine political success and failure. The swiftly moving events release for the first time a ripple of comedy in the counterpoised scenes of Sejanus' and Macro's intrigues. The fluid Elizabethan stage becomes the perfect medium for expressing vivid contrasts and ironies of plot and counterplot. If Sejanus' bombast still falls short of the heroic, he reacts swiftly and courageously to the calamity of the statue. Macro's return to Rome, however, shakes his confidence, and the averting of the god's face brings a hysterical defiance. At this anxious moment Macro's announcement of the "tribuniciall dignity" is a shattering psychological coup. The ever-wary Sejanus succumbs completely to relief and lowers all defenses: the sacrificial wolf has been prepared for the slaughter.

Like *Volpone*, *Sejanus* ends with a scene of judgment. The hero-villain is denounced, condemned by the Senate, and executed by the populace whom he oppressed. The perpetrator of inhuman outrages is at last punished in a fearful measure for measure. But "justice" in Sejanus' instance means only that one cutthroat annihilates another while the master criminal goes free. Moreover Sejanus' fall brings no moral resolution. His ruin does not herald the end of political corruption, nor does it positively counterbalance the portrait of decadence developed throughout the play. On the contrary, Sejanus' execution is a final revelation of the hopeless decay of the state. When he walks into Macro's trap, the fawning Senators scramble to flatter him. Spineless, perfectly conditioned sycophants, they sit bewildered by Tiberius' last and most brilliant letter, which (for the audience) recapitulates his Machiavellian use of Sejanus. Under the pretense of considering rumors, which are not to be believed, Tiberius thrusts all guilt for their coöperative villainies on Sejanus, lamenting that Sejanus' "loyal fury" would make Tiberius' intended mercy seem like "wearied cruelty." Hinting the vaguest doubt of Sejanus' innocence, motivated only by concern for the common good, Tiberius orders Sejanus stripped of position and authority, until the Senate can investigate the malicious charges. The Senators turn and twist with every calculated contradiction in the letter. As they waver Macro enters on cue to fire the tinder which Tiberius has prepared. While the ruined Sejanus moans that it has "beene otherwise, betweene you, and I," Macro leads the Senators in the officially sanctioned direction of mob violence. Their passions inflamed, their reasons lost in a hysteria of fear and hatred, they condemn Sejanus without evidence or trial. Then the crowd, following Macro and shouting "Liberty, liberty, liberty," butchers and mutilates Sejanus' body. Piling horror on horror, the "wittily and strangely-cruell" Macro devises the rape and murder of Sejanus' innocent chilren. As the play ends, choric commentators exclaim against the many-headed multitude and the wanton caprice of Fortune. They warn the insolent statist

> Not to grow proud, and carelesse of the gods:
> It is an odious wisedome, to blaspheme,
> Much more to slighten, or denie their powers. (V. 899–901)

This pious moralizing, like the tags which punctuate the close of Webster's tragedies, is not without point; still we know that Sejanus' catastrophe was neither a turning of Fortune's wheel nor an act of divine retribution. Behind the insensate fury of the mob lay the calculating ambition of Macro; behind Macro's witty cruelty, the genius of Tiberius, the secular god in the empire of Rome who rigs Fortune's wheel and punishes overreaching ambition when it threatens his own security. The spasm of brute passion purges nothing except the pent-up anger of the populace, who, in high Roman fashion, have been given a spectacle and a scapegoat, and who have been made partners in crime with their oppressors.[8] At the end of *Sejanus* the players change but the political drama remains the same. As one favorite falls, another rises who bids fair to become "a greater prodigie in *Rome*, then he/That now is falne." The Senators compete in their flattery of the "Newest Man." The absent Tiberius wallows in his unnatural lusts and the present crisis forebodes an even more terrifying issue because the "hope" of Rome lies in the sons of Germanicus, whom Tiberius has adopted: Nero and Caligula.

Only if Jonson had been willing to sacrifice historical fact for didactic purpose could he have contrived a naïvely moralistic drama out of his chosen materials. And yet a deeply moral interpretation of the relationship between Sejanus and Tiberius was possible without falsifying history. For Tacitus describes Tiberius as a tormented, superstitious criminal, who lashed out at Sejanus in a frenzy of terror.[9] Jonson's Tiberius is no less complex, but his "anxieties" are calculated poses of a masterful politician; his "ayenbite of inwit" is only one of many superb Machiavellian hypocrisies.

If, as has been suggested,[10] Jonson sought to portray in *Sejanus* the tragedy of civic decadence, then he could have given that tragedy a personal poignancy by depicting the fall of a Silius rather than a Sejanus. If he sought to portray the tragedy of overreaching ambition, then he should have allowed Sejanus some of Volpone's grandeur and accepted Tacitus' characterization of Tiberius. As it is, the play is neither a tragedy of civic decadence nor one of insatiable ambition. We are not allowed to pity and we are not moved to fear. Because Jonson does not clarify his tragic theme, the smoldering intensity of emotion that lies beneath the surface of *Sejanus* never bursts into flame.

Catiline his Conspiracy (1611)

The Jacobean public, which did not especially admire *Sejanus*, had even less stomach for Jonson's second essay in tragedy when it appeared eight years later. Whether this surprised Jonson we do not know, but his venomous address to the "Reader in Ordinarie" indicates that despite his contempt for the mob he was not willing to accept its displeasure. Obviously he made no attempt to woo the groundlings in *Catiline*. Its style is more rhetorical and sententious than that of *Sejanus*; it has an even greater proportion of oratory to dramatic action and an even more deliberate dedication to a "classical" mode. Thus it is easier to admire Jonson's convictions than to read his play. He had the courage to be deliberately and terribly wrong, which by artistic canons is not a redeeming virtue.

Had he been content merely to force the gruesome story of Catiline's conspiracy into a five-act structure adorned with ghosts and choruses his play might have rivalled the most lurid contemporary melodrama, for Catiline was born to play the lead in a Jacobean revenge tragedy. According to Sallust he was guilty of almost incredible crimes of sensuality and violence; he was infatuated with murder and revenge as well as with power. He plotted with a desperate band of malcontents a Wagnerian immolation of Rome, on whose ruins he planned to build a personal empire. Here was a subject that could have made *Volpone* seem like a Sunday-school pageant, but significantly Jonson could not rise (or descend) to it. Although his conspirators seal their pact with a draught of human blood, they lack the first fine careless rapacity of the Jew of Malta. Their hunger for destruction produces only a stale hyperbole; their very inhumanity is dull. And their braggadocio merely accentuates their hollowness of spirit that in crisis borders on sheer cowardice. We cannot thrill to conspirators plotting the ruin of their city who crumble at the first opposition. The would-be assassins run when Cicero names them. Catiline is ruined, as Caesar shrewdly observes, by words alone, by his inability to outbrave Cicero's eloquent accusations.

If all the characterizations in *Catiline* were as crudely melodramatic, the inadequacies of the conspirators would be less noticeable. But unfortunately Catiline and his fellow cutthroats inhabit a bizarre Senecan demimonde in a larger, more realistically conceived Roman society. Their crude psychologies jar against the more sophisticated portraits of Cicero and Cato, even as their theatrical Machiavellianism clashes with the more astute policy of Caesar and Crassus. Whereas the contrast of Machiavel and pseudo-Machiavel in *Sejanus* serves to define the relationship between Sejanus and Tiberius, the disparate modes of characterization in *Catiline* actually threaten the unity of the play. It is as if by some strange mishap the villains of *The Revenger's Tragedy* had stumbled into a performance of *Chabot*.

The diversity of characters and of threads of plot in *Catiline* creates the impression that Jonson faced an overwhelming task in shaping diffuse historical materials into a unified fable. It is disillusioning to discover, therefore, that just the opposite was true—that Jonson's tragedy blurs Sallust's lucid, coherent narration and interpretation of Catiline's career. To Sallust the conspiracy is a symptom of the inner rot which afflicted an overprosperous Republic. He explains Catiline's hunger for power and wealth as an extreme criminal manifestation of the vicious appetites nurtured by luxury. He makes it clear that many of the noblest sons of Rome rallied to Catiline's cause. Jonson also attempts to identify the conspiracy with civic decadence.

Cicero and the Choruses recite the Polybian theory of cyclical decay; they lament the extravagance and sloth that are sapping the once virile Roman spirit. Nevertheless Jonson's conspirators seem more like the spawn of *The Spanish Tragedy* than Roman decadents. Their thirst for destruction is purely instinctive; they are not so much fallen aristocrats as psychological and moral aberrations.

Jonson, it would seem, was willing to moralize about Roman decadence but not to drive the moral home by uniting choric commentary, characterization, and dramatic action. He allows Catiline to dominate only the first half of the tragedy; thereafter Catiline plays an increasingly minor role until he finally disappears in the fourth act. Only the first half of *Catiline* dramatizes the inner rot of conspiracy; the second half portrays the patriotic struggle to preserve the state and introduces a second hero, the noble Consul Cicero. Possessing two heroes in one play, Jonson is content to drop Catiline before the last act, especially since unity of place demands that the dramatic action remain in Rome after Catiline has fled. With the experience of *Sejanus* behind him, Jonson now seems intent upon emphasizing a moral resolution which history provides; he has found in Cicero a political hero worthy of admiration and he makes much of him.

In casting Cicero as the protagonist of the latter half of *Catiline*, Jonson dramatizes an essentially Chapmanesque conflict between Stoic hero and corrupt society. Indeed, Cicero is in many respects a near relative of Clermont, Chabot, and Pompey. From his earliest appearance he is wrapped in the spiritual loneliness that haunts Chapman's heroes. He has, like Chabot, risen to high position through merit alone, but that very fact isolates him from the aristocracy, to which Catiline, Caesar, and Crassus belong. Cicero, not Catiline, is the upstart. His own brother lacks faith in him and suspects that he is exaggerating the danger of the conspiracy. Only a few men about him understand the mortal danger that faces Rome; the city as a whole is indifferent to the infection that is raging within it.

In Chapman's drama, moral victory does not depend upon public success; it resides in a private philosophical triumph over the temptations and adversities of a disordered world. In Jonson's tragedies, however, the moral issues are public and the moral resolution must also be public. Evil must be defeated upon the stage as well as in the mind. We

can therefore understand why Jonson chose to divide his play between two protagonists and why he amplified the role of Cicero, who
is a minor figure in Sallust. But it is hard to see why he sacrificed dramatic unity to achieve a moral resolution that is at best tentative if not
completely illusory. In an excellent study of Jonson, J. A. Bryant, Jr.
describes *Catiline* as the tragedy of a state that is "spiritually
doomed."[11] Its action, he remarks, "is roughly analogous to a sick
man's detection and treatment of an annoying symptom while the
fatal cancer eats patiently away at a vital organ" (p. 272). Cicero,
"naïvely comforted at the destruction of Catiline" palliates the disease
but does not cure it, for though the immediate threat to the Republic
is annihilated, Caesar and Crassus, the guiding spirits of the conspiracy,
are free to continue their subversion of the state (pp. 269–72).

Although I agree in the main with Professor Bryant's interpretation of *Catiline* I see no evidence of naïveté in Cicero's handling of the
conspiracy. On the contrary, the deepest irony in the play is the total
lack of naïveté in Cicero's motives and in his acceptance of a partial
victory over the forces that threaten Rome. A political realist,
he willingly accepts the disparity between moral ends and political
means—between his high ideals and the ambitions of those who help
him to destroy the conspiracy. Cicero does not shatter Catiline by
eloquence alone; he uses spies and informers, bribes and threats; he
appeals to greed as well as to altruism. How strange in fact is the con-
federacy of motives that defeats Catiline: Cicero's and Cato's selfless
patriotism, Fulvia's vanity, ambition, and envy of Sempronia, Curius'
prodigality, lust, and unscrupulousness. The scene in which Cicero
convinces Curius to turn his coat a second time is a quaint emblem of
a society in which the expedient sham of patriotism must be accepted
at face value. Fulvia urges Curius to take the safer way to advancement by becoming Cicero's spy. Cicero outlines "what thanks, what
titles, what reward" will be heaped on the true patriot. While Cicero
follows virtue for its own reward, he unhesitatingly buys the "loyalty"
of Fulvia, Curius, and the wavering Antonius, who receives Cicero's
province. Shrewd, disillusioned, and disingenuous, he "anticipates"
Machiavelli in his basic premise:

> 'Tis well, if some men will doe well, for price:
> So few are vertuous, when the reward's away. (III. 479–80)

It is not naïveté that keeps Cicero from accusing Caesar and Crassus, even though they are obviously part of the conspiracy and potentially more dangerous than Catiline. When Cato suggests that Crassus and Caesar would ring hollow if tested, Cicero agrees but adds "if that we durst prove 'hem." Although he suspects Caesar, Cicero would not have the Senate at this perilous time dare

> an unprofitable, dangerous act,
> To stirre too many serpents up at once.
> CAESAR, and CRASSUS, if they be ill men,
> Are mightie ones; and, we must so provide,
> That, while we take one head, from this foule *Hydra*,
> There spring not twentie more.
> . . . .
> They shall be watch'd, and look'd too. Till they doe
> Declare themselves, I will not put 'hem out
> By any question. There they stand. Ile make
> My selfe no enemies, nor the state no traytors. (IV.528–37)

We cannot tax Cicero's policy and call it cowardice. He agrees with Machiavelli that it is wiser to temporize with evil ambitions, "instead of violently attacking them; for by temporizing with them they will either die out of themselves, or at least their worst results will be long deferred. And princes or magistrates who wish to destroy such evils must watch all points, and must be careful in attacking them not to increase instead of diminishing them, for they must not believe that a fire can be extinguished by blowing upon it. They should carefully examine the extent and force of the evil, and if they think themselves sufficiently strong to combat it, then they should attack it regardless of consequences; otherwise they should let it be, and in no wise attempt it."[12]

Cicero would not aggravate the present danger to the state by forcing Caesar and Crassus into open rebellion. He prefers the mockery of allowing them to debate with the Senate the most judicious way of punishing traitors. When the full scope of the conspiracy is bared, however, he is confronted with actual evidence of Caesar's complicity. The serpents have already stirred, they are coiled to strike; the question now is whether to attack them or to turn one's back upon them for the moment. Turning his back, Cicero buys time for Rome by suppressing the evidence of Caesar's guilt. He prevents the incriminating letters to Caesar from being read before the Senate. He dismisses (to prison) as a "lying varlet" the messenger who implicates Crassus. Praising the enemies of Rome, he refuses to believe the accusations of his own trusted spy, the twice-turned Curius. Such "prudence" is not wholly voluntary; it is enforced by Caesar's shrewd criticism of Cicero's use of spies and informers. When Curius' "libell" against him is announced, Caesar responds:

> It shall not [trouble me], if that he have no reward.
> But if he have, sure I shall thinke my selfe
> Very untimely, and unsafely honest,
> Where such, as he is, may have pay t'accuse me. (V.361–64)

Under the surface mockery of this speech lies a deeper irony: the very methods Cicero employs to purge the state limit the scope of his action. His Machiavellian means of intelligencing and bribery qualify his moral ends; and, as in *Byron's Tragedy*, the preservation of the state against unlawful conspiracy is tainted by moral compromise.

If we assume that Jonson's controlling purpose in tragedy was a scrupulously faithful reproduction of history, then it is difficult, if not impossible, to account for his Machiavellian portrait of Caesar. Sallust's attitude towards Caesar is completely favorable. He brands the charges of Caesar's complicity in the conspiracy as false and views Caesar and Cato as pillars of the tottering state.[13] Even Plutarch, who condemns Caesar's political ambitions and methods, acknowledges that his part in the conspiracy was only rumored.[14] Thus we face the curious fact that Jonson undercuts the moral resolution of his tragedy, not through a stern dedication to historical truth, but through a deliberate revision of his sources. Like Sejanus, Catiline gloats over his mastery of the political situation, even though he is another politician's tool. It is Caesar who delivers the brilliant Machiavellian oration on the techniques of conspiracy. And after Catiline is denounced, it is Caesar who brazens out his Iago-like claim to honesty, keeping himself free for the future thrust towards empire which was to destroy the republic which Cicero temporarily shored. Again we are left with the impression that Jonson chose the wrong protagonist. Depicting Caesar as the intellectual leader of the conspiracy, he takes as his ostensible hero

Caesar's dupe. Again we watch the "tragedy" of a Roman Buckingham while the Roman Richard lurks in the background.

To point out Jonson's crucial alterations of his sources is not to ridicule his claim to "truth of Argument." No other contemporary sought or achieved so authentic a reproduction in art of the classical world. And when Jonson departed from his sources he sacrificed a recorded fact or opinion in order to clarify what seemed to him a larger truth of political history. He sacrificed the opportunity to impose naïve moralistic interpretations on his subject matter in order to convey, implicitly at least, the fundamental amorality of political conflict, in which success is not to the virtuous but to the cunning and the strong. The weaker politician goes to the wall; the Sejanuses and Catilines fail but the Tiberiuses and Caesars achieve, if only temporarily, political mastery.

I do not mean to offer too simple an explanation of the unique qualities and failings of Jonson's tragedies. No theory of moral vision will account for the frequent shallowness of his characterizations, for the staggering burden of his rhetoric, for the narrowness of his sympathies, and for the sheer monotony of his portrayal of evil. Nevertheless it does seem to me that there is a void of ethical meaning at the heart of Jonson's tragedies which the great bulk of moralizing commentary only emphasizes. The body politic is stretched out upon Jonson's dissecting table; an expert scalpel lays bare the inner rot and metastasized corruption. But the lesson in anatomy offers in the end only a Machiavellian understanding of who's in and who's out. The light of the spirit gleams fitfully in *Sejanus* and *Catiline* and is gone. Cicero, who was to the Renaissance the noblest and most eloquent moral instructor of antiquity, must descend into the market place of political loyalty to chaffer for the security of Rome.

Even had they been more successful on the stage, it is doubtful that Jonson's tragedies would have inspired imitation. Political tragedy as a form distinct from the conventional history play or tragedy required an intellectual motive and insight that was rare in the drama of the period. Only Marlowe and Shakespeare among the Elizabethan playwrights had the genius to explore the hidden realities of political conflict. Lesser talents were content to exploit patriotic themes, spectacle, and the grandeur or romantic adventure of popular history. It is quite possible, as we shall see, that the ironic technique of *Volpone* left its impress on Tourneur's imagination and that Jonson's comic vision of respectability was an indirect influence on *Women Beware Women*. But because interest in historical drama waned rapidly in the Jacobean theaters, Jonson's Roman plays could have had little effect on the further development of tragedy. It is curious that the one great tragedian who admired Jonson enough to borrow some of the lines and dramatic situations of *Sejanus* is, by all appearances, the least likely son of Ben—John Webster. Yet the romanticism of *The White Devil* and the classicism of *Sejanus* have, as we shall see, certain common grounds, and there is good reason to believe that Jonson's tragedies provided some of the inspiration for *Appius and Virginia*.

Of course Jonson's closest affinities in tragedy were with Chapman, whose artistic journey led to a more positive conclusion than *Catiline*. Indeed, had Jonson been more like Chapman he might have felt the need to write yet a third Roman tragedy in which the jarring tensions of *Sejanus* and *Catiline* are harmoniously resolved. But he was not driven to "reconstruct philosophy" in art, partly because he did not see his tragic theme steadily, and partly because, like the Cicero he admiringly characterizes, he could accept the eternal divorce of moral ideals and political realities. His disillusioned awareness of the many stages on which the Machiavellian drama has unfolded attenuates rather than deepens his sense of outrage. His "detachment" is not that of a playwright dramatizing remote political issues but that of a Jacobean intellectual who perceives, almost against his will, that contemporary attacks on policy are protests against history itself.

CHAPTER IV

Cyril Tourneur

STUDIED individually *The Revenger's Tragedy* and *The Atheist's Tragedy* seem curious monuments to the diversity of
Jacobean tastes. Studied together as works attributed in the seventeenth century to a single author, they pose a unique critical problem
because they seem to express totally opposite moral viewpoints and
artistic talents. The problem vanishes, of course, if we agree with
eminent scholars that *The Revenger's Tragedy* was written by Middleton. But this solution leads in turn to an equally vexing question of
interpretation, for *The Revenger's Tragedy* is, I think, more alien in
spirit to Middleton's art than to Tourneur's. It is difficult, in fact, to
believe that the poised, detached observer of life who gave us Middleton's comedies and tragedies could ever have felt the moralistic passion
that informs Vindice's lines.

My reasons for assigning *The Revenger's Tragedy* to Tourneur
are set forth in the present chapter and, to some extent, in my later
discussion of Middleton. Compared to the precise scholarship of those
who argue for Middleton they may seem unscientific; but I do not
expect here to settle a controversy that hangs in such even balance as

to permit only personal conclusions. If the stylistic evidence in favor of Middleton is impressive, so too is the stylistic and bibliographical evidence supporting the traditional attribution to Tourneur. Moreover while the parallels of expression in *The Revenger's Tragedy* and Middleton's plays may suggest influence or imitation, they do not establish a single authorship.[1]

Approaching the question from another direction, I would suggest that the artistic relationship between *The Revenger's Tragedy* and *The Atheist's Tragedy* has not been adequately explored because the latter play has not received the close, careful critical attention lavished on the former. When we study in detail the polemical intention and achievement of *The Atheist's Tragedy*, however, we find strong evidence that it is a product of the same mind and talent which created *The Revenger's Tragedy*. Indeed, as we shall see, Tourneur's success as a melodramatist is the chief clue to his failure as a didacticist.

Although a just appreciation of Tourneur's artistry has replaced the nineteenth-century celebration of him as a master of satanic revels, recent critical attention has centered more upon explaining the mind that created *The Revenger's Tragedy* than upon analyzing the play as dramatic literature. But the purists need not complain; for after paying homage to Tourneur's poetic and dramatic powers, critics must inevitably attempt to relate his vision of licentiousness and depravity to some realm of normal experience. Not surprisingly Tourneur has divided the critics as well as the bibliographers. Miss Ellis-Fermor and Harold Jenkins speak of Tourneur's instinctive awareness of universal evil.[2] John Peter and Samuel Schoenbaum place Tourneur in the tradition of the medieval moralists.[3] Michael Higgins finds in Tourneur a Calvinistic revulsion against man's depravity.[4] And lurking behind most recent discussions of *The Revenger's Tragedy* is Mr. Eliot's influential opinion that the play expresses an adolescent hatred of life.[5] Such diversity of opinion suggests that before we can celebrate the wedding of moral vision and artistic form in Tourneur's drama we must first carefully distinguish between the two.

Unlike Chapman and Jonson, Tourneur is completely at ease with the techniques of popular melodrama and totally uninterested in political themes and problems. *The Revenger's Tragedy* lacks even the shadowy political background which provides a framework of great events for the sensationalism of *The Spanish Tragedy* and *The Jew of Malta*. Like Chapman's heroes and like Jonson's Cicero, Vindice is pitted against a decadent society, but one that is corrupted by sensual appetites, not by political opportunism or tyranny; its villains are, for the most part, ambitious only in their lusts. Like Bussy, Vindice is a malcontent, isolated from society, who faces the problem of virtuous action in an evil milieu and who finds that he must flank policy with policy to gain revenge. In *The Revenger's Tragedy*, however, there is no disjunction of moral argument and revenge fable, for Tourneur's ethical vision is perfectly imaged in the dramatic action; his moral argument and his plot are one.

Inspired by the literary and scholarly idealism of Renaissance humanism, Chapman and Jonson find their tragic fables in the pages of history. Untouched by their classicism, Tourneur finds the materials of tragedy in the popular myth of Italianate evil, which had already become a common property of the stage. It is a tribute to Tourneur's powers that with all our knowledge of dramatic convention we still feel that *The Revenger's Tragedy* expresses an intensely personal view of reality, though we know its setting is the Italy of the *novella* and of Elizabethan Protestant imaginations, the Italy described so vividly by Ascham and others as a sink of atheism, luxury, and sensual abandonment. In other Jacobean tragedies, Italianate settings are used more or less as backdrops for such glorious villains as Brachiano or Ferdinand. Tourneur's characters, however, do not transcend the Italianate; they epitomize it. His imagination triumphs over nature and reality by distilling the essence of Italianate horror, by pre-empting and refining a conventional image of sensuality and violence.

At the same time that Tourneur's genius presents the Italianate image in all its lurid perfection, his artistic discipline (a rare attribute in Jacobean dramaturgy) makes it difficult to penetrate beyond the image to the mind that created it. Other Jacobean playwrights universalize the action of their dramas by philosophical reflection. Tourneur admits none in *The Revenger's Tragedy* unless we call Vindice's choric commentaries "philosophical." Other dramatists use traditional parallels and correspondences to enlarge their dramatic scene; their characters, vehicles for philosophical and moral attitudes, are archetypal Stoics or politicians. Tourneur's allegorical method of characterization paradoxically denies universal importance to such automata of evil as the Duke and Lussurioso, for though they personify particular vices they are no more than samplings of a depraved world. They cannot vary or develop; they cannot step momentarily out of character to comment on their world because their existence in the reader's imagination depends upon the consistent pulse of the vicious passion which they embody.

Actually Tourneur suggests the existence of his dramatic universe not by philosophical expansion of his immediate scene, but by the use of perspective. He draws a group of characters who are, depending upon their prominence in the play, "large" or "small," distinct or vague. In the foreground are Lussurioso, the Duke, and Vindice; slightly "behind" them are the Duchess, Spurio, and Hippolito. Further in the background, and therefore smaller and less distinct in outline, are Ambitioso and Supervacuo. Almost fading into the background itself is Junior, the "yongest sonne," and behind him are all the shadowy figures of the court. But there is no essential difference between the Duke, "the yongest sonne," and any of the lesser courtiers, except that the Duke's villainy is writ large, while the courtiers' lusts and assignations are only vaguely sketched. Tourneur cannot convince us that his tragic universe holds a mirror up to nature, but he skillfully creates an illusion of depth in his two-dimensional scene by suggesting that the Duke's court extends and merges imperceptibly with a larger world which, if brought into the foreground, would be no different from the group of sensualists which Tourneur examines in detail.

Even as Tourneur isolates his Italianate scene from contact with normal experience he places upon it the stamp of his unique temperament. The ruling passions of his characters swell not from within, but from one central, inexhaustible reservoir of emotion that animates virtuous and vicious alike and that gives the play its superb unity of tone. Cynicism, outrage, loathing, and horror are fused in *The Revenger's Tragedy* by Tourneur's morbid fascination with the erotic. To the mind that created Vindice's world, the sexual is as intriguing and repelling as a hideous disease. The most characteristic and memorable lines in the play are concerned with some facet of illicit sexual desire or bawdry. There are of course other vices in Vindice's society, but they are ancillary; the lust for murder is almost always a desire to avenge some rape, adultery, or incest. Like the medieval satirist, Vindice castigates the frailty and concupiscence of women, but unlike the medieval satirist, he is amused by their sly tricks. Knowing their coy whoredoms, he trusts no woman's virtue, not even his mother's or sister's. His erotic imagination transfigures even his dead mistress' skull as he recalls when

> 'twas a face
> So farre beyond the artificiall shine
> Of any womans bought complexion
> That the uprightest man, (if such there be,
> That sinne but seaven times a day) broke custome
> And made up eight with looking after her.[6] (I. i. 23–28)

Similarly Vindice cannot think of night without imagining strange and fulsome lusts:

> Night! thou that lookst like funerall Heraulds fees
> Torne downe betimes ith morning, thou hangst fittly
> To Grace those sins that have no grace at all.
> Now tis full sea a bed over the world;
> Theres iugling of all sides; some that were Maides
> E'en at Sun set are now perhaps ith Toale-booke;
> This woman in immodest thin apparell
> Lets in her friend by water, here a Dame
> Cunning, nayles lether-hindges to a dore,
> To avoide proclamation.
> Now Cuckolds are a quoyning apace, apace, apace, apace.
> And carefull sisters spinne that thread ith night,
> That does maintaine them and their bawdes ith daie! (II. ii. 149–61)

This is far removed from Elizabethan paganism. Vindice's thoughts do not hover on feminine beauty or on the physical pleasures of sex. He is aroused and revolted not by what is seen, but by what is imagined—by the huggermugger, the backstairs work, the juggling behind the arras, and the stealing away by torchlight. He is fascinated with stealth rather than with sex. He is the Peeping Tom turned moralist and moralizing with the fevered sexual images dwelt upon by the impotent or the frustrate.

If the eroticism of *The Revenger's Tragedy* were confined to

Vindice's speeches, we might credit Tourneur with a penetrating study of psychological abnormality. But actually the erotic is woven into the total fabric of the play, present as it is in every act and in almost every scene. Indeed, we find in both of Tourneur's tragedies a consistent association of the sexual and the macabre, a lingering over "fulsome lusts" and assignations in graveyards and with skulls. We cannot, however, view the hectic sexuality of *The Revenger's Tragedy* as an unconscious Freudian revelation when in fact it is a superbly fashioned poetic and dramatic motif. Despite the intense feeling that animates Tourneur's lines, his ironic intellect is always in control. We would never, for example, mistake Vindice's attacks on luxury and sensuality for the spontaneous overflow of powerful moral feelings. Addressing the skull of Gloriana he says:

> . . . here's an eye,
> Able to tempt a greatman—to serve God,
> A prety hanging lip, that has forgot now to dissemble;
> Me thinkes this mouth should make a swearer tremble,
> A drunckard claspe his teeth and not undo e'm,
> To suffer wet damnation to run through e'm.
> Heres a cheeke keepes her colour; let the winde go whistle,
> Spout Raine, we feare thee not, be hot or cold
> Alls one with us; and is not he absurd,
> Whose fortunes are upon their faces set,
> That feare no other God but winde and wet? (III. v. 57–67)

Vindice's sermon is brittle and premeditated; each word and image falls perfectly into place. Some kind of moral frenzy is implicit, but it is a frenzy that has been transmuted into detached bitterness. Some shock of intense disillusion and horror has given way to the cynicism that turns all of life into a sardonic joke. It is not the vanity of evil alone that amuses Vindice; it is the utter futility of a life in which there are only three kinds of human beings: the completely abandoned, the hypocritical, and the rare, impecunious, malcontented good.

That Vindice serves as Tourneur's moral chorus we cannot doubt, but he is more importantly a character in the play, one whose moral perceptions are slightly distorted at the beginning and, in the end, perverse. It is fittingly ironic that Vindice, the cynic, should uphold morality in his world, and that it should be the task of one who is contemptuous of all feminine modesty to protect virginity and to avenge murdered innocence. Vindice loathes vice, yet he has no faith in virtue. He makes a jest of religion as of everything else. "Save *Grace* the bawde," he remarks, "I seldome heare *Grace* nam'd!" And when Gratiana insists that all the riches in the world could not make her an unnatural bawd, he answers:

> No, but a thousand Angells can;
> Men have no power, Angells must worke you too't,
> The world descends into such base-borne evills
> That forty Angells can make fourescore divills. (II. i. 98–101)

Vindice wittily imbues a conventional Elizabethan pun with new meaning. These are the angels whose potency he does not doubt. When he speaks later of the heavenly angels and their "Christall plaudities," he is much less convincing. His opposition to evil, though violent, lacks philosophical conviction and an ultimate moral goal. Although he uses the phraseology of religion and moral philosophy, and although he complains that evil is unnatural, his cynicism springs from an awareness that his world has irrevocably departed from its natural course.

Within his society Vindice represents the only possible moral order, one that is warped in nature and eminently corruptible because it has no higher purpose than the accomplishment of revenge. Vindice sees himself as the instrument of divine justice, which he interprets as a *lex talionis* that gruesomely requites villainy with villainy. When the tortured Duke screams, "Is there a hell besides this, villaines?" Vindice answers:

> Villaine?
> Nay heaven is iust, scornes are the hires of scornes,
> I nere knew yet Adulterer with-out hornes. (III. v. 197–99)

To be sure, the Vindice who says this is not the Vindice who originally set out to revenge his murdered love. Although he can save his mother and sister from shame, he cannot save himself from his own cynicism. After murdering the Duke, he can watch with satisfaction an innocent man condemned for telling the truth, because such travesty of justice vindicates his own "moral" viewpoint. By the end of the play, little semblance of Vindice's moral purpose remains; he and Hippolito are hardly distinguishable from the men they slaughter. Murder piles on murder, revenge upon revenge, as hate, lust, and ambition set lechers, adulterers, and assassins at each others' throats. When the carnage ends, Vindice and Hippolito are sent off to execution, not because the moral order is restored or because the goddess Astraea returns to earth, but only because Antonio is a politic ruler who fears that those who killed the old Duke may also kill him. The royal lechers have paid for their crimes, but we do not feel that their blood has cleansed the Augean filth of the court.

To all appearances, then, the ending of *The Revenger's Tragedy* is quite amoral. In the last judgment, life and death—all's one. Two self-satisfied murderers unexpectedly "go to it" because of a final ironic twist of fate. Evil (or at least some evil) is purged adventitiously but in the process the once virtuous agents of retribution are corrupted. The fact that the stage is littered with corpses does not convince us of the existence of some higher moral order, for in Vindice's society the good die as horribly as the evil, and the triumph of justice requires something more than balanced double entries in the ledger of Death. We must have a deeper understanding of the "why" of Vindice's fall —we must recognize some pattern of ethical causality in the loathsome incidents of the plot—if we are to believe that *The Revenger's Tragedy* draws to a moral conclusion. Such a pattern of causality does emerge; in fact it grows more distinct with every step of Vindice's descent into criminality, until at last we see that far from exploiting irony for irony's sake, *The Revenger's Tragedy* is cast in an ethical design as sophisticated and intellectual as that of Jonson's greatest comedies.

The apparent imitations of *Volpone* in *The Atheist's Tragedy* support my belief that *The Revenger's Tragedy* was also influenced by Jonson's play. The same dark, cynical, satiric spirit broods over *Volpone* and *The Revenger's Tragedy*. Both plays center on the conflict between a pair of cunning, knavish minds. They have similar allegorical characters, ironic reversals, and uses of disguises and deceptions. Like Volpone's, Vindice's disguises reveal more of the inner man than they hide, since a mastery of deception requires some natural affinity for the assumed role.[7] "*I have* considered," Jonson writes in *Discoveries*, "our whole life is like a *Play:* wherein every man, forgetfull of himselfe, is in travaile with expression of another. Nay, wee so insist in imitating others, as wee cannot (when it is necessary) returne to our selves. . . ."[8] Here in sober commonplace is the moral "lesson" of *Volpone* and *The Revenger's Tragedy*.

Throughout Tourneur's play a malicious Fate seems to thwart the best laid plans of sensualist and revenger alike. But on no other character does irony weigh more heavily than on Vindice. Seeking only to revenge himself upon the Duke, he is hired first to procure his sister for Lussurioso. Then he is engaged to pander for the Duke, and lastly he is employed by Lussurioso to murder Piato, i.e., to kill himself. In his most trying moments, however, Vindice appreciates the comedy of his situation, for it is the kind his intellect can savor. Above all he enjoys his superior knowledge and position in the deadly game of pretending that he must play. He can always see through Lussurioso's pretenses, but his own disguises are impenetrable. He always knows Lussurioso's masked motives, but his own are inscrutable. Thus his outbursts against Lussurioso are tempered by an unholy enjoyment of the battle in which he is (or so he believes) always master.

In Vindice's society seclusion and retreat are the only ways to preserve one's integrity against the degrading temptations or coercions of the court. Seclusion, however, breeds its own spiritual ills—among them "discontent," the nobleman's consumption. Vindice's opening soliloquy reveals that bitterness and cynicism have already eroded his moral beliefs. He has already seen too much of the world—his own beloved murdered, virgins surrendered, families destroyed, all that men prize bought and sold like so much merchandise. Obsessed with vengeance, he broods in isolation and castigates the court from a distance until Hippolito brings word that Lussurioso has asked him

> To seeke some strange digested fellow forth:
> Of ill-contented nature, either disgracst
> In former times, or by new groomes displacst,
> Since his Step-mothers nuptialls, such a bloud
> A man that were for evill onely good;
> To give you the true word some base coynd Pander. (I. i. 84–89)

Here is an irresistible temptation to assume, for a little while, the way of the world in order to obtain revenge. Seizing the opportunity Vindice decides to disguise his true self in a mask of evil; he will "put on that knave for once" and be "a man a'th Time." Adopting his temporary role Vindice jestingly asks Hippolito, "Am I farre inough from my selfe?" and he calls upon Impudence,

> Thou Goddesse of the pallace, Mistris of Mistresses
> To whom the costly-perfumd people pray,
> Strike thou my fore-head into dauntless Marble;
> Mine eyes to steady Saphires: . . . (I. iii. 6–9)

Perfect in his disguise Vindice plays the villain so brilliantly that it would almost seem he has a natural talent for it. He is shocked to learn, however, that he must launch his new career by procuring his own sister for Lussurioso. He complains to Hippolito that they are made "strange fellowes," "innocent villaines." And yet the idea of testing his sister's and mother's virtue is not wholly repellent to his distrusting nature. Again he plays the role of scoundrel so well that he converts his mother, Gratiana, into an unnatural bawd. Later defending herself, Gratiana claims that only the disguised Vindice could have suborned her. And it is hard to disagree, for there was no one better fitted to play the pander.

With Vindice's success as a pander, the richer irony of his disguises begins to unfold. When we witness his fiendish murder of the Duke, we realize that this "innocent villain" has put on the knave not for once but for all time. He has indeed gone far from himself, and yet he must go even farther. After the Duke's murder the game of seeming becomes so hectic that Vindice is forced to assume disguise upon disguise, until he literally forgets himself. Hippolito sees more clearly what is happening, and when Lussurioso hires Vindice to kill Piato (Vindice's "former self"), he cries out, "Brother we loose our selves." But Vindice brushes aside this fear, for he now sees the opportunity for perfect vengeance, and he finds the humor of the situation irresistible:

> Thats a good lay, for I must kill my selfe.
> Brother thats I [the Duke's body]: that sits for me: do you marke it,
> And I must stand ready here to make away my selfe yonder—I must
> sit to bee kild, and stand to kill my selfe, I could varry it not so little
> as thrice over agen, tas some eight returnes like Michelmas Tearme.
> (V. i. 3–7)

Vindice does not yet know that he is the butt of his own joke. When Lussurioso curses over his father's body, Vindice exults in his continued triumph, in his knowledge that with the game nearly over, Lussurioso has "lost." He does not see that Lussurioso has in his own way triumphed as well. Lussurioso sought to hire a villain and he succeeded. He sought to hire a cunning pander and he succeeded in that too. Finally he hired Vindice to kill himself and Vindice does so, because he comes to love the game of evil for its own sake and to relish the murder rather than its "moral" purpose. By the end of the play he has learned so well the roles that Lussurioso hired him to play that his "outward shape, and inward heart/ Are cut out of one piece." And it is altogether fitting that Vindice, who hated the revels of the court, becomes in the end one of the court masquers. This is his last disguise, and he goes to his death precisely because of the courtly impudence which he once mockingly assumed. He exits annoyed but unpenitent, chiding Hippolito:

> May we not set as well as the Dukes sonne?
> Thou hast no conscience, are we not revengde?
> Is there one enemy left alive amongst those?
> Tis time to die, when we are our selves our foes. V. iii. 151–54)

Since he is a man who is "for evill onely good," Vindice does not know how meaningful these last words are. But before he leaves the stage, he seems to glimpse the design of past events and to penetrate for the first time beyond the immediate irony of the situation:

> This murder might have slept in tonglesse brasse,
> But for our selves, and the world dyed an asse;
> Now I remember too, here was *Piato*
> Brought forth a knavish sentance once—no doubt (said he) but time
> Will make the murderer bring forth himselfe.
> Tis well he died, he was a witch.
> And now my Lord, since we are in for ever:
> This worke was ours which else might have beene slipt.
>
> (V. iii. 157–64)

Vindice has not lost his sense of humor. Knowing that it is he rather than the world that dies an ass, he joins in the off-stage laughter that has greeted every successive act of his "flawless" knavery.

Like Jonson, Tourneur depicts a world of rogues and scoundrels in which there is no true regard for moral principles. Yet governing this world is a moral order, detached and ironic, which operates through the inevitable processes of human psychology. In *Volpone* the operation of the moral order produces comedy—the comedy of futility, of the Seven Deadly Sins—which establishes, if only by inference, that God's in his heaven though all's not right with the world. No laughter, however, can purify Vindice's deeds. The moral order governing his universe is like Tourneur himself: unerring in its craftmanship, disillusioned in its view of life, but orthodox in its values. It is in keeping with the "comic spirit" of the play that Vindice's one moment of redeeming joy produces the cruelest jest of all. Upon reforming his fallen mother, he allows himself a stolen interlude of happiness, only to be reminded by Hippolito that he forgets his task of revenge. Vindice answers:

> . . . ioye's a subtill elfe,
> I think man's happiest, when he forgets himselfe. (IV. iv. 92–93)

We do not have to resort to psychoanalytical conjectures to understand how a mind capable of this moral subtlety could have spent such artistic care on, and poured such intense conviction into, a bizarre portrait of decadence. For Tourneur's Italianate portrait, like Chapman's vision of political decadence, is a poetic protest against the decay of long established moral and social ideals. Despite his sophisticated Jacobean artistry, Tourneur's intellectual and spiritual roots were in a pre-Renaissance past. The medieval cast of his thought is evident in all of his works—in his satiric passion, his predilection for allegory, and in his use of the themes of *vanitas* and *memento mori*. L. G. Salingar has very effectively argued that Tourneur's pattern for society was feudalistic and that he viewed the decay of the manorial system as the disintegration of the moral order itself.[9] In Vindice's society abundance has replaced sufficiency as the goal of men's lives; the new Deadly Sin of Trade has replaced the ancient sin of Avarice, and the love of money has corrupted the love of the soil. "Why are there so few honest women," Vindice asks his mother,

> but because 'tis the poorer profession? that's accounted best, thats best followed, least in trade, least in fashion, and thats not honesty—beleeve it, and doe but note the loue and deiected price of it.
>
> (II. i. 250–53)

Tourneur has the scorn and indignation of medieval satirists, not their religious or moral security. His faith, attached as it was to the material "facts" of God's universe, may well have been shaken when these "facts" failed—when economic change destroyed the immemorially stable, feudal agricultural scheme. Even in *The Revenger's Tragedy* we can see that he hungered for the kind of literal reassurances which *The Atheist's Tragedy* offers to the believer. That is to say, the depravity of Vindice's world is measured by its divergence from a medieval conception of the universe as the theater of God's judgment. Why has virtue no "revenewe"? complains Castiza. Vindice wonders:

> Why do's not heaven turne black, or with a frowne
> Undoo the world—why do's not earth start up,
> And strike the sinnes that tread uppon't? (II. i. 275–77)

And after hearing Lussurioso's murderous plans he exclaims:

> Is there no thunder left, or ist kept up
> In stock for heavier vengeance? (IV. ii. 223–24)

Without identifying specific lines of the play with Tourneur's personal thoughts, I would suggest that his was a mind that lingered with satisfaction on the medieval *De casibus*. To the modern reader D'Amville's death in *The Atheist's Tragedy* is a bit preposterous; to Tourneur it was simply an example of inevitable divine retribution. When the bad bleed, then is Tourneur's tragedy good.

It would not be difficult to link the attack on "luxury" in *The Revenger's Tragedy* with the orthodox moralism of *The Atheist's Tragedy*, which emphasizes the association of atheism and sensuality. A mind that could see in "patrimonyes washt a pieces" a deterioration of moral order would have been even more profoundly disturbed by the real or imagined spread of disbelief in the early seventeenth century. But there is no reason to assume that the atheism which Tourneur conventionally refutes explains the satanic vision of his first tragedy. And there is certainly no evidence that his second tragedy expiates an earlier sin of disbelief. If the terms of religion and moral philosophy seem empty commonplaces in *The Revenger's Tragedy* (especially when mouthed by abandoned sinners), their conspicuous presence indicates a traditional frame of reference which Tourneur did not easily cast off. And if heaven seems a remote possibility, sinners like the Duke find their hell on earth; for Tourneur exercises the artist's prerogative of creating in literature the pattern (in this instance, the moral pattern) missing in life. We need not posit, then, that Tourneur experienced a religious "conversion" between *The Revenger's Tragedy* (1607) and *The Atheist's Tragedy* (1611). More than likely the latter play simply chronicles a return to the orthodoxy that was Tourneur's fundamental position after a temporary disillusionment which he immortalized in Italianate metaphor.

The Atheist's Tragedy

If tradition did not associate Tourneur's name with *The Revenger's Tragedy*, it is not likely that many readers would be interested in *The Atheist's Tragedy* today. Its artistic virtues are genuine enough yet not so dazzling as to make us forget its wooden characterizations and its heavy-handed moralism. Here the artist in Tourneur gives way to the didacticist, and the moral lesson can persuade only those who require no persuasion. T. S. Eliot remarks that Tourneur's genius "is in *The Revenger's Tragedy*; his talent only in *The Atheist's Tragedy*";[10] I would add that Tourneur's genius and talent are very closely related, for *The Atheist's Tragedy* is most effective when it most resembles *The Revenger's Tragedy*. Its most convincing portraits are of Levidulcia and Sebastian, who would be equally at home in Lussurioso's society; its most brilliant poetic passage is D'Amville's Vindicean soliloquy in the graveyard. Curiously, however, the inspiration of *The Atheist's Tragedy* is as peripheral as it is sporadic. Its liveliest characters are minor figures and, worse still, its most awkward and unconvincing moments occur at crucial points in the dramatic action. This is so, I suspect, because Tourneur's subject, though congenial enough to his moralizing temper, was quite beyond his artistic capacities.

Tourneur's art leans consistently towards the hyperbolic and the bizarre. *The Transformed Metamorphosis, The Revenger's Tragedy,* and *The Atheist's Tragedy* all give evidence that he possessed a fantastic imagination which required the impetus of great feeling to avoid vulgarity and absurdity. He had the kind of brilliant technique which could triumph over its limitations in a tour de force like *The Revenger's Tragedy*, but which was not suited for all dramatic occasions. Quite understandably, his allegorical method was more successful in characterizing an abnormal obsession than a normal personality. The beleaguered Castabella, for example, is a more convincing portrait of femininity than is the acrid-tongued, steely-edged Castiza, but like Charlemont, Castabella always threatens to become a purely conventional emblem of virtue. Inflexible in his dramatic methods, Tourneur paints D'Amville with the same brush that depicted Lussurioso even though the fable of *The Atheist's Tragedy* demands a hero-villain of Faustian proportions. Like the automata of *The Revenger's Tragedy*, D'Amville is an abstraction impelled by a monomaniacal lust, only his is (theoretically at least) intellectual rather than sensual. There are such men in the world around us, but they are rarely driven, as D'Amville is, to commit rape to vindicate their philosophies.

Had Tourneur been able to free himself from the satiric obsessions of *The Revenger's Tragedy*, he might have created a more successful hero in his second tragedy. It would seem, however, that the portrait of D'Amville incarnates the same protests against superfluity and economic opportunism that we find in Tourneur's earlier play. On its practical level, D'Amville's materialism is that of a New Man, a Jacobean parvenu with a criminal appetite for wealth and status. Indeed, were it not for D'Amville's atheistic naturalism and his sneers at Languebeau Snuffe, we might easily believe that he is at heart a Precisian, for his "piety," his moneylending, his mercantile vocabulary, his equation of material success and providential aid, and his deification of "industry" smack more of the elect than of the damned. No wonder then that D'Amville seems neither fish nor flesh. While his ideology "dignifies" his policy, his crass ambitions cheapen his blasphemy, so that all in all he is—as Tourneur no doubt intended—a feeble opponent of an omnipotent God.

If the moralizing spirit of *The Revenger's Tragedy* prepares us somewhat for the didacticism of *The Atheist's Tragedy*, it does not prepare us for the painfully obvious and labored moralism which blankets the latter half of Tourneur's second tragedy. Even if we assume (as I think we must) that *The Atheist's Tragedy* is a polemic—

a dramatic counterpart of Renaissance confutations of atheism—we can still say that the polemic is too crudely handled to be convincing. But while saying this, we have to keep in mind that a very literal faith in providential order was as much a part of intellectual Calvinism as of popular belief. Moreover while D'Amville may seem to modern readers a ridiculous straw man, he is, as I have shown,[11] an archetypal Renaissance atheist, synthesized from commonplace opinions about the character and career of disbelievers. He had, if nothing else, a mythic reality for Tourneur's audience.

One might even argue that the polemical intention of *The Atheist's Tragedy* demanded the sacrifice of the subtlety which Tourneur demonstrates in *The Revenger's Tragedy*. In both plays he relies heavily on irony for dramatic effect. Just as the ironic reversals of *The Revenger's Tragedy* culminate with Vindice's self-denunciation, so too the ironic reversals of *The Atheist's Tragedy* culminate with D'Amville's confession of guilt and self-murder on the scaffold; both heroes, we note, bring down upon themselves an unlooked-for but perfect judgment. Compared to Vindice's unconsciously willed self-destruction, however, D'Amville's peripetia is a crude *coup de théâtre*. Could not Tourneur have found a more convincing way of having his villain hoist with his own petard? The answer, I think, is that Tourneur could not allow D'Amville to effect his own destruction in the way that Vindice does, because D'Amville is not an overreacher who is victimized by his own ego. An enemy of religion, he is struck down at the height of his prosperity by God, who is, according to Renaissance apologists, the implacable foe of atheists, and who accomplishes the honest man's revenge. But since God does not actually appear in Tourneur's play His intervention must be made unmistakable to the audience. Tourneur must literally explicate his fable so as to make clear that when the bad bleed—when D'Amville knocks out his brains in a preposterous accident—then is God's power revealed. In other words, the essential point of *The Atheist's Tragedy* would be lost if the plea for divine vengeance in *The Revenger's Tragedy* were not answered with a vengeance—if we were not made to feel the "unnaturalness" and miraculousness of D'Amville's catastrophe.

On the other hand, we cannot apologize for the artistic failings of *The Atheist's Tragedy* by arguing that it was not intended to be a work of art. Since it was written for the stage and aspires to the laurels of tragedy, it must be judged by literary criteria. Actually we cannot say that Tourneur's genius was enslaved by his subject matter, because Marlowe found in the *Faustbook* approximately the same ideas about atheism which Tourneur incorporates in his play. If Tourneur had written *Doctor Faustus*, Faustus would no doubt resemble D'Amville, and if Marlowe had written *The Atheist's Tragedy*, D'Amville would no doubt possess a Faustian splendor. To put it simply, a broader talent than Tourneur's was needed to realize the potential grandeur of his chosen theme.

There is an implicit confession of inadequacy in Tourneur's heavy reliance on other men's artistic ideas in *The Atheist's Tragedy*. That he studied literature more than he studied life is apparent even in *The Transformed Metamorphosis* and *The Revenger's Tragedy*,[12] but he did not need to borrow extensively from other dramatists in *The Revenger's Tragedy* because his ingenious mind could work a score of variations on the revenge formulas of earlier plays. For *The Atheist's Tragedy*, however, he had no archetypal pattern to follow except perhaps that of *Doctor Faustus*, and the emphasis of Marlowe's play falls more upon the hero's superhuman aspiration than on his denial of Christianity. It is true that Tourneur derived all his ideas about atheism from contemporary prose confutations, in which the atheist is described as an arrogant, villainous blasphemer who recognizes no power above nature, who thirsts for pleasure and power, and who is tormented by a cowardly fear of death. Indeed, the very pattern of D'Amville's fate was suggested by the apologists' assertion that most atheists suffer unnatural deaths (the wages of their sins) and die confessing their sins and their folly of disbelief.[13] Still Tourneur had to translate these ideas into dramatic form, and for better or worse he chose to imitate playwrights who possessed the philosophical breadth he personally lacked.

To dramatize the atheist's preoccupation with death, Tourneur borrows and transforms the graveyard themes of *Hamlet*. To dramatize the atheist's disillusionment with nature, he turns to *King Lear*. The distracted D'Amville, who has lost his faith in nature and who cries out for judgment, is quite obviously modeled on the crazed Lear. Somewhat less obvious is D'Amville's kinship with Edmund, though

we can trace the line of descent in such passages as his request for
Charlemont's body after execution:

> I would finde out by his Anatomie;
> What thing there is in Nature more exact,
> Then in the constitution of my selfe.
> Me thinks, my parts, and my dimensions, are
> As many, as large, as well compos'd as his;
> And yet in me the resolution wants,
> To die with that assurance as he does. (V. ii. 161–67)

Although the speech as a whole echoes Lear's desire to anatomize
Regan, its middle lines specifically recall Edmund's early assertion that
"my dimensions are as well compact,/ My mind as generous, and my
shape as true, as honest madam's issue." We can also compare D'Amville's exultation after his brother's murder ("Here's a sweete Comedie.
T'begins with O *Dolentis,* and concludes with ha, ha, he."—II. iv.
101–2) with Edmund's "theatrical" aside about Edgar (". . . and Pat!
he comes, like the catastrophe of the old comedy. My cue is villainous
melancholy, with a sigh like Tom o'Bedlam. O, these eclipses do por-
tend these divisions! Fa, sol, la, mi").[14] Like Edmund, D'Amville
hungers for a title and conspires against his own brother. Like Edmund, he is an emancipated intellectual who takes nature for his goddess and laughs at superstitious credulity. It is not accidental, moreover, that D'Amville compares himself with Charlemont in the same
terms that Edmund compares himself with Edgar, for Charlemont is
merely a Gallic version of Edgar. Like Edgar he is robbed of his
inheritance by a close relative, and like Edgar he is falsely condemned
as a criminal. If we wish further evidence of Charlemont's ancestry,
we need only compare his pious Stoicism with Edgar's speeches in the
storm and deep conviction of divine justice.

Tourneur's direct imitation of Marlowe is less extensive than his
imitation of Shakespeare, but he probably derived his conception of
plot from the celebrated and often reprinted *Doctor Faustus.* The
dialectical opening of *The Atheist's Tragedy* seems to be modeled on
Faustus' great opening soliloquy, even as the crazed D'Amville's yearning for annihilation echoes Faustus' dying thought:

> O were my body circumvolv'd
> Within that cloude; that when the thunder teares

His passage open, it might scatter me
To nothing in the ayre! (IV. iii. 277–80)

It is even possible that D'Amville's grotesque catastrophe was suggested to Tourneur by Thomas Beard's account of Marlowe's death, for in Beard's narrative as in Tourneur's play the judgment of God falls on a villainous atheist who, in attempting to kill another man, is mortally wounded in the head with his own weapon.[15]

Like *Faustus*, *The Atheist's Tragedy* dramatizes an atheist's harrowing journey towards the spiritual and moral knowledge which is gained by less arrogant minds through a simple act of faith. Tourneur's hero, however, begins his journey from an intellectual position that is diametrically opposite to Faustus'. D'Amville has no Faustian hunger for forbidden knowledge; on the contrary, he arrogantly assumes at the beginning of the play that he knows all answers and completely understands the nature of man and the universe. Only when the deaths of his sons ruin his grandiose ambitions does he question the adequacy of his philosophy; and then through personal despair he also learns a very elementary and obvious cosmological truth—that there is a power above nature that controls its force. Faustus, we might say, is the intellectual demon of an Elizabethan world awakening relatively late to the intellectual adventure of the Renaissance and rebelling against the confines of medieval thought. D'Amville, in contrast, is the demon of a seventeenth-century world that has swept away medieval assumptions and seeks a new intellectual adventure in scientific reason. While Faustus' *hybris* denies the limitations on human thought, D'Amville's *hybris* imprisons man's mind within the phenomenal universe. While Faustus seeks to penetrate arcane mysteries, D'Amville denies that any mysteries lie beyond the scope of mundane experience and empirical reason. While Faustus aspires to be a god—to gain the power of a prime mover over nature—D'Amville rejects the possibility of any higher power than nature, which is to him the ultimate reality of the universe.

Because D'Amville is philosophically complacent, Tourneur faced a more difficult problem than did Marlowe in translating the atheist's heresy into effective plot, for Faustus' hunger for knowledge provides an immediate intellectual cue to action which is lacking in Tourneur's hero. The villainous goals of pleasure and power are, of course, appropriate to D'Amville, but, as Tourneur recognized, these goals do not in themselves define the unique ungodliness of an atheist. Tourneur therefore relates D'Amville's politic ambitions to a more fundamental and richly ironic obsession: his ruling passion is the very hunger for immortality which, being universal in men, was to the orthodox mind an evidence of the immortality of the soul. Unlike the Christian believer, however, D'Amville seeks immortality in the continuance of his line. He erases through a dynastic vision the fear of death which the orthodox mind eradicates through a vision of eternal spirit.

In D'Amville's immortal longings Tourneur achieved a more sustained motive for dramatic action than Marlowe found in the *Faustbook* or, so far as we can tell, was able to invent. But his inspired stroke is so faultily delivered that (like D'Amville's axe-blow) it almost knocks out the brains of the play. Whereas Marlowe elevates the conventional libertinism of the atheist to heights of exquisite poetry, Tourneur stages D'Amville's ideologically inspired passion as one of several unnatural graveyard lusts. Requiring heirs, D'Amville attempts to seduce his daughter-in-law, Castabella, and manages thereby to reduce the sensational libertine plea for unconfined love to a dull pronouncement:

> Incest? Tush.
> These distances affinitie observes;
> Are articles of bondage cast upon
> Our freedomes by our owne subiections.
> Nature allowes a gen'rall libertie
> Of generation to all creatures else. (IV. iii. 139–44)

When the horrified Castabella counters with her own philosophical arguments, D'Amville attempts to rape her, but is frightened away by Charlemont, who is providentially lurking in the graveyard dressed in a ludicrous disguise.

The wild improbabilities of the graveyard scene are one evidence of a flagging imagination. Another is the increasing reliance in the latter half of the play on material derived from other dramatists. Compared, let us say, to the imitations of *Othello* in *Love's Sacrifice*, Tourneur's borrowings are creative, but like Ford's imitations, they are an abdication of artistic responsibility. The attempted rape fortuitously prevented is, I think, a reminiscence of *Volpone*, as is more certainly

D'Amville's glorification of his gold at the beginning of the fifth act. Like Jonson's hero, D'Amville finds an unlooked-for justice in a court of law, where true judgment is meted out despite the frailties of human wisdom. To flesh out the situation borrowed from Jonson, Tourneur refashions Lear's mad scenes. Like Lear the distracted D'Amville cries out for justice to support his belief in the universe. Like Lear he discovers through suffering that man truly needs, not wealth and power, but patience—the resolute assurance in the face of calamity that comes only to the untroubled conscience.

Increasingly indebted to other writers' inspiration in the latter half of *The Atheist's Tragedy*, Tourneur is also increasingly willing to sacrifice credibility to didactic effect. Charlemont's and Castabella's unexpected drowsiness in the graveyard is absurd, but their chaste slumber on a pair of skulls is a vivid contrast to D'Amville's unnatural lusts and morbid fear of death. In the last act the ironic contrasts grow more and more heavy-handed. As D'Amville gloats over his gold the corpses of his sons are brought on stage. When he tries to buy back their lives with his all-powerful wealth, the Doctor laughs. As he quakes with fear of death, Charlemont and Castabella cheerfully leap to the scaffold. He requires wine to bolster his failing spirits, but Charlemont keeps up his pluck with a glass of water.

I may exaggerate the lameness of the closing scene of *The Atheist's Tragedy*. What seems painfully contrived on the page may be far more effective in the theater, and a fine actor could no doubt endow D'Amville's distraction with some element of pathos. But I doubt that Tourneur intended D'Amville to seem pathetic, for Tourneur does not feel Marlowe's sympathy for the aspiration he condemns, nor does he make us feel, as Marlowe does, the grandeur as well as the absurdity of his hero's denial of God.[16] At his most poignant moment, when he begs the Doctor to restore his sons' lives, D'Amville is, as he recognizes, ridiculous. Similarly, when conscience first strikes him (in the graveyard scene), he is reduced to comical and quaking fears. By the end of the play it is obvious that he is more of a farcical dupe than a tragic protagonist.

In *Doctor Faustus* the arch-atheist Marlowe demonstrates that the tragic and the religious view of life are not necessarily antithetical. Tourneur's religious viewpoint, however, almost explicitly denies the possibility of tragedy. It makes of the world a theater of judgment in which the only conceivable dramatic action is a divine farce if not a divine comedy. In this setting the central question of *The Revenger's Tragedy*—that of action in an evil world—is not so much confronted as annihilated, for Charlemont does not have to take action, nor can he be corrupted by discontent. There is no inexplicable suffering, no tormenting sacrifice of innocence, no unbearable personal agony to shake his faith in this best of all possible worlds.

Because *The Atheist's Tragedy* was based on a secondhand and academic conception of atheism, it does not convince us that D'Amville's atheism posed a more immediate or alarming threat to Jacobean morality than did the sensuality which Lussurioso represents. But then Tourneur's play was probably not intended as a call to arms against ungodliness. It is true, as E. A. Strathmann points out, that more often than not the Renaissance apologists describe the atheist as a naturalist, "who, through overmuch study of nature, was inclined to exalt her, only the agent of creation, to the role of creator."[17] And there are enough references to naturalists outside the confutations to suggest that there were men in Tourneur's age who did not accept Bacon's limitations on the scope of scientific reason or who sought to attribute all phenomena to natural causes.[18] Still it seems to me that Tourneur's play, like the usual Jacobean prose confutation of atheism, is primarily a testament of faith; it is the kind of cautionary work, filled with sound and profitable doctrine, that would have been written even if there had been no fear at all of the spread of atheism. It is not so much a refutation of a dangerous contemporary ideology as a celebration of the eternal order of Providence.

And in fact D'Amville's view of nature is not completely refuted in *The Atheist's Tragedy*. He does not learn that the ultimate reality of nature is rational moral order; instead he learns that his view of nature is incomplete—that reasoning "meerely out/Of Nature" does not produce a valid interpretation of the cosmos. The very orthodoxy of Tourneur's religious position makes all the more significant the fact that the Elizabethan identification of nature and moral law is shattered in *The Atheist's Tragedy* and never restored. It is true, of course, that D'Amville and Levidulcia are not casually permitted to usurp nature as the justification of their sensual appetites. When D'Amville argues for unconfined love, Castabella retorts that his libertine view of nature degrades man to the level of animals.[19] Nevertheless D'Amville and Levidulcia are not condemned as unnatural for the simple reason that they are the representatives of nature in the play. And the very fact that nature proves to them a false goddess simply confirms the impression that nature is not a reliable guide to the proper conduct of men's lives. Corroborating evidence in *'Tis Pity She's a Whore* indicates that as the Jacobean age wore on it became increasingly difficult to deny outright a naturalistic view of the universe.[20] It was possible only to insist upon the limitations of naturalistic explanations and upon the validity of the higher truths of religion and morality, which lie beyond the reach and attack of empirical reason. Thus though its viewpoint is antipodal to that of the *De Augmentis*, *The Atheist's Tragedy* bears indirect witness to the encroachment of a scientific epistemology on the classical and medieval assumptions which underlay the moral philosophy of the sixteenth century.

Extremes of cynicism and moralism, of high and pedestrian art, are not rare in the works of the Jacobeans, whose tragic inspirations were short-lived and whose descents into mediocrity were often precipitous. The unique problem of Tourneur's drama, however, is that we have only two seemingly disconnected points of reference with which to chart the progress of his art. It is as if we had to piece together Chapman's personality from only *Bussy D'Ambois* and *Caesar and Pompey*, or Donne's personality from one song and one sermon, or T. S. Eliot's personality from only *The Waste Land* and *The Cocktail Party*. The apparent pattern of Tourneur's drama—the retreat (or return) from skepticism to orthodoxy—is common enough in the literature of ages of anxiety, but we lack other works, other artistic coördinates, which might confirm the pattern. That the mind and talent which created *The Revenger's Tragedy* found an artistic resting place in *The Atheist's Tragedy* seems to me perfectly plausible. Whether there is any trace of that mind and talent in *Women Beware Women* and *The Changeling* the reader will have to decide for himself at the close of Chapter VII.

CHAPTER V

John Webster

Although it is possible now to patronize the misguided William Archer, the specter of his criticism still hovers over Webster's plays. For however inadequate Archer's critical theories were, his attacks on the formlessness of Webster's tragedies contained an irreducible kernel of aesthetic truth. More sympathetic and judicious critics may not complain of Webster's "ramshackle looseness of structure," but they must agree with J. A. Symonds that

> we rise from the perusal of [Webster's] Italian tragedies with a deep sense of the poet's power and personality, an ineffaceable recollection of one or two resplendent scenes, and a clear conception of the leading characters. Meanwhile the outlines of the fable, the structure of the drama as a complete work of art, seem to elude our grasp. The persons, who have played their part upon the stage of our imagination, stand apart from one another, like figures in a *tableau vivant*.[1]

Of course the same observation has been made of other Elizabethan and Jacobean plays. As F. L. Lucas remarks, Shakespeare's contemporaries were not concerned with logical causality or consistency in plot. They worked in scenes and wrote for an audience that wanted "a succession of great moments"—"great situations ablaze with passion and poetry."[2] Still we cannot say that the highest reach of Elizabethan dramatic art was a "succession of great moments" or that the architectural failings of Webster's tragedies are "conventional." All things considered, the plotting of *The White Devil* is not more episodic than the plotting of *King Lear;* it seems more episodic because *The White Devil* lacks the moral emphasis and focus which unifies the sprawling structure of Shakespeare's play. The relationship of form and vision is even more complex in *The Duchess of Malfi,* where Webster seems again and again to sacrifice dramatic structure to tragic idea. As we shall see, the Duchess must die "too soon," because her death is a touchstone as well as a turning point in the lives of the other characters.

Judging *The White Devil* to be Webster's finest achievement, Mr. Lucas explains the customary preference for *The Duchess of Malfi* as resulting from irrelevant moral considerations.[3] Yet the "moral" preference for the *Duchess* may have its aesthetic basis. Undoubtedly *The White Devil* is a more brilliant and vigorous play; in contrast to the anticlimax of the *Duchess,* it rushes to a spectacular and supremely theatrical conclusion like a mighty river hurling itself over a fall. Still we ask from tragedy more than an unwearying display of human vitality or a thrilling clash of personalities. We expect a depth of vision that penetrates the surface violence or anarchy of life to illumine the underlying pattern and meaning of man's fate. Despite its errors and inconsistencies of plot,[4] the *Duchess* is a greater play than *The White Devil* because it offers a more coherent and profound interpretation of experience. Its action has a rightness and inevitability that makes the unflagging energy of *The White Devil* seem, by comparison, artistically unpurposed.

Because Webster wrote the last Jacobean tragedies of heroic proportion, one is tempted to read a larger significance into the twilight and horror-ridden world of the *Duchess.* Here, one might say, is a vision of evil beyond which tragedy could not go and from which Webster and Jacobean drama as a whole retreated into tragicomedy. The truth, however, is that Webster's tragedies were not greatly admired or influential in their own time and were written after the vogue of tragicomedy had begun. Moreover the *Duchess* is not as flawed or illogical a play as critics have suggested; certainly it was not written by a playwright so unnerved by his nightmare intuition that he could not manage his plot. Take, for example, the notorious "absurdity" of Ferdinand's delayed revenge. In Act II, scene v, Ferdinand, maddened by news that his sister has had a "bastard" child, describes an insane plan of vengeance to the Cardinal. He promises to "sleep" until he knows his sister's lover and then leap to a furious revenge. Yet according to the conversation between Antonio and Delio in the next scene, the rash and hysterical Ferdinand "sleeps" several years and does not actually stir until his sister has had two more children. Then he confronts the Duchess *before* he knows who her lover is.

How ridiculous this all seems when we consider the plot in our studies. When the *Duchess* is staged, however, there is no impression of delay or absurd lag in action; immediately after Ferdinand announces his intended revenge (in II. v), he appears at the Duchess' court (in III. i) and begins the systematic torture of his sister. Thus time moves in the *Duchess*, as in some of Shakespeare's plays, at more than one rate; for Webster must, on the one hand, stress Ferdinand's irrational fury, and, on the other hand, emphasize the careless indifference of the Duchess and Antonio to their ignominious position. Webster achieves these cross-purposes by allowing the action to move forward uninterruptedly even as time is stretched out in the dialogue. The simultaneous rush and delay of Ferdinand's revenge is a remarkable bit of artistic legerdemain: the ear contradicts the eye but the mind is not insulted nor is integrity of character sacrificed. Thus what has been described as a symptom of weakening powers or carelessness might better be taken as evidence of Webster's grasp of his materials— of his bold willingness to be "inconsistent" in order to obtain the precise moral discriminations which are lacking in *The White Devil*.

To speak of the lack of moral discriminations in *The White Devil* is not to accuse Webster of the ethical confusion we find in *Bussy D'Ambois*. In Webster's tragedies there is no tampering with traditional values or philosophical attempts to disguise vice as virtue. Murder is called murder; lechery is condemned as lechery. Webster's immoralists are warned that the wages of sin are death and when the moral reckoning falls due, they admit the justness of their fates. The dying Vittoria announces:

O my greatest sinne lay in my blood.
Now my blood paies for't.[5] (V. vi. 240–41)

The dying Cardinal in the *Duchess* exclaims: "Oh Justice:/ I suffer now, for what hath former bin." Similarly Ferdinand takes leave of life with a memorable moralistic epigram:

"Whether we fall by ambition, blood, or lust,
"Like Diamonds, we are cut with our owne dust. (V. v. 91–92)

In both plays choric figures recite the final moral lesson. For Delio the bloody catastrophe of the *Duchess* proves that *"Integrity of life, is fames best friend."* Giovanni, scanning the holocaust of Lodovico's revenge, warns:

Let guilty men remember their blacke deedes,
Do leane on crutches, made of slender reedes. (V. vi. 302–3)

Although these sententious aphorisms are not irrelevant to what preceded them, they seem a bit like annotations by another hand— Christian glosses, as it were, on a pagan epic of courage and consuming passion. They do not suddenly crystallize a moral judgment embodied in Webster's portrayal of character, nor do they capture the essential significance of the lives on which they comment so weightily. Just before she dies Vittoria exclaims:

O happy they that never saw the Court,
Nor ever knew great Man but by report. (V. vi. 261–62)

This facile commonplace of the Elizabethan courtier would no doubt appear to advantage on Vittoria's tombstone, but like most tombstone verse it is dedicated to the living rather than the dead.

Unlike Shakespeare's Edmund, Webster's villains are not suddenly touched by moral feeling at their deaths. If they expire with sententious commonplaces on their lips it is because they are accustomed to playing the moral chorus at other men's tragedies. Francisco de Medicis, the master politician of *The White Devil*, is also the scourge of lechery and the defender of the sanctity of marriage. The Cardinal, Ferdinand, and Bosola are responsible for most of the ethical exhortation in the *Duchess*. In Shakespearean tragedy the hypocritical moralizing of Iago or Edmund emphasizes the deceptive surface of personality and the vulnerability of those who trust in human nature. The hypocritical moralizing in Webster's drama is more deeply subversive of ethical conviction because it is not intended to deceive. As there is no effective moral order to oppose them, Webster's immoralists can be frank in their duplicity. When Francisco and Brachiano or Vittoria and Monticelso confront one another with pious accusations and denials of guilt, their cards are on the table. They play with consummate skill the Machiavellian game of moral pretense that the world demands. They make the right gestures and speak the right words because while their society does not insist upon the reality of virtue, it insists upon the illusion. Not ready to take open vengeance on Vittoria, Francisco and Monticelso devise a trial in which they are both prosecutor and judge, and though it is not a fair trial it has the form of legality, and the form suffices. Indeed, if Vittoria's defiance seems to nullify the charges hurled against her, it is not because she is more than innocent, but because innocence and guilt are not the primary issues in her arraignment.

There are few Jacobean tragedies in which innocence and guilt seem as irrelevant as in *The White Devil*. Despite the obliquity in *Bussy D'Ambois* there is a surge of moral passion that exceeds the demands of art and that overwhelms the conventionally contrived dramatic situations. In *The White Devil* the opposite seems true: the scorn and bitterness in its lines seem inadequate to the terror of the dramatic situations; even murders seem, to use Lodovico's phrase, no more than "flea-bytinges." Morally sensitive characters like Isabella and Marcello are weak and ineffectual, too easily silenced, murdered in dumb show or by a casual sword thrust. Those like Flamineo who effectively dissect the corruption of their world are part of that corruption and too perverse in their values to comprehend moral truths. Because their choric commentaries lack the moral accent of Vindice's speeches, we leave the play with the impression that the harshest reality of Flamineo's world is not the ruthless destruction of innocence but the ingratitude of princes and the venality of their underlings. In *King Lear* the perversion of the feudal bond of loyalty by servants like Oswald is a recurrent subject of moral commentary and a symbol of the annihilation of traditional moral and political values. But in *The White Devil* there are no faithful Kents to remind us that in the past servants did not always pander to their masters' wills. In the tragedies of Chapman, Jonson, and Tourneur, the decadence of the present scene is directly or indirectly contrasted with a previous norm of aristocratic values. But in *The White Devil* there is no suggestion that the courts of princes were once less corrupt or that the hunger for wealth, position, and sensual pleasure was not always the norm of human existence.

On the other hand, Webster does not deny the reality of virtue in *The White Devil*. He does not suggest that Isabella's devotion to Brachiano is sham or that Vittoria is the pattern of womanhood. Virtue does exist untainted and uncompromised, but it is impotent and ultimately meaningless—swept away into the same mist that enshrouds the fates of assassins and adulterers. The foolish, harmless Camillo exists only to be got rid of. The right-thinking Marcello is unable to break away from Brachiano's court and is killed as soon as he decides to oppose his brother. Isabella is effective only when she assumes Brachiano's guilt, and Cornelia, the moral chorus who prophesies retribution, lacks the strength to condemn Flamineo for the sin of Cain. Moreover while virtue is not an illusion, it breeds disastrous illusions about the meaning of marriage or the bonds of family love. It is defenseless against the violence that threatens it because it depends on words for protection against the passions of men who have contempt for words and who have no illusions about themselves or others.

One can understand why Webster's studies of sensual passion, his cynicism, and his taste for Italianate intrigue and horror have wed his tragedies to Tourneur's in the minds of critics and in the pages of anthologies. But we should not let a marriage of editorial convenience blind us to the profound differences between the two dramatists. In *The Revenger's Tragedy* and in *The Atheist's Tragedy*, reality is interpreted, as it were, through plot—through the concatenation of events that reveals an underlying moral purpose and order. In so far as he is capable, Tourneur delineates the nature of man's universe through the patterning of dramatic incidents. Webster, in contrast, seeks the meaning of existence in the supreme moments of agony and duress that lay bare the soul; the incidents of his plots serve primarily to bring his characters face to face with their mortal destinies. Like Tourneur he uses revenge as a motive to conclude his fable, but the routine appearances of the ghosts in *The White Devil* and the use of a minor figure (Lodovico) as the instrument of retribution suggest that his mind is engaged in other passions.

If Webster had a master in tragedy other than Shakespeare, it was Jonson, not Tourneur. Scornful of sham and pretense, Webster, like Jonson, seeks beneath moral illusion for the truths of experience that are scaled by hammer-blows of fate and refined in the incandescent crucible of violence. There is perhaps more of *Sejanus* in *The White Devil* than first meets the eye in Webster's imitations and in his prefatory lip service to Jonsonian classicism.[6] In both tragedies virtue is unarmed; Machiavellian strength and cunning determine men's fates. In both tragedies the master politician achieves his Machiavellian goal and escapes the catastrophe that ensnares his henchmen. Like Jonson, Webster has no interest in philosophical issues or metaphysical ideals. There are occasional references in his plays to the philosophy of Padua and the atheism of antiquity, but they are incidental if not accidental. Like many of his contemporaries he borrowed freely from Montaigne without being influenced by Montaigne's view of life. He was impressed by Montaigne's acute observations of detail and by the vividness of Florio's prose, not by the ironic attack on moral assumptions in the "Apologie." It is amusingly characteristic of Webster's "philosophical" attitudes that Hooker's metaphysical postulate, "Obedience of creatures to the Law of Nature is the stay of the whole world," is subordinated (in *The Devil's Law-Case*) to the cynical observation, several times repeated in Webster's drama, that nature is kind to bastard children.[7]

I do not mean that Webster, like Fletcher, had no apparent intellectual interests and no genuine concern with ideas. His attitude towards philosophical questions suggests derision rather than neutrality. He presents in art the skeptical, pragmatic nominalism of the late Renaissance, the weariness with meaningless abstractions and endless debates over words. In his tragedies the Elizabethan faith in didacticism —in the moral power of words—is blown away by the first gust of violence. Humanistic learning is represented by a fool, a malcontent, and a madman. The stupid, impotent Camillo is the Aristotelian scholar of *The White Devil*. Bosola is spoken of as a "fantasticall" Paduan scholar,

Like such, who studdy to know how many knots
Was in *Hercules* club, of what colour *Achilles* beard was,
Or whether *Hector* were not troubled with the tooth-ach—
He hath studdied himselfe halfe-bleare-ei'd, to know
The true semitry of *Caesars* nose by a shooing-horne,
And this he did
To gaine the name of a speculative man. (III. iii. 50–57)

Even more fantastic is the Stoic "rationality" which enables an insane
Ferdinand to place philosophy in perspective before he dies:

. . . the paine's nothing: paine many times is taken away with the
apprehension of greater, (as the tooth-ache with the sight of a Barbor,
that comes to pull it out) there's Philosophy for you. (V. v. 78–80)

There is no reference in *The White Devil* to the rational cosmic
order set forth by Renaissance philosophy. Perhaps men would like to
believe that the institutions of religion, law, and family are expressions
of universal decorum; but these institutions seem fragile defenses
against the anarchy of human passion. Justice, as Lodovico points out,
is indeed for the weak and the poor because the rich and the powerful
escape judgment or bend the law to their purposes. Religion is the last
refuge of whores and panders (witness Vittoria and Flamineo) and
provides the sacrament and mask for Lodovico's vengeance. Before
sexual and mercenary appetites and before the brutal coercions of
wealth and place, traditional sanctities are meaningless: *brother, sister,
husband, wife* become empty terms. Brachiano poisons his wife; Vittoria incites the murder of her husband. Flamineo panders his sister
and kills his brother, and only Lodovico's intervention prevents Flamineo and Vittoria from destroying one another. When the customary
ties of devotion slip, only the passions of lust and ambition bind men to
each other and then only for self-gratification. Not surprisingly the
great moments in *The White Devil* are those of individual assertion
and defiance. At the trial Vittoria and Brachiano do not defy the world
together nor do they defend their love against its judgment. Brachiano
interrupts the proceedings momentarily to announce his personal defiance and then he leaves Vittoria to her fate. Vittoria will not admit
that she loves Brachiano, although she is willing to confess that he
attempted to seduce her. Brachiano is strangled while Vittoria waits
in another room. She weeps at his death but when Flamineo threatens

to kill her, all thought of her late husband vanishes as she concentrates on the immediate problem of survival. She dies in the company of Flamineo and Zanche, yet quite alone, like them unable to turn her thoughts outward from herself. "I doe not looke," says the dying Flamineo,

> Who went before, nor who shall follow mee;
> Noe, at my selfe I will begin and end.
> "While we looke up to heaven wee confound
> "Knowledge with knowledge. ô I am in a mist. (V. vi. 256–60)

One might say that the power of *The White Devil* is its dramatization of the *isolated* criminal will shattering moral restrictions. The opening scene introduces Lodovico, enraged by banishment, spurning the consolations of philosophy offered by Antonelli and Gasparo. They recall his riotous past and remind him of the crimes for which he has been justly sentenced. "Worse then these," Gasparo adds,

> You have acted certaine Murders here in Rome,
> Bloody and full of horror. Lod. 'Las they were flea-bytinges:
> Why tooke they not my head then? Gas. O my Lord
> The law doth somtimes mediate, thinkes it good
> Not ever to steepe violent sinnes in blood,
> This gentle pennance may both end your crimes,
> And in the example better these bad times.
> Lod. So—but I wonder then some great men scape
> This banishment, ther's *Paulo Giordano Orsini*,
> The Duke of *Brachiano*, now lives in Rome,
> And by close panderisme seekes to prostitute
> The honor of *Vittoria Corombona*,
> *Vittoria*, she that might have got my pardon
> For one kisse to the Duke. Anto. Have a full man within you,
> Wee see that Trees beare no such pleasant fruite
> There where they grew first, as where they are new set.
> Perfumes the more they are chaf'd the more they render
> Their pleasing sents, and so affliction
> Expresseth vertue, fully, whether trew,
> Or ells adulterate. Lod. Leave your painted comforts,
> Ile make Italian cut-works in their guts
> If ever I returne. (I. i. 31–52)

We cannot take Antonelli and Gasparo too seriously here, because they are Lodovico's henchmen, who are working to repeal his banishment and who later aid him in his bloody vengeance. Nevertheless they have a professed code of ethics. They try to placate their master with a pious phrase, a snatch of Boethius, an edifying simile from natural history. But he rips apart their cant with the logic of an experienced murderer who knows that dukes need not fear "gentle pennance." The other heroic figures in *The White Devil* are cut to Lodovico's measure. They listen impatiently to the voice of morality as one listens to the foolish babbling of a child; and when they answer, they silence it. When Isabella warns that Brachiano's adultery will anger heaven, he replies, "Let not thy Love/ Make thee an unbeleever." When Cornelia protests against Flamineo's pandering, he answers, "Pray what meanes have you/ To keepe me from the gallies, or the gallowes?" After Monticelso has expounded Vittoria's whoredom to the court at great length, she contemptuously replies:

> These are but faigned shadowes of my evels.
> Terrify babes, my Lord, with painted devils,
> I am past such needlesse palsy—for your names,
> Of Whoore and Murdresse they proceed from you,
> As if a man should spit against the wind,
> The filth returne's in's face. (III. ii. 150–55)

Webster's villains are not gulled by words or placated by painted comforts. They know how to use pious phrases as well as how to accept them. Flamineo is a master of sanctimony; Brachiano announces at the trial that his interest in Vittoria is prompted by "charity. . . . To orphans and to widdows." It is also for charity's sake that Brachiano's murderers bar Vittoria from the room in which he is being strangled. And as Vittoria, Flamineo, and Zanche trade religious sentiments, we wonder if moral precept has any meaning at all.

In his "glorious villains" Webster creates heroic characters who escape the restrictive bonds and illusions of morality only to be swept to disaster by the irresistible tide of their desires. They are not slaves of passion in any ordinary sense, confused and blinded by uncontrollable appetites. In a strangely perverse way they know themselves better than do Cornelia and Isabella, but that self-knowledge is a tyranny as well as an emancipation. Because they see their goals so clearly they recognize no alternatives, and although they create the circumstances of their lives they never transcend them. Their exist-

ences are momentary, their reactions conditioned reflexes. Not burdened by sorrows or fears (except for temporary flashes of remorse)
they respond vigorously to the stimuli of the immediate moment. But
because they are completely absorbed in the tumultuous present they
never see beyond it; they never lift their eyes to the larger horizons visible to Chapman's heroes. Those like Flamineo who understand the essential nature of their society are peculiarly unable to solve the problems of their own destinies. When at the threshold of death they gain a
brief respite from the perpetual crisis of their lives, they glimpse only
the pattern of their own fate, which becomes for them the eternal
design of man's existence. They are all, like Brachiano, quite lost from
the beginning despite the fierce energy that impels them onward.
"Fate's a Spaniel," Flamineo decides at last,

> Wee cannot beat it from us: what remains now?
> Let all that doe ill, take this precedent:
> *Man may his Fate foresee, but not prevent.* (V. vi. 178–81)

In a sense the blind determinism of the emancipated will is the
great unrecognized theme of *The White Devil*—the key to the otherwise incomprehensible futility of Flamineo's dramatic career. That
there was joy in Flamineo's making we cannot doubt, for he is the
most engaging and brilliant of Webster's villains: high-spirited, volu-
ble, quick with scorn or admiration, so frank in his enjoyment of evil
that we are perhaps a little ashamed of our uninspired virtue. Flamineo
has, as Mr. Lucas observes, "more humour, a quicker wit, a deeper
cynicism even than Iago."[8] He has also more pride and candor. Unwilling to fawn or pretend virtue, he soothes his lacerated ego by parading
his contempt for Brachiano. And yet his motives are contemptible
beside the satanic hunger for destruction engendered by Iago's nig-
gardly spite. Even the crude Machiavels of the Elizabethan stage had
more grandiose ambitions for wealth, power, or bloodshed than
Flamineo, who commits the basest crimes against his own blood to gain
a paltry advancement. To secure himself against the gallows, he spends
his life running the vile errands of men inferior to himself in mind and
spirit. And even as his goal is incredibly mean his cynical "realism" is
hopelessly naïve. Knowing from experience that those who serve
"great men" will be discarded when they have served their purpose, he

schemes feverishly to ensure the reward that will bring him Brachiano's security against the law. But his politic mind has no better answer to Marcello's challenge than a cowardly sword-thrust that binds him forever to Brachiano's "mercy." Only at his death does he realize that he engaged in a ludicrous attempt to avoid a self-imposed fatality, and then he sees the absurdity of all endeavor, not of his politic ambitions.

If Flamineo is a baffling character, it is not because Webster did not understand him, but because he suspected, even in *The White Devil*, that the Machiavellianism which seemed to release man's heroic potentialities was ultimately a negation rather than a fulfillment of life. Fearful of confounding knowledge with knowledge, Flamineo shuts his eyes to everything except the "necessity" which his own mind creates. Despite his intellect he pursues a base irrational goal, and like Webster's later Machiavels ends in a little point, a kind of nothing, playing desperate games with Vittoria before he is slaughtered, apparently without resistance, by his enemies.

I do not wish to deny the superb poetry and theatricality of Flamineo's death scene. For sheer dramatic impact it has no equal in Jacobean tragedy; yet it stuns the emotions without involving or moving them very deeply. It calls forth an instinctive gasp of pity and admiration for untamed, undaunted animals surrendering to the hunter's knife. We are not "engaged" in the fates of Flamineo and Vittoria because we do not share their emotional responses, which are not only different in degree from normal feeling but different in kind as well. In the *Duchess* the strength and dignity of Webster's heroine are set off by contrast to Cariola and Bosola. In *The White Devil* there is no heightening contrast between Vittoria and her assassins or even between Vittoria and Zanche. It may be that instinctive fearlessness, however thrilling on the stage, does not lend itself to fine distinctions; one lioness at bay is like the next. In the very act of asserting their individuality Flamineo, Vittoria, Zanche, and Lodovico lose it: they imitate one another. Because Webster's dichotomies of strength and weakness are artistically and morally primitive, tragic heroine and whorish servant, noble aristocratic lady and silly cuckold exit alike into the mist.

Although Francisco's revenge imposes a conventional pattern on the final scenes of *The White Devil*, Lodovico's entrance is more of an interruption than a consummation of the drama of Vittoria's and Flamineo's lives. He wields a knife cunningly but his skill might have been spared, for Flamineo and Vittoria were already at each other's throats. In *Sejanus* the fall of the underling and the escape of the master politician are the final revelation of the amorality of politics. In *The White Devil* it does not seem to matter very much that Lodovico is apprehended while Francisco escapes, because both are no more than instruments of plot. It is only an accident of lust that makes Lodovico Brachiano's nemesis and only a chance insult that turns him against Flamineo. One misses in the denouement of *The White Devil* that sense of ironic inevitability which orders the sweepstake carnage of *The Revenger's Tragedy*. When the grand design of Webster's play should be finally elucidated, we see nothing more than a series of exterminations that temporarily rid Giovanni's court of vermin.

The Duchess of Malfi

Because the *Duchess* appeared only a year or so after *The White Devil* it is dangerous to speak of the "development" of Webster's tragic art. Mr. Lucas thinks the *Duchess* a weaker play; Clifford Leech finds in it evidence of declining artistic powers.[9] I am convinced only that it is a much more mature play than *The White Devil*—the work of a dramatist who now sees life more clearly, more steadily, and more compassionately. It is not so much the expression of a personal, nihilistic disgust with life as a relatively detached study of the moral cowardice that robs life of meaning. Significantly enough, there are no glorious villains like Lodovico in the *Duchess;* the triumph and defeat of the emancipated will no longer hold the center of the stage. Evil still has a heroic facade but the facade crumbles eventually to reveal madness and womanish cowardice; the sheer bestiality of criminal desire, emphasized continually by animal imagery, assumes a graphic reality in Ferdinand's lycanthropy. Innocence is still defenseless against the onslaught of Machiavellian violence. Yet only the defenseless victim, the Duchess, has the strength to endure—the cardinal and redeeming virtue in Webster's tragic universe—and her self-possession in the face of death is a spiritual victory rather than a glorious defeat. Whereas the greatest moments in *The White Devil* are gestures of amoral defiance, the greatest moments in the *Duchess* are the moral discoveries at the close of the fourth act, which make the bloody catastrophe seem anticlimactic.

This is not to say that Webster turned didacticist in his second tragedy. We falsify his conception of character when we try to judge the Duchess by the socially unreal, pietistic standard expressed in the "character" of "a vertuous Widdow."[10] Only Ferdinand and the Cardinal speak of the sin of marrying twice and they do not convince us that the Duchess should be condemned as unfaithful to a nameless, dead husband, who is mentioned casually in passing. Nor do they convince us that she earns her torments by breaking the laws of social decorum. Her marriage to a man unworthy of her is a disastrous mistake, yet one she never regrets and which she redeems by the beauty and selflessness of her devotion. Moreover, it is not the marriage itself which is shameful but the moral compromise involved in hiding it. Deeply religious before her death, the Duchess sees her agony as heaven's scourge; but Ferdinand and Bosola, her "judges" and executioners, declare her innocent. If she is to serve as a cautionary example we must assume that had she not married she would have been safe from the animality of her brothers—as safe perhaps as Othello would have been had he chosen Iago instead of Cassio as his lieutenant.

The moralist teaches men how to avoid catastrophe; Webster is concerned only with how they accept it. The moralist explains the justice of men's falls; Webster does not reassure us that measure for measure is the law of existence. Armed with the doctrine of free will the moralist cannot believe in fatality; but in the hideous mist of error that enshrouds Webster's characters, no man can be called master of his fate, and no choice is clear until circumstances force men's decisions. Webster dramatizes the mystery of the irrational will without moralistic gloss. He offers no simple explanation of why Antonio, who is called a brave soldier, always chooses a coward's way or why Bosola obeys his baser instincts. If critics emphasize the irrationality of Ferdinand's motives rather than the Cardinal's, it is because the Cardinal does not attempt to explain his goals, while Ferdinand calls attention to the nightmarish confusion of his mind. Even as Goneril and Regan have no reason to torture Lear, so Ferdinand has no reason to torture his sister, unless a frenzied egomania is "reason" enough.

But for all the references to Fortune in the *Duchess*, Webster's characters are not the playthings of a capricious goddess. Nor are they like the heroic characters of *The White Devil* swept blindly to their graves. For the unreflecting villains of Webster's first tragedy there is no hope of redemption, no chance of moral illumination before their deaths. For Bosola, Antonio, and the others the redemptive moment is possible; the moral opportunity is real and within their grasp. They have the chance to protect, spare, or rescue the woman who is the center of their lives. Some form of moral awareness comes to all of them (even to the Cardinal), and when they awaken too late from the sordid dreams of their past they despair, not of life itself[11] but of their contemptible selves. For Antonio and Bosola the burden of self-knowledge is almost as terrible as it is for Ferdinand. Even though it gives them the strength to try to change their lives, it warps their actions as they move through death-in-life towards the grave.

In Antonio and Bosola we confront again, but with deeper understanding, the paralysis of will that committed Flamineo to a career which he knew was hopeless. We see now that it is not conscience which makes cowards of us all but a hunger for personal safety; we discover with Bosola that security is the suburb of Hell. In *The White Devil* only the pious were deluded by false securities; in the *Duchess*, however, those who seem to see the world most clearly are most deeply infatuated with nonexistent safeties. "Realism" is itself an illusion that robs men of the strength to accomplish their purposes.

On the surface Antonio and Bosola are moral opposites, one a loyal, virtuous servant, the other a despicable Machiavellian intelligencer. Bosola decries an age in which virtue is its own reward; Antonio boasts that he has "long serv'd vertue,/ And nev'r tane wages of her." Bosola is chosen to be Ferdinand's informer because Antonio is incorruptible—the "worthy," the "good man." When Antonio sets out to face the Cardinal, Delio exclaims, "Your owne vertue save you," but neither Antonio's honesty nor Bosola's policy secure them against their fates. And it is hardly an accident that they cause each other's death, for in life they were brothers under the skin, men who committed spiritual suicide before a sword-thrust ended their miserable lives.

Like Flamineo, Bosola is a malcontent, embittered by experience, and hungry for the security which advancement will afford. He lacks Flamineo's high-spirited wit but he is capable of true moral feeling, and although he can for a time relish his Machiavellian successes he is finally appalled by Ferdinand's insane revenge upon the Duchess. He would like to be "honest" in Antonio's way, but he knows himself and the world too well to try, and he can never escape the self-pitying anger of the "neglected" man. Early in the play he complains to his former master, the Cardinal:

> I have done you better service then to be slighted thus: miserable age, where onely the reward of doing well, is the doing of it! (I. i. 32–34)

This ironic mockery of the ideal of virtue for its own sake is completed by the knowledge that Bosola's "good service" was murder. He recognizes only two ways of "doing well": either through profitless virtue or by profitable villainy. Thus when Ferdinand offers gold, he immediately asks:

> So:
> What followes? (Never raind such showres as these
> Without thunderbolts i'th taile of them;) whose throat must I cut?
> (I. i. 264–66)

He is tempted to refuse these corrupting gifts which would take him "to hell," but unable to refuse he accepts his servitude in a pathetic and revealing speech:

> I would have you curse your selfe now, that your bounty
> (Which makes men truly noble) ere should make
> Me a villaine: oh, that to avoid ingratitude
> For the good deed you have done me, I must doe
> All the ill man can invent: Thus the Divell
> Candies all sinnes o'er: and what Heaven termes vild,
> That names he complementall. (I. i. 295–301)

If Bosola does not yet have a conscience, he has certain moral needs. He is genuinely outraged, it seems, by the hypocrisy and sanctimony that delight the more deeply cynical Flamineo. And unlike Flamineo, who serves to be free from service, he seeks to give meaning to his life by loyal service—first to Ferdinand and then to Antonio. Assuming, however, that moral service is impossible when great men are not noble, he chooses a cutthroat's honor, a scrupulous adherence to the bargain that gold seals and reward justifies. Too poor to look up to heaven, he asks Antonio's leave "to be honest in any phrase, in any complement whatsoever—shall I confesse my selfe to you? I look no higher then I can reach . . ." (II. i. 90–92). This is the "realist's" defeatist credo. Too cowardly to aspire to virtue, Bosola will dare any criminal act before he dares to assume control over his own destiny. So long as he believes that he will save himself by loyal service, he remains true to his politic code. But when Ferdinand rewards him with a curse for murdering the Duchess, his cynicism disintegrates into plaintive questioning:

> Let me know
> Wherefore I should be thus neglected? sir,
> I serv'd your tyranny: and rather strove,
> To satisfie your selfe, then all the world;
> And though I loath'd the evill, yet I lov'd
> You that did councell it: and rather sought
> To appeare a true servant, then an honest man. (IV. ii. 353–59)

Bosola is the feudal liege man brought up to Jacobean date; he is a man o' the times who yearns like Kent to be "acknowledged." Left alone with the Duchess' body he recoils from his own depravity and decides to redeem his life by dedicating it to Antonio. (Although he lectured to his Duchess on the vanity of life, it was she who taught him "how to die.") Despite his new-found moral courage, however, Bosola never escapes from the mist of error that enshrouds his life. The Cardinal's Machiavellian tenacity temporarily blunts his moral purpose and causes him to stab Antonio, whom he would have saved. He dies still gnawed by "neglect," happy only that he has fallen "in so good a quarrell."

For Antonio there is not even this satisfaction. His contemptible death is appropriate for one who felt trapped by circumstances at the moment of his greatest happiness. When he jests with the Duchess about the deceptive joys of marriage, his lines ring pathetically true. Too knowledgeable and wary, he lacks the sublimely illusory confidence that love brings to his wife. Overwhelmed by Ferdinand's fury, he tries repeatedly to shape some safety for himself and thus he is, in spite of his soldierly abilities, ineffectual in every crisis. "Lost in amazement," he confides his fears to Delio; and though he speaks bravely of

confronting Ferdinand he ignores his opportunity. When at Loretto
the Duchess suggests that they part, he replies, "You councell safely";
even then he speaks of himself as spiritually dead.

When he is infinitely weary of his "pore lingering life" and
despairs of saving himself by halves, he seeks a "pardon" from the
Cardinal. His hope for mercy is suicidal, but he seems to know this;
indeed, he is more than half in love with easeful death. He has opened
inward on himself the doors of death which have such "strange geo-
metrical hinges"; and when Bosola completes the agonizing mortification by degrees Antonio plays his own tragic chorus:

> In all our Quest of Greatnes . . .
> (Like wanton Boyes, whose pastime is their care)
> We follow after bubbles, blowne in th'ayre.
> Pleasure of life, what is't? onely the good houres
> Of an Ague: meerely a preparative to rest,
> To endure vexation. (V. iv. 75–80)

Here is Flamineo's testament of futility softened by pathos and regret.
The pity of Antonio's fate is not that he could have saved the woman
he loved, but that he knew too well the hopelessness of his situation.
Content to stave off disaster as long as he can, he protects his secret
marriage by lies and deceptions. He grows rich "the left hand way"
while rumors spread that his wife is a whore. He takes shameful ways
to avoid shame because he cannot accept with dignity the fatal consequences which he so clearly foresaw.

In Bosola and Antonio, Webster cuts across conventional distinctions to illuminate the anguish of men whose lack of illusion is the
greatest illusion of all. Perplexing as these characters seem to modern
readers, they were no doubt recognizable to Webster's audience, who
saw at court many men similarly fascinated with their dooms, flutter-
ing like moths around the candle of advancement and hoping even in
the Tower for a return to favor or a royal reconciliation, until the
executioner's axe brought an end to uncertainty.

In Brachiano and Flamineo, Webster admired heroic villains who
to themselves were "enough"; he sought the meaning of life in the
Troll morality. We cannot judge Bosola, however, by the standard of
the Gyntian self, for his mind is so divided that he is never truer to
himself than when he vacillates between cynicism and compassion for

the Duchess. If, as we are told, Webster celebrates the religion of self in the *Duchess*,[12] then his high priest is Ferdinand, who like the lunatics in *Peer Gynt* achieves the total absorption in self possible only to the insane. Even before his mind gives way Ferdinand lives in a continual fever of egoism that is alleviated by the complete subjugation of Bosola and his sister. We do not have to exaggerate the faint suggestions of incestuous desire to motivate Ferdinand's fury at the Duchess; even more terrible than any hints of unnatural lust is his frenzied conception of "Honor," his pitiless identification with his sister. To him her greatest sin lay in her blood, the same blood that runs through his aristocratic veins.

The Cardinal is a complementary portrait of the buried life: his diseased ego is satisfied not by a brute assertion of will but by a rational mastery of Machiavellian arts. He pursues, it would seem, the ultimate intellectual refinement of Machiavellian technique that becomes an end in itself. He does not have the Elizabethan Machiavel's instinctive appetite for horrendous crime. He has a connoisseur's taste for flawless villainy, for security in evil. On the surface he is nerveless, emotionless, so much the master of himself that even Bosola must admire his seeming fearlessness. But what appears at first to be a mastery of passion is finally revealed to be a deficiency of normal feeling, an emotional lifelessness. Delio has heard that the Cardinal is

> a brave fellow,
> Will play his five thousand crownes, at Tennis, Daunce,
> Court Ladies, and one that hath fought single Combats.
>
> (I. i. 154–56)

Antonio knows better: "Some such flashes superficially hang on him, for forme: but observe his inward Character: he is a mellancholly Churchman" (I. i. 157–58). Apart from these superficial flashes the Cardinal has no commitment to life. He spends his last hours troubled by a dull headache of remorse and bored by the whisper of his conscience. Together with Ferdinand he represents the collaboration of sadistic fury and intellectuality that lies behind the totalitarian savagery in *Lear* and in the world around us. If there is a heavy-handed irony in the manner of his death, his sudden display of cowardice is not surprising in one so expert at murdering defenseless women. Although he seemed fearless, the prospect of death unnerves him.

Cringing, begging to be spared, he tries to buy off Bosola, who answers:

> Now it seemes thy Greatnes was onely outward:
> For thou fall'st faster of thy selfe, then calamitie
> Can drive thee. (V. v. 56–58)

Though mortally wounded himself, Bosola is satisfied that the Cardinal, who

> stood'st like a huge Piramid
> Begun upon a large, and ample base,
> Shalt end in a little point, a kind of nothing. (V. v. 96–98)

If the Cardinal has any virtue it lies in the final knowledge of his insignificance—in his request to be laid aside and forgotten.

Webster's search for a nobility that rises above enslaving circumstances, unsatisfied in the glorious villains of *The White Devil*, is consummated in his portrait of a fragile, tormented young woman kneeling before her murderers. Only he among the Jacobeans dared to find a tragic heroism in a vain, willful girl, who until her dying moments is careless of her name and blind to the responsibilities which accompany prerogative. In temperament she is a heroine of Shakespearean romantic comedy, graceful, witty, wanton and innocent at the same time, who woos and wins her husband in spite of himself. She capriciously ignores the challenge of an aristocratic life, but the challenge of death— the supreme challenge in Jacobean tragedy—she accepts boldly and triumphantly. There is a beauty in her death that makes the ugliness of Ferdinand's life unbearable and that shakes the cynical nihilism which is Bosola's defense against conscience. What begins as a vicarious purge of the filthiness of Ferdinand's mind becomes in the end a conflict of inner strength between the Duchess and her torturers. Caught in the trap that Fortune set for her she ceases to be Fortune's slave. Her murderers would drag her down and open her eyes to the "realities" which they perceive; they would have her share the horror of their lives. They bring her to her knees, but it is the posture of heaven. They surround her with assassins but it is she who gives the last command:

> Go tell my brothers, when I am laid out,
> They then may feede in quiet. (IV. ii. 243–44)

From the lips of a woman who has gone beyond despair we learn the annihilating truth that the power to oppress and kill is an ultimate value only to those who find death "infinitely terrible."

For the Duchess no gesture of defiance is needed to obliterate the terror of death. It is against the attempt to despoil her humanity that she flings her celebrated assertion of individuality, "I am Duchesse of *Malfy* still." Perhaps we tend to exaggerate the heroic ring of this line, which could be justly interpreted as a tremor of meaningless pride. But even if it is an expression of that quality which Chapman called "noblesse," there is no justification for removing the line from its context as *the* quintessential moment of the play. The Duchess' strength is not a lonely existential awareness of self but a remembrance of love, expressed in her parting words to Cariola and in her answers to Bosola. The spirit of woman that once betrayed now sustains her, for she knows that the fragile, "illusory" joys of devotion are the deepest certainties of human existence. Webster's other heroes and heroines die obsessed with their sins and follies, projecting their individual experiences as the pattern of man's fate. The Duchess is the only one to move out of self, to turn her thoughts outward upon those she loves and upward in serene religious faith.

More than a conventional artistic "solution," the Duchess' piety seems an intuition of a realm of values obscured by the corruption of the Church (in which the Cardinal is a Prince) and by the cant that passes for religious conviction. Yet Webster does not allow us to share the Duchess' conviction of the providential nature of her torments. As in *Lear* the characters in the *Duchess* interpret their tragic experiences in various and contradictory ways. And if any one character speaks for Webster at the close, it is not Delio, the outsider, but Bosola, who was an actor "in all the maine of all":

> Oh, this gloomy world,
> In what a shadow, or deepe pit of darknesse,
> Doth (womanish, and fearefull) mankind live!
> Let worthy mindes nere stagger in distrust
> To suffer death, or shame, for what is just——(V. v. 124-28)

It is not the courage to be greatly evil which Bosola commends, but the courage to be greatly good in a world which offers a hundred crooked subterfuges and which demands the sham, not the reality, of virtue.

When we look in Webster's later plays for a more positive note we find little worthy of the genius that created *The White Devil* and the *Duchess*. So far as we can see Webster said all that he had to say artistically in these two plays. The rest should have been silence because when he returns to earlier themes in *Appius and Virginia* (1625–27) his lines are unconvincing. Yet the play is interesting in that it seems to confirm Jonson's influence on Webster's tragic art. One might expect that collaboration with Heywood would soften the harshness of Webster's muse, that *Appius and Virginia* would linger on the sweet pathos of the ancient tale. One finds, however, that the acrid spirit of *Sejanus* reigns,[13] that pathos gives way, even in the final scene (attributed by Mr. Lucas to Heywood), to an appreciation of the heroic fortitude of a Machiavellian villain. The scenes of military life and dissension may well have been inspired by *Coriolanus*, but the portrait of Appius is clearly modeled on Jonson's Roman politicians, who also corrupt the law and tyrannize over a decaying state. Unfortunately the attempt to follow Jonson's Roman way is soon obscured by melodramatic scenes of confrontation and reversal. Because the choric commentaries on tyranny, on fortune, and on politic ambition are purely rhetorical, we cannot take Icilius and Virginius seriously as saviors of a tottering Roman state. In fact the theatricalism of the latter half of the play makes one suspect that Mr. Lucas is too optimistic in assuming that here "Webster escapes from the influence of Fletcher."[14]

Less conclusive is the evidence of Jonson's influence on *The Devil's Law-Case* (1620), though the climactic trial scenes do suggest that Webster returned to Marlowe's Barabas by way of *Volpone*. Closer in spirit to Webster's masterpieces than to *Appius and Virginia*, *The Devil's Law-Case* shows momentary flashes of Webster's earlier brilliance, but its Machiavellian hero, Romelio, is too bourgeois to stand beside Flamineo and Bosola and his engagingly cynical candor is almost completely submerged in the crosscurrents of a swirling plot. One senses in the careless entanglements of the fable Webster's impatience with the petty venal world he derisively portrays. Like Antonio, the disappointed Leonora awakens wearily from her illusions to confront the emptiness of her past. She remarks to her maid:

> Thou hast lived with me
> These fortie yeares; we have growne old together,

As many Ladies and their women doe,
With talking nothing, and with doing lesse:
We have spent our life in that which least concernes life,
Only in putting on our clothes. (III. iii. 418–23)

These lines are as memorable in their own fashion as many of the great speeches in the *Duchess* and *The White Devil;* they are touched by a sudden, unexpected compassion that turns the edge of satire against itself. Yet Webster is too contemptuous to enter fully into the mind of Leonora or to enjoy the bitter-sweetness of unheroic aspiration and frustration. Had he more of Shakespeare's tolerant appreciation of the minutiae of life he might have escaped the gloomy pit of his tragedies into more sunlit horizons. But the virtues which he admired and which called forth the supreme effort of his genius flowered only in the darkness of mortal agony. He lived in such imaginative communion with death that perhaps he could not respond to the beauty of spring without also remembering the mocking fragrance and beauty of a decked hearse.

It is not for us, however, to pity the personal anguish that finds expression in immortal art. Whatever horror is projected in the imagery and action of the *Duchess,* its most vivid and memorable scene is the triumph of the Duchess over adversity—a triumph of mind and spirit which we do not find again in tragedy until Ford's portrait of Penthea in *The Broken Heart.* Because of its melancholy twilight mood and its haunting portrayals of spiritual despair, the *Duchess* seems to us a "late" play, one that is burdened with the entire weight of the Jacobean tragic experience. But if with *Caesar and Pompey* it marks the passing, or rejection, of the heroic vision of early Jacobean drama, it also signals (as will become clear in Chapter VII) a new and vital emphasis in tragedy which was to mature in the plays of Middleton and Ford. And if it is true that the *Duchess* is a threnody for the dying Renaissance, then it is altogether fitting that it should reaffirm that ineffable quality of the human spirit which the Renaissance defined as the dignity of man.

CHAPTER VI

John Marston
Beaumont & Fletcher

Only the tactlessness of scholarship would impose the uncouth Marston on so suave and congenial a pair as Beaumont and Fletcher. Crowded in a little room they form an uncomfortable trio, so different in talent and temperament that it is hard to believe that they were contemporaries who wrote for the same audiences. We cannot imagine Fletcher committing Marston's artistic atrocities, nor can we imagine Marston losing himself in Fletcher's Arcadian dreamworld. As tragedians, however, they stood approximately equidistant from the "center" of Jacobean tragedy; men of considerable talents and little vision, they were in touch with, but not involved in, the tragic issues of their greater contemporaries. In the next chapter we will have occasion to study the unique character of *The Maid's Tragedy*. But here we are concerned not with Marston's and Beaumont and Fletcher's achievements in tragedy but with their respective roles as prologue and epilogue to the first golden decade of Jacobean tragedy. Whereas Marston's plays heralded in crude form

the finer achievements in tragedy that were to follow, Fletcher guided
Jacobean drama from Shakespearean heights to a valley of mediocrity
in which the only artistic landmarks were the tragedies of Middleton
and Ford.

Critics who have no taste for Marston's virtues have no charity
for his vices, and in truth it is often difficult to distinguish the two.
Like most experimenters he revels in the "original" stroke; his most
reliable weapon is surprise. His lack of propriety is the breach in the
wall of convention through which his wit sallies in pursuit of a novel
effect. One never feels that Marston's muse was difficult or crabbed as
Webster's is reputed to have been. Though his tragic style is labored,
it was probably not labored over. Even in his least successful plays he
writes with a genuine theatrical instinct, with a knack for racy dialogue of a somewhat unrespectable nature. In his comedies he is
avowedly an entertainer, who seeks to delight and not instruct, and
whose modest aim is to amuse without offending.

Nevertheless Marston has offended some critics, particularly Professor Harbage, who finds in his plays the moral and artistic eccen-
tricities characteristic of the "coterie" drama.[1] More recently Samuel
Schoenbaum has delineated the "precarious balance" of Marston's
mind: his "maladjusted" morbid fascination with sex, disease, bodily
functions, and filth.[2] Without denying Marston's linguistic outrages, I
would still suggest (if psychological inferences are in order) that
Marston was probably one of the more stable personalities who wrote
for the Jacobean stage. He accepted the orders of the Church, I
imagine, with a relatively clear conscience because his greatest artistic
sins were committed in invincible ignorance and often with high
seriousness; moreover they were primarily sins against good taste
rather than premeditated assaults on moral values.

From a broad cultural viewpoint, taste and morality may be inseparable, but in a specific literary instance, discrimination between
the two is possible and necessary because standards of propriety vary
more widely than do standards of morality. The bawdy puns in Shakespeare offended Victorians, and the Chaucerian fabliaux are no longer
suitable for mixed company, even among the disinterested students of
literature in coeducational universities. Although the invention of the

flush toilet sweetened the literary imagination, a concern with bodily functions has arisen again in the fiction of the twentieth century, and the love of an off-color joke has been from Chaucer to James Joyce a sign of robust literary talent. Marston's bawdry, unfortunately, is neither as witty as Joyce's nor as artistically appropriate as Shakespeare's. It has nothing to recommend it except sheer exuberance and the undeniable accent of truth. Too frequently, moreover, Marston's style is the raw hyperbole of the Elizabethan popular satirist. His intention is quite obviously to shock the sensibilities, to obtain the phrase with the proper "intestinal" effect. And yet his grossness seems wholly naïve and boisterous and utterly free of the calculated prurience which mars Fletcher's far more genteel art. We can well believe that the sophisticated wits who frequented the private theaters enjoyed Marston, because he is a literary curiosity, an "original" who possessed the kind of rough vitality which is patronized even today by some esoteric literary circles. And although his intellectual capacities were negligible, he filled his plays with modish ideas, especially with the newly coined literary gold of Florio's Montaigne.

While Shakespeare's or Webster's imitations of Montaigne are only indirectly illuminating, Marston's wholesale plagiarism of the *Essays* (which was remarkable even in an age of copybooks) is an immediate revelation of his artistic interests and habits. We cannot say that he was influenced by Montaigne, because there is little evidence that he assimilated intellectually the passages which he copied from the *Essays;* and like Webster he was attracted to Montaigne's incidental observations, not his philosophical thought. Marston was a merchandiser of Montaigne's ideas, content to take an immediate profit in the flavor that they added to a casual spot of dialogue. His goal was not to enrich his mind with Montaigne's urbane wisdom but to salt the thin vein of his wit with the polished gems of Florio's prose. Without transmuting that prose into poetry, he incorporated it so skillfully in his plays that we are scarcely aware of the use of scissors and paste. He also has a certain skill in reshuffling materials from the *Essays* to fit a particular dramatic context. An observation on nature is neatly grafted on a discussion of policy. A comment on the social hypocrisies of feminine modesty is cleverly reoriented to apply to a nuptial scene.[3]

Because Marston gathered other men's ideas with a kind of journalistic curiosity, his plays are valuable mirrors of current opinions. But by the same token, it is almost impossible to piece together Marston's own viewpoints by excerpting passages from his plays. By snipping out lines here and there, one can offer a fascinating variety of "Marstons," none of them perhaps true to the total impression of his personality which we derive from the plays. Compared to Webster, of course, Marston seems easily accessible. He does not brood behind the masks of his *dramatis personae;* he seems to have nothing to hide or nothing that he cares to hide. And yet he is so inured to his literary trade that he can scarcely write without calculated effect and without assuming a professional stance. In the *Satires,* where he pretends to unpack his heart with words, he creates a dramatic personality which is in some ways as artificial as any of the characters in his plays. He comes before us as the traditional satirist: blunt, outspoken, caustic, contemptuous, a fearless moral critic of the time. His targets—the social follies and vices of London citizenry—are as conventional as his method of attack. He has the popular controversialist's command of invective and finds no subject within his narrow range too petty or vulgar for commentary. At the same time he is acutely conscious of the noble purpose of satire and fiercely defends his high "calling."

Because Marston very slenderly knew his literary purposes, it is difficult to assess the sincerity of his literary attitudes and emotions. Yet even if we assume the worst about the intention of *Pygmalion,* we need not conclude that the attacks on sexual vices in the *Satires* and the plays are hypocritical. There is a difference between a poem of the pure (or impure) imagination and a poem or play which deals with "life."A writer who apologizes for his wanton muse—for sophisticated eroticism in art—may be honestly revolted by carnality in the world around him. And Marston's entry into the Church would suggest that the contempt for Precisians expressed in the *Satires* and the moral passion of *The Malcontent* (1604) are more than conventional.

Of course, it is all too easy to mistake an effectively wrought line for an outburst of personal feeling because the impression of sincerity depends so largely on aesthetic effect, on the diction and tone of a passage. We must remember that Marston, like Tourneur (and like all successful writers), has the ability to exploit his own feelings for artistic purposes. Indeed one would judge from the totality of

Marston's works that he was an "artist" first, a moralist second. *The Malcontent* is a relatively fine play because Marston's literary purpose is perfectly attuned to his moral sensibility. His melodramatic intention creates so weird a confusion of ethical values in *Antonio's Revenge* (1601), however, that the ending of the play has served many critics as an illustration of Jacobean obliquity.[4] While Antonio and his fellow assassins pluck out the tongue of Piero, a Senecan tyrant, the ghost of Andrugio exclaims:

> Bless'd be thy hand! I taste the joys of heaven,
> Viewing my son triumph in his black blood.[5] (V. ii. 67–68)

And when after a quaint variation of the Thyestian feast, the much tortured Piero is finally killed, the Ghost sighs:

> 'Tis done, and now my soul shall sleep in rest:
> Sons that revenge their father's blood are blest. (V. ii. 114–15)

The Ghost is not mistaken. Instead of the hangman, Antonio and the other gloating revengers face a group of public-spirited citizens, who laud their achievements and hope that their "honours live/ Religiously held sacred, even forever and ever" (V. ii. 127–28). Antonio, who has butchered an innocent child in cold blood, listens modestly and then decides with his companions to continue his pious efforts in "holy verge of some religious order" as "most constant votaries."

If we did not see in Marston's other plays a lack of discipline and a willingness to sacrifice artistic unity for immediate dramatic effect, we might well suspect that the closing scene of *Antonio's Revenge* is a sardonic travesty of Christian sentiment. A familiarity with Marston's literary methods suggests, however, that the ethical intention of *Antonio's Revenge* is not confused but rather as peripheral as that of *Titus Andronicus*. Incapable of Fletcher's frivolity, Marston approached tragedy with as serious a purpose as Chapman, but he aspired to a "Senecan" ideal that was, if anything, less sophisticated than Kyd's and that equated tragic grandeur with rhetorical bombast and gruesome melodrama. The proud boast in Antonio's valedictory speech that "Never more woe in lesser plot was found" indicates the nature of Marston's dramatic intention. It is not the tears in things that he seeks to express; it is the "rarity of Art," "the pur'st elixed juice of rich conceit," which in practice meant an almost grotesque hyperbole. Confusing exaggeration with elevation, he gives his protagonist and villain heroic proportions by sheer inflation. Since Piero's tyranny is diabolically inhuman, Antonio's revenge must be appropriately fiendish. In a sense Marston's melodramatic instinct was correct; nothing short of the rack would have been a just punishment for Piero. But when Piero has received the appropriate Senecan tortures, Marston, shopping around for the obligatory moral ending, perfumes the butchery with the odor of sanctity. If he intended the monastic decision to symbolize the revengers' unfitness for normal life, then he would have been wiser to allow Antonio to die, unless of course he kept him alive with a vague thought of yet another sequel to *Antonio and Mellida*.

Had Marston been a more sensitive and disciplined craftsman, he might have chosen a more fitting conclusion for *Antonio's Revenge*. At the same time, however, he might also have excluded from the play much that is fascinating as well as irrelevant. The intrusion of Stoic philosophy in the *Revenge*, for example, is strictly speaking fraudulent. It adds a "philosophical" complication that has no organic purpose in Marston's fable. Yet the pitting of Senecan philosophy against Senecan revenge motivation is in itself an inspired innovation which later dramatists (e.g., Chapman and Tourneur) make dramatically and morally significant. As a matter of fact Marston's protagonist has need of Stoic resignation. His father has been murdered by the man who is forcing his mother into marriage. His fiancée has been accused of foul lust. Advised to be patient, he retorts that "Patience is slave to fools." Told that " 'tis reason's glory to command affects," he rejects painted comforts. He is passion's slave personified until rebuked by the Stoical Pandulfo, who has mastered similar cause for grief and rage. For a time Marston threatens to write finis to the revenge convention by anticipating Tourneur's and Chapman's "rejection" of its ethic; Pandulfo advises Antonio:

> 'Tis not true valour's pride
> To swagger, quarrel, swear, stamp, rave, and chide,
> To stab in fume of blood, to keep loud coils,
> To bandy factions in domestic broils,
> To dare the act of sins, whose filth excels
> The blackest customs of blind infidels.

No, my lov'd youth: he may of valour vaunt
Whom fortune's loudest thunder cannot daunt;
Whom fretful gales of chance, stern fortune's siege,
Makes not his reason slink, the soul's fair liege;
Whose well-pais'd action ever rests upon
Not giddy humours but discretion. (I. ii. 325–36)

If Pandulfo's philosophy prevails, the mounting atmosphere of Senecan horror and premonition of bloody catastrophe will lead to the most exasperating anticlimax in the annals of drama. Fortunately reason rather than revenge is vanquished. Seeking spiritual "physic" in Seneca, Antonio finds only hackneyed precepts and meretricious platitudes. After a few lines of *De Providentia*, he exclaims:

Pish, thy mother was not lately widowèd,
Thy dear affièd love lately defam'd
With blemish of foul lust, when thou wrotest thus;
Thou wrapt in furs, beaking thy limbs 'fore fires;
Forbid'st the frozen zone to shudder. Ha, ha! 'tis nought
But foamy bubbling of a fleamy brain,
Nought else but smoke. (II. ii. 49–55)

Finally Pandulfo breaks down in the very act of delivering a sermon on fortitude and admits that he has merely hidden his natural weaknesses behind a Stoical facade:

Man will break out, despite philosophy.
Why, all this while I ha' but played a part,
Like to some boy that acts a tragedy,
Speaks burly words, and raves out passion;
But, when he thinks upon his infant weakness,
He droops his eye. I spake more than a god,
Yet am less than a man.
I am the miserablest soul that breathes. (IV. ii. 69–76)

So much for philosophy! With this confession Pandulfo drops his Stoic pose and assumes the more "natural" role of bloodthirsty revenger.

Although one could interpret this "rejection" of reason as an example of the Jacobean belief in psychological determinism, it seems more accurate to describe Pandulfo's reversal as a utilitarian device of plot. Despite the quotation from *De Providentia*, Marston's concern with Stoic philosophy never rises above the stale libel of Seneca's voluptuousness, repeated in *The Malcontent*. Indeed, Marston's "unconventional" rejection of Stoic rationality is quite conventional; he is the first Jacobean to exploit dramatically the skepticism about Stoic self-sufficiency expressed by Erasmus and Montaigne and implicit in the moral philosophy of the Elizabethan age.[6]

Marston's treatment of Stoicism is characteristic. It promises at first more than it finally delivers. It presents a current opinion in its lowest common denominator. Elsewhere in his plays there are interesting suggestions of a contemporary weariness with intellectual controversy that faintly adumbrates the more significant "nominalism" of Webster's tragedies. His mockery of philosophy is frequently a conventional attack on pedantry; but now and then Marston's satiric wit cuts below the surface of casual observation. In *What You Will* (1601) the discontented Lampatho expresses a conventionally Montaignesque disparagement of reason:

> In Heaven's handiwork there's naught,
> None more vile, accursed, reprobate to bliss,
> Than man: and 'mong men a scholar most.
> Things only freshly sensitive, an ox or horse,
> They live and eat, and sleep, and drink, and die,
> And are not touched with recollections
> Of things o'er-past, or stagger'd infant doubts
> Of things succeeding. (II. ii. 128–35)

Then he adds a more immediate and pregnant comment on "vain philosophy":

> I was a scholar; seven useful springs
> Did I deflower in quotations
> Of cross'd opinions 'bout the soul of man.
> The more I learnt the more I learnt to doubt:
> Knowledge and wit, faith's foes, turn faith about.
> .   .   .   .
>   philosophers
> Stood band[y]ing factions all so strongly propp'd,
> I stagger'd, knew not which was firmer part;
> But thought, quoted, read, observ'd, and pried,
> Stuff'd noting-books; and still my spaniel slept.
> At length he waked and yawn'd and by yon sky,
> For aught I know he knew as much as I. (II. ii. 151–80)

Lampatho, like Flamineo after him, knows the infinite vexation of thought, of confounding knowledge with knowledge. Having wasted his youth on the idle questions which engrossed the Paduans and the Christian apologists, he at last turned to more fruitful endeavors.

When Marston touches on a significant moral or philosophical question it is, generally speaking, by way of minor characters. In *Sophonisba* (1605–6), for example, an impressive refutation of Machiavellian doctrine (cribbed from Montaigne) is given to Gelossa, and the servant maid Zanthia argues, like Chapman's Machiavels, that wedlock or virtue "Are courses and varieties of reason,/ To use or leave, as they advantage them" (III. i. 83–84). In *The Malcontent* Maquerelle expresses the libertine argument that honesty is but a fable devised to "wrong our liberty" (V. ii. 108–11). In the first scene of *The Fawn* (1604–6), Duke Hercules pleads for the "appetite of blood" with a familiar libertine dialectic:

> And now, thou ceremonious sovereignty—
> Ye proud, severer, stateful compliments,
> The secret arts of rule—I put you off;
> Nor ever shall these manacles of form
> Once more lock up the appetite of blood.
>
> .   .   .   .
>
> Shall I, because some few may cry, "Light! vain!"
> Beat down affection from desirèd rule?
> He that doth strive to please the world's a fool.
> To have that fellow cry, "O mark him, grave,
> See how austerely he doth give example
> Of repressed heat and steady life!"
> Whilst my forced life against the stream of blood
> Is tugg'd along, and all to keep the god
> Of fools and women, nice Opinion,
> Whose strict preserving makes oft great men fools,
> And fools oft great men. No, thou world, know thus,
> There's nothing free but it is generous. (I. i. 40–65)

But a reader who anticipates a torrid portrait of unconfined love will be disappointed, because the Duke casts off the "manacles of form" to become a satiric scourge of villainy.

The Dutch Courtezan (1603–4), Marston's most successful and "philosophical" comedy, offers in the midst of gutter slang and bawdry the first extensive treatment of libertine ideas in Jacobean drama. From its opening a somber note is struck by Malheureux, a puritanical moralist, who is revolted by the casual sensuality of his friend Freevill. Freevill, a libertine more by inclination than by conviction, has sowed his wild oats and is ready to marry and "settle down." As a joke he takes his moralizing friend on a farewell visit to his whore, Franceschina. Doomed by the most venerable cliché of Elizabethan comedy —Cupid's revenge—Malheureux falls promptly in love with her. Only here the venerable cliché takes on a new meaning because Malheureux falls victim to what the moral philosophers of the late Renaissance called "natural passion." Freevill, amused by Malheureux's infatuation, regards it as a vindication of his own incontinence, and he mockingly turns Malheureux's words against him:

> Go your ways for an apostata! I believe my cast garment
> must be let out in the seams for you when all is done.
>   Of all the fools that would all man out-thrust,
>   He that 'gainst Nature would seem wise is worst.
>
> (I. ii. 268–72)

Malheureux does not enjoy the joke. Although he cannot easily shrug off his moral habits, his awakened sensuality threatens his puritanical convictions:

> Is she unchaste—can such a one be damn'd?
> O love and beauty! ye two eldest seeds
> Of the vast chaos, what strong right you have
> Even in things divine—our very souls!
> .   .   .   .
> Are strumpets then such things so delicate?
> Can custom spoil what nature made so good?
> Or is their custom bad? Beauty's for use—
> I never saw a sweet face vicious! (I. ii. 234–46)

Malheureux's scruples are beginning to waver. Like Ford's lovers he finds Neoplatonic sophistries to justify his lust, but he does not yet abandon the traditional moral view of custom and nature. He still believes that virtue is natural, and vice an "unnatural" product of vicious custom. He is no longer sure that Franceschina is evil, but if she is, it is because evil habits have corrupted her natural goodness. In theory, at least, he is still true to moral philosophy.

Like all romantic agonists he struggles vainly against irresistible passion:

> Soul, I must love her! Destiny is weak
> To my affection.—A common love!—
> Blush not, faint breast!
> That which is ever loved of most is best.
> Let colder eld the strong'st objections move,
> No love's without some lust, no life without some love.
>
> (I. ii. 248–53)

As his desire mounts, his casuistry becomes more subtle and ingenious, until at last, weary of rationalizing, he joins with the libertine naturalists in complaining against the tyranny of custom:

> [Birds] have no bawds, no mercenary beds,
> No polite restraints, no artificial heats,
> No faint dissemblings; no custom makes them blush,
> No shame afflicts their name. O you happy beasts!
> In whom an inborn heat is not held sin,
> How far transcend you wretched, wretched man,
> Whom national custom, tyrannous respects
> Of slavish order, fetters, lames his power,
> Calling that sin in us which in all things else
> Is Nature's highest virtue.
> *O miseri quorum gaudia crimen habent!*
> Sure Nature against virtue cross doth fall,
> Or virtue's self is oft unnatural. (II. i. 72–84)

No longer convinced of Franceschina's wickedness, Malheureux decides that tyrannical custom has falsely condemned her natural (and, therefore, "good") beauty. Inverting the traditional antithesis of custom and nature, he agrees with the libertines that despite artificial laws, man is still nature's creature, in whom sexual desire is "Nature's highest virtue." Malheureux still believes that virtue exists, but he sees that nature and virtue clash, that man's tragedy is his inability to practice the morality he is capable of idealizing:

> O accursed reason,
>
> How many eyes hast thou to see thy shame,
> And yet how blind once to prevent defame! (II. i. 89–91)

Because "raging lust" controls his fate, Malheureux kneels before Franceschina, who demands as the price of her favors Freevill's murder. Proclaiming "there is no hell but love's prolongings," Malheureux agrees, but finds it impossible to rationalize murder by naturalistic arguments:

> To kill my friend! O 'tis to kill myself!
> Yet man's but man's excrement—man breeding man
> As he does worms; or this, to spoil this nothing.
> The body of a man is of the self-same mould
> As ox or horse; no murder to kill these.
> As for that only part which makes us man,
> Murder wants power to touch't. O wit, how vile!
> How hellish art thou, when thou raisest nature
> 'Gainst sacred faith! Think more: to kill a friend
> To gain a woman! to lose a virtuous self
> For appetite and sensual end, whose very having
> Loseth all appetite, and gives satiety! (II. ii. 213–24)

Put to this crucial test Malheureux's libertine philosophy disintegrates, for analogies between men and animals reduce men to worse than brutishness. And even Freevill, who refused to take Malheureux's passion seriously, now sees that lust is a most deadly sin. Overhearing Franceschina's plot, he exclaims:

> O, thou unreprievable, beyond all
> Measure of grace damn'd irremediably!
> That things of beauty created for sweet use,
> Soft comfort, as the very music of life,
> Custom should make so unutterably hellish! (V. i. 63–67)

In Freevill's speech the wheel comes full circle. Although there is some recognition that reason and nature have divided, nature and custom neatly return to their traditional places in the moral scheme. When the plot is finally untangled all ends happily. Virtue is preserved, villainy punished, and even the conycatching Cocledemoy is revealed to be an "innocent wag."

If *The Dutch Courtezan* is a weightier play than Marston's other comedies, its treatment of libertine naturalism is nevertheless superficial. The illumination which D'Amville obtains through mind-shattering catastrophes comes facilely to Malheureux, whose passion is a temporary quirk in a repressed, Angelo-like temperament. The wooden rhetoric and transparent speciosity of Malheureux's arguments make it difficult to take his libertinism seriously or to connect it with any larger or more serious questioning of the traditional moral view of nature. But then we should not expect high seriousness from Marston's comedies, which he dismissed as "slight hasty labours." All in all he strikes an agreeable bargain with the reader; he offers more than he demands in return. And those with a taste for the intellectual gossip of the Jacobean literary world might spend a few profitable though not very edifying hours in his company.

Beaumont and Fletcher

Even as Marston's drama is, in many respects, an induction to Jacobean tragedy, so the plays which go under the authorship of Beaumont and Fletcher form its recessional. When the tragic impulse faded, Fletcher and his collaborators reigned through the long grey period that preceded the appearance of Ford. Fletcher's artistic talents were considerable, perhaps superior to his goals. His dramatic techniques were so fluent as to make one long at times for Marston's roughness, for the crudity and boisterousness which at least flowed in the common muddy stream of Jacobean life. After a while one grows slightly tired of interchangeable characters, plots, and situations, of pasteboard heroes and heroines who are suitable for all dramatic occasions because they have no inner reality or individuality. Questions of honor, chastity, and loyalty arise, but they are so woven into the rhetorical texture of the plays that they do not trouble the intellect. The climactic scenes of Webster's tragedies are those in which his heroes and heroines face the challenge of death. The climactic moments of Fletcher's tragicomedies occur more often than not in boudoirs when honor or courtly love is in rhetorical question. The chaste heroine lures her would-be lover on only to insist upon her virtue when we can no longer believe in it.

Because the ethical frivolity of Fletcher's drama (the toying with moral as well as erotic feeling) is thoroughly premeditated and in fact the work of a highly skilled and disciplined craftsman, it is far more disturbing and reprehensible than Marston's inane amalgam of Senecan horror and religious sentiment. There were, no doubt, Elizabethan theatrical hacks who would have taken Fletcher's path had they been able to; but irresponsibility in an artist of Fletcher's talents, who dominated the English stage in the second decade of the century and whose achievements (in some contemporary eyes) overshadowed Shakespeare's, is not a common occurrence. It would seem to indicate both a decline of artistic standards and a debasement of the audience's taste.

Miss Ellis-Fermor suggests that the popularity of Fletcherian tragicomedy stemmed from "a desire to escape from the weight and profundity of tragic thought no less than from the accuracy and exactness of comic portraiture."[7] Compared to earlier tragedies Fletcherian romance is of course "escapist," but in an absolute sense it is no more escapist than the chivalric romances which held the early Elizabethan stage. One doubts, moreover, that Fletcher's audience felt any need to escape the burden of tragic thought, because that burden was felt only by a few gifted dramatists and shared by their audiences only for some brief hours in the theaters. Perhaps the bitter remarks in the preface to *The White Devil* indicate that by 1612 audiences had lost their taste for high tragedy, but all that we can say with certainty is that few great tragedies were written after the first Jacobean decade.

Fletcher's pre-eminence in the second Jacobean decade, I suspect, represents the accident of a lesser artist dominating and transforming a literary tradition that had been created by greater writers. He conquered the Jacobean theater for much the same reason that Marlowe and then Shakespeare conquered the Elizabethan stage—because with all his defects, he was the most versatile and prolific dramatist of the second decade. His audience preferred (and perhaps with reason) the relatively novel "escapism" of his romances to uninspired rehashings of the materials of tragedy and comedy. He won the laurel by the default of other men's genius.

I do not mean that Fletcher's pre-eminence was purely an accident, or that the decline of Jacobean drama was without cultural implications. Fletcher's ascendancy in Shakespeare's company marked the victory of the private theater sensibility in the once public playhouse. From a broadly popular art the English drama rapidly diminished to a courtly diversion performed for a "select" and sophisticated audience.[8] Yet in a larger perspective Fletcher did not radically alter the development of the stage. He represents instead the final stage of a long-continuing evolution that transformed the drama from an amateur communal undertaking in provincial cities and towns into a capitalistic enterprise, a very skilled, professional, and commercial entertainment centered in the metropolis of London and influenced to varying degrees by the taste and patronage of the court. Only during the relatively brief score of years when Shakespeare's genius flowered did the drama become artistically significant and retain its popular character. For he alone had the comprehensiveness and fecundity to create many plays of truly universal appeal that did not require an intellectually sophisticated audience and yet met the highest standards of disciplined and refined taste. It is not quite accurate to say that Shakespeare's art prospered at the Globe because it expressed the views of the predominantly middle-class audience. Shakespeare won his audiences by sharing with them a vision of life that transcended the parochial views of any particular class. And because he brought the relatively crude art of the popular stage to an unparalleled level of aesthetic achievement, he unwittingly helped to extinguish it.

Professor Harbage suggests quite rightly that Puritan opposition could not have silenced the stage in 1642 had not the drama first alienated itself from the general populace. Why that alienation occurred, Professor Harbage does not precisely say, except to suggest that the King's Men moved to the Blackfriar's in a shortsighted attempt to steal the thunder and the audiences of the "select" companies, who were not then a serious threat.[9] If this were true, then we must believe that the hardheaded, eminently successful businessmen of Shakespeare's company chose, by altering their repertory, to jeopardize and finally sacrifice the secure income they gained from the public theater in order to obtain an appreciably smaller and uncertain profit from the private audience.[10] It is much easier to believe that by 1608 the income from the public theaters was no longer large and secure and that the move of the King's Men was not a tactical victory over the private companies but a very strategic retreat before the actuality or imminent threat of a dwindling popular audience.

One clear reason for the decline of the public theaters would seem to be the mediocrity of their playwrights after Elizabeth's death. The plays which Heywood and Dekker wrote for the Red Bull between 1609 and 1613[11] might have satisfied an audience whose fondest memories were of *Cambises* but not an audience whose tastes were schooled by the great period of drama that had preceded. Against the rising tide of Puritanism, the competent mediocrity of Heywood and the hack writing of Dekker could not retain the interest of the vast diversified audience required to make the public playhouse a profitable enterprise. I would suggest without any cynicism that it was much easier to give up Heywood or Massinger for religious convictions than it was to give up Marlowe, Shakespeare, the early Dekker, Greene, and Jonson.

The repertory of the King's Men from 1609 to 1913 is equally revealing. During this period Shakespeare contributed only three new plays (excepting the collaborations with Fletcher) as against eight in the preceding four years. In fact, it is quite possible that between 1608 and 1611 he contributed no plays at all. As their mainstay—the one dramatist who could hold the popular stage against odds—grew silent, his company turned to Fletcher, and for survival rather than additional profit shifted their operations to the private theater.

Had Shakespeare continued to write with his previous fecundity or had a new Shakespeare arisen, the popular dramatic tradition might have survived until the Civil War. But even this is doubtful. Once the Puritan opposition to the stage gathered momentum it produced a self-intensifying and irreversible cultural reaction against the drama, which was furthered by the mediocrity of the popular playwrights. As the drama retreated from middle-class disapproval, that disapproval inevitably hardened. An entertainment that had been familiar and popular but condemned now became one that was "alien," unpopular, and condemned; and indeed condemned because it was "alien." Still we can no more successfully explain (or moralize) the decline of Jacobean drama than we can explain the decline of Romantic poetry. There is no mystery in the failure of Elizabethan drama to perpetuate itself indefinitely. The mystery lies rather in the rare moment of genius that created the only significant body of tragedy that exists outside the classical drama of Greece.

Similarly we cannot explain Fletcher's artistic methods by reference to the ethos of late Jacobean society.[12] His is the kind of skilled formularized technique that has been employed by writers in every age since the printing press, the growth of literacy, and the commercial stage made the practice of literature a profession rather than an avocation. The closest parallel to Fletcher's techniques can be found today not in the "coterie" off-Broadway theater but in the daytime radio serial with its stereotyped characters and situations, its improbable melodrama, and its calculated exploitation of the housewife's escapist desire for romance and adventure. I imagine that if Fletcher were writing in this age of prose drama, it would not be for the critical, urbane Broadway audience that applauds Tennessee Williams and Arthur Miller but for Hollywood, which for decades has supplied a diversified national audience with a modern version of the theatrical unreality Fletcher so skillfully produced.

It is characteristic of Fletcher's professionalism that he does not go outside the bounds of drama for his "intellectual" material. When his immoralists complain that "no chain of deity or duty" can restrain their "furious desires," we recognize easily enough the literary convention of irresistible passion. When his immoralists justify their lusts with libertine sophistries, the dramatic situation is usually reminiscent of an earlier play; and the very appearance of naturalistic ideas in Fletcher's drama indicates that they had become familiar literary materials stripped of philosophical significance. The climactic situation in *The Knight of Malta* (1618–19), for example, recalls D'Amville's attempted rape of Castabella in the graveyard, and Collona echoes Levidulcia in arguing that sexual desire is natural in women,

> Since they are all born *Sophisters* to maintain
> That lust is lawful, and the end and use
> Of their creation.[13] (III. iii)

The plot of *The Captain* (1609–12), centering around the prostitute Lelia and two friends, Julio and Angelo, is a fairly obvious recollection of *The Dutch Courtezan*. One glance at Lelia prompts Angelo to Malheureux's libertine complaint against "confin'd" love:

> 'Tis true, she's excellent,
> And when I well consider, *Julio,*
> I see no reason we should be confin'd
> In our affections; when all Creatures else
> Enjoy still where they like. (III. iv)

The climactic scene of *The Captain*, however, introduces a disgusting prurience not found in Marston's play. Not recognizing her disguised father, Lelia attempts to seduce him. When he reveals himself, her

ardor is not quenched; and when he exclaims against the unnaturalness
of incest she replies:

> You are deceiv'd, Sir, 'tis not against nature
> For us to lye together; if you have
> An Arrow of the same Tree with your Bow,
> Is't more unnatural to shoot it there
> Than in another? 'Tis our general nature
> To procreate, as fire is to consume,
> And it will trouble you to find a stick
> The fire will turn from; if't be Natures will
> We should not mix, she will discover to us
> Some most apparent crossness. . . . (IV. iv)

Lelia carries the libertine appeal for unconfined love to its obscenely
animalistic conclusion that the only "natural" barrier to desire is an
incompatibility of sexual organs.

Compared to *The Captain, A King and No King* (1611) is a
work of consumate moral delicacy and grace. It has the usual incredible plot, cardboard characters, and specious theatrical gestures. But its
central theme of incestuous love is handled with a restraint that for a
time smacks of high seriousness; Fletcher seems genuinely concerned
with portraying the conflict between moral knowledge and intuitive
feeling. As in *The Dutch Courtezan* the progress of illicit passion is
charted by the coördinates of libertine ideology. Arbaces has at first
no illusions about his love for his sister:

> Such an ungodly sickness I have got,
> That he that undertakes my cure, must first
> O'erthrow Divinity, all moral Laws,
> And leave mankind as unconfin'd as beasts,
> Allowing 'em to do all actions
> As freely as they drink when they desire. (III)

Arbaces' self-accusations do not, however, settle the problem of moral
judgment, for his love has more extenuating circumstances than Giovanni's in *'Tis Pity*. Shared by Panthea, it is not in the beginning lustful or loathsome in character, although moral law condemns it as unnatural. Indeed, it is the apparent "arbitrariness" of moral law that
turns Arbaces' once chaste affection into a raging lust. Frustrated by
the "meer sounds" of brother and sister, he finds Malheureux's solace
in a naturalistic complaint against reason:

> Accursed man,
> Thou bought'st thy reason at too dear a rate,
> For thou hast all thy actions bounded in
> With curious rules, when every beast is free:
> What is there that acknowledges a kindred
> But wretched man? (IV)

By the end of the fourth act, however, the weight of such moral earnestness is more than Fletcher will bear. Instead of seeking a genuine ethical solution to Arbaces' conflict, he falls back on the ever-useful trumpery of romance; we learn through a fantastic revelation that Arbaces and Panthea are not brother and sister at all. And as if to prove that Arbaces' skepticism about moral "words" were justified, vice becomes virtue by a simple twist of plot.

So far we have looked at those aspects of Fletcher's plays which indicate all too clearly the decline of the Jacobean stage after its first golden decade. It would be unjust, however, to leave the impression that Fletcher's influence on the drama was merely harmful or to fail to distinguish between his art and Beaumont's more significant contribution to seventeenth-century tragedy. If the worst of Fletcher may have led the way to the eroticism and obliquity of *Love's Sacrifice*, the delicacy of his finest work prepared the Jacobean and Caroline sensibility for the fragile beauty and pathos of Ford's masterpiece, *The Broken Heart*. Even more immediate, though less obvious, was Beaumont's influence on Middleton—an influence that will be examined in the next chapter. Like Marston, Beaumont was a transitional figure who looked back on an earlier mode of tragedy even as he helped to shape a new one. And, as we shall see, his limited achievement in tragedy was to suggest a new range of dramatic possibility for a writer of much greater genius.

CHAPTER VII

Thomas Middleton

THE FIRST decade of Jacobean tragedy spent its genius freely. The second inherited a glorious tradition and a dwindling artistic capital, which for better or worse was invested primarily in tragicomedy. Ten years after the death of Elizabeth, Shakespeare, Chapman, Beaumont, Marston, and Tourneur had deserted the stage; Jonson and Webster had completed their great works. No bold new talents came forward to take their places and to continue the creative experimentation of the first decade. As the audiences dwindled, the dramatists found safety in numbers; fluent collaborators, they accepted the fact that romance was the most negotiable product in the shrinking market place of the theater. Yet when the drama seemed hopelessly committed to the trivial and the mediocre, *Women Beware Women* (ca. 1621) and *The Changeling* (1622) appeared to revive momentarily the greatness of the Jacobean stage.

Why Middleton assumed the tragic mask at so belated and inauspicious a time is a difficult question to answer, particularly if we assume that the tastes of the audiences determined Jacobean dramatic practice. It is conceivable that his ambitions in tragedy matured very slowly or that, long inured to the writing of comedy, he had first to experiment with the sensationalism of *Hengist* before he accepted the greater challenge which tragedy offered. There is some evidence that he attempted tragedy very early in the century,[1] but it is not difficult to understand why in the golden period of tragedy he found his metier as a comic satirist. His ironically detached, unheroic view of life was not attuned to the heroic passions of early tragedy; his psychological and sociological interests could not embrace the epic cosmological themes of Marlowe or Chapman. While his contemporaries pondered man's tragic relation to the universe, Middleton studied the comic relation between human appetites and the social environment which conditions them. Significantly, he did not turn to tragedy until it had acquired a shape more pleasing to his talent; however much he learned from Shakespeare or Jonson, he drew his immediate inspiration from *The Maid's Tragedy*, a play which heralds the romantic and psychological bias of later Jacobean tragedy.

It is only by comparison to the plays of Beaumont, Webster, Middleton, and Ford that we realize the completely masculine emphasis of early Jacobean tragedy. The women in Chapman's, Jonson's, and Tourneur's plays are, generally speaking, minor, conventional figures. Shakespeare's heroines are, of course, superb, but only Lady Macbeth has a commanding part in tragedy and she only for the first scenes of the play. Like Marston's Sophonisba, Cordelia and Desdemona play sacrificial roles; their deaths are not tragic in themselves but in their effects upon the heroes who loved and betrayed them. The later Jacobean tragedians shift the tragic emphasis from hero to heroine, from betrayer to betrayed. It does not matter very much why Ferdinand and Ithocles betray their sisters; all that matters is the pathos of the tragic heroine, who proves herself stronger and nobler than the men who torment her. When Ford rewrites *Othello* in *Love's Sacrifice*, his tragic protagonist is Bianca, not Caraffa. When Beaumont imitates *Hamlet* in *The Maid's Tragedy*, Ophelia becomes (as Aspatia) the nominal protagonist, Hamlet is reduced (as Amintor) to posturing impotence, and the sensual Gertrude becomes (as Evadne) so powerful a figure that she actually usurps the traditionally masculine role of revenger.

There is no single obvious explanation for the rise of the heroine in later tragedy. No doubt Beaumont and Fletcher's influence helped to turn the drama away from the masculine arenas of politics and history towards the study of intimate, emotional relationships. We can suppose too that in the decades following *Tamburlaine* the heroic vein of tragedy had been so exhaustively worked that dramatists sought new ideas and materials. It is striking that they "discovered" the tragic heroine at the very time that serious interest was developing outside the drama in the place and role of women in contemporary society.[2] When they dramatize the anguish of enforced or forbidden affections, Beaumont, Webster, Middleton, and Ford make clear the helplessness of women in a world ruled by men and masculine ideals. Their heroines long for freedom from the tyranny of family and convention; they are sacrificed at the altars of masculine "honor" and ambition. Of course the Jacobean playwrights are not social reformers. Just as Elizabethan patriotic fervor and anxiety gave impetus to the history play, so too, I think, Jacobean debate over the status of women suggested to the playwrights a fruitful subject for psychological investigation—the emotional drama of women restricted by the mores and conventions of society to a subservient and passive role, to a life of reaction rather than action. Unable to shape the circumstances of their lives, the Jacobean heroines are at the mercy of father, husband, or brother. Excluded from the worlds of action in which men may realize their potentialities, they are more absorbed in and dependent upon emotional relationships: their fulfillment must lie in love and in marriage. Even in revolt against convention, they are totally dependent upon men for their happiness, security, and protection; and thus they are vulnerable to the unexpected brutalities of the masculine will. They are most admired for those qualities—innocence, delicacy, fragility, softness—which leave them defenseless against the superior male, for whom they are both romantic subjects and sexual objects.

After the epic sweep of early tragedy, the later Jacobeans return, as it were, to the romantic themes of the Elizabethan stage. Ford imitates *Romeo and Juliet* directly in *'Tis Pity* and more obliquely in *The Broken Heart*. Webster's Duchess would, in an earlier decade, have wooed her husband in the forest of Arden. Middleton's "romanticism" is far more deeply and grimly ironic. He finds his Juliets in Bianca Capello and Beatrice-Joanna, and he uses Reynolds' sordid tale for

The Changeling, I imagine, because it offers a mocking parallel to Shakespeare's tragedy of star-crossed love. Like Juliet, Beatrice is drawn by love-at-first-sight from the safety of an arranged marriage into a world of subterfuge, clandestine passion, and violence; indeed her secret meetings with Alsemero recall the lines as well as the dramatic situations of Shakespeare's play. In addition to the Petrarchan themes of *Romeo and Juliet*, Middleton borrows its paradoxical motifs of loving-hate and death-breeding marriage, and he richly embroiders its central image of poison, the fatal "cure" for hopeless passion.[3]

I do not wish to labor parallels which very likely would not have been noticed in a theater, even by an audience quite familiar with *Romeo and Juliet*. To understand *The Changeling* we need not see its probable relation to Shakespeare's play, although that relation adds another dimension of meaning to Beatrice's tragedy. But to grasp the fundamental ironies of *The Changeling* we must, I think, recognize its indebtedness to *The Maid's Tragedy*, for Beaumont's masterpiece[4] was the enchanted glass which changed Elizabethan Petrarchanism into the matter of Jacobean tragedy.

One receives the impression from literary histories that *The Maid's Tragedy* (1611), though enormously successful in its own time, was a sterile mutation of the "tragedy of blood," a play that could not possibly have had noble descendants. Most critics who admire it do so condescendingly. Those who praise its emotional rhythm succeed only in begging the question of seriousness in art; for if we applaud Beaumont's ability to play upon his audience's emotional responses, how can we condemn a modern sentimentalist who exploits purer sentiments—our love of puppies or our memories of puppy love? John F. Danby is rare among the critics of Beaumont because he can admire the brilliance of *The Maid's Tragedy* at the same time that he condemns its neuroticism and speciosity. In *Poets on Fortune's Hill*, he carries the ancient charge of Beaumont's decadence to an ultimate but refreshingly different conclusion. Where earlier critics defined Beaumont's decadence as a frivolous escape from reality, Mr. Danby considers his drama an expression of the decadent reality of Cavalier society. Where earlier critics complained that Beaumont's characters are artificial stereotypes, Mr. Danby maintains that Amintor and Philaster are accurate projections of the Stuart courtly personality, which is both neurotic and adolescent, divided in its allegiances and driven by blind, absolute loyalties.[5] I do not think that we can quarrel with Mr. Danby's analysis of Beaumont's artistic methods, but I suspect that his concern with cultural values blinds him to the very high comedy of Beaumont's plays.[6]

Because Beaumont was, in the best and worst senses of the term, a "professional dramatist," we must assume that his first and primary consideration was always theatrical success. Perhaps he was drawn to *Hamlet* because he saw its hero as a paradigm of the contemporary "splintered" personality; more likely, however, he admired its quintessential theatricality and recognized that Hamlet is Shakespeare's most fascinating character, a master of a hundred moods and poses, who knows not what seems. Evidently no scene in Elizabethan and Jacobean tragedy impressed Beaumont's and Middleton's imaginations as did the closet scene in *Hamlet,* for the most effective moments in their tragedies are, as we shall see, restagings of this climactic scene of moral and psychological tension, when a hero, torn by love and hate, pity and contempt, indignation and cynicism, forces an impercipient, irresponsible heroine to face her own vileness.

Of course the "echoes" of *Hamlet* in *The Maid's Tragedy* merely accentuate the emptiness of its ethical and political issues. Its agonizing reappraisals of honor and loyalty are merely words, words, words; its characters are doomed by the unpredictable quirks of their deranged personalities, not by the inexorable consequences of their acts. And yet there is, as Mr. Danby demonstrates, an intellectual, even a "metaphysical," unity in Beaumont's play.[7] Each of its melodramatic scenes is a variation on a central Petrarchan theme of love and honor; each is a dramatic conceit which "acts out" the metaphysical contrarieties of love and hate, desire and death, the bridal bed and the bier.

One must admit the sheer dramatic power with which Beaumont constructs the witty conceit of Amintor's wedding night. The sinister imagery of the masque creates a subtle mood of uneasiness, which is heightened by Amintor's remorse at having betrayed Aspatia. Meanwhile Evadne's restlessness and indifference prepare us for the horrifying revelation that she is no blushing, modest virgin but a coldly contemptuous, experienced wanton. Stunningly theatrical, the scene surprises the intellect as well as the emotions by its intricate web of ironies. Most obviously it is a travesty of a natural, virginal consummation of the marriage vow. At the same time, it also travesties the vow itself, for Evadne insists that she will not sleep with Amintor because she has taken a religious vow of fidelity to the King. Looked at from another direction, the scene is a parody of Petrarchan and Neoplatonic ideals. Expecting sensual bliss, Amintor is forced to climb the ladder of love to a more spiritual devotion which does not require consummation. At first the youthful, courtly egotist cannot believe that Evadne does not love him. When she resists his embraces, he romantically envisions her as a cruel fair to be won by devoted service and as a wronged maiden whose honor he will lovingly revenge. Evadne mockingly accedes to the literary pretense by demanding the ultimate Petrarchan service of murder. (Only later does Amintor discover the necrophilic "joke" of her assurance that she will kiss the sin of blood from his lips.) It is an easy step from the pseudo-religiosity of courtly love to the really blasphemous essence of the dramatic conceit—a witty revision of the legend of St. Cecelia. Like Chaucer, Beaumont tells of a husband who learns on his wedding night that his bride has taken a religious vow of chastity, only now the religious vow is that of a whore to her seducer.

Amintor's perverted bridal is a many-faceted theme capable of ingenious variations. The revelation of Evadne's nature does not reunite appearance and reality, for Amintor, unable to revenge himself on the King, must assume the degrading pretense of satisfied husband. Because this role soothes as well as lacerates his throbbing ego (because he would and would not confess his humiliation) he overplays it, so much so in fact that the King, who cast it, thinks Amintor's pretense of sexual satisfaction too genuine. This brilliant twist of plot turns the Petrarchan triangle and the moral situation upside down. The lecherous King now assumes Amintor's stance of disillusioned Petrarchan idealist. Bitterly complaining that there is no faith in sin, he accuses Evadne of having cuckolded him by sleeping with her husband. The wanton Evadne now becomes what she before pretended to be: a betrayed innocent, who appeals to Amintor to tell the truth so as not to breed dissension between lovers. Amintor becomes the heartless slanderer—the Don John, the Iago—who in the final throes of degradation must admit the reality of his pretense to the man who enforced it and who redeems the ideality of Evadne's whoredom by confessing himself a frustrate cuckold.

Many Jacobean poets play ingeniously with the antithetical meanings of "die" (the consummation of the flesh in orgiastic pleasure or in the rot of the grave); but only Beaumont literally dramatizes the pun by translating verbal ambiguity into ironic peripetia. First Amintor, expecting nuptial bliss, learns that Evadne can love him only when he is dead. Next the King, awaiting Evadne in his bed, learns that she can pity him only when he is a corpse. Then Evadne, who jokingly set murder as the price of her love, demands Amintor's love for having killed the King. And when she cannot "die" with him—when he will not take her to his bed—she accepts the substitute gratification of death, even as Aspatia ends her agony of frustration by forcing Amintor to slay her.

We may wish that Beaumont had possessed a more wholesome imagination, or we may admire his acute perception of the pathological sublimation of sexual desire in sadistic (or masochistic) acts—a sublimation imaged in the recurrent phallic symbolism of a sword plunging into human flesh. Melantius, who glosses this symbolic action with a threat that his sword will be Evadne's lover, encourages his sister to find in revenge a satisfaction greater than that of being the King's whore. Under his guidance she reenacts the bridal scene with the King in Amintor's place, but nothing changes except (as before) the sides of the Petrarchan triangle. Now Evadne hates the King with the cold fury she showed to Amintor in the first bridal scene. And the act of revenge, which her repeated dagger thrusts turn into an inversion and perversion of the sexual act the King anticipated, is not satisfying to Evadne unless Amintor will kiss the sin of murder from her lips and take her to his bed.

Evadne is not an isolated portrait of perversity. Her volcanic nature brings to the surface the vein of morbidity which underlies most of the action of the play. Without Evadne's presence Aspatia's death scene would be a lyric swan song of innocent passion and undying love. But even as Evadne's lustful passion for Amintor contrasts with Aspatia's purer devotion, the juxtaposition of her suicide and Aspatia's points to the unconscious, morbid sexuality of Aspatia's death wish. In the midst of perversity and neuroticism, Melantius would seem a tower of normality. A blunt, honest soldier uncorrupted by the lasciviousness of the court, and a devoted friend, he can, unlike Amintor, translate his sense of honor into effective action. Yet at the close of the play the shocking contrast between Melantius' indifference to Evadne's death and his boundless grief for Amintor sheds a strange light on preceding events. Before, we accepted as inevitable the ironies of Melantius' "reformation" of Evadne, a reformation that turned a whore into a murderess. Now we wonder if Melantius' motive in the "closet scene" was a pure scruple of family honor or a desire to sacrifice a sister for a friend. Now we perhaps understand the great care with which Melantius dissuaded Amintor from the vengeance which should have been their joint duty. Only Beaumont could have "rewritten" *Hamlet* so as to make Horatio appear a latent homosexual!

These intimations of warped sexuality do not complicate Beaumont's characters as similar intimations complicate the "motiveless malignity" of Iago or Webster's Ferdinand. For here the pathological suggestions are completely divorced from, and counter to, the surface impression of character. Ironic wit offers not a deeper insight into character but an alternative view of character to that created by the rhetorical and emotional texture of the dialogue. Indeed, one scarcely knows what attitude to take towards Beaumont's characters. Are we supposed to surrender so completely to dramatic illusion that we do not feel the theatricality of their postures and passions? Or are we to recognize that they rarely communicate with one another because they are too busy unpacking their hearts in words, too busy dramatizing their self-conscious awareness of their emotional states? Are we really asked to admire the vacillating Amintor, who is as obtuse as he is sensitive, who speaks of honor but is totally absorbed in his vanity, and whose royalism is as instinctive a reflex as a knee-jerk? All the evidence would suggest that Amintor is a pitiless and, at times, comic study of immature, unstable egotism. Yet unless we accept Amintor's "nobility" at face value, the emotional structure of the play apparently collapses since he is the mover of Evadne's, Melantius', and Aspatia's passions. If he is ridiculous, then Evadne's suicide, Aspatia's death wish, and Melantius' devotion are worse than meaningless. Perhaps to be moved by the play we must see Amintor through their uncritical eyes and admire the very poses which Beaumont ironically discounts.

Before we conclude that Beaumont wishes us to take these characters more seriously than he does himself, we should look at the less complex problem of *Philaster*, whose hero is Amintor's twin, a poor man's Hamlet, exquisitely sensitive, infinitely courageous and totally ineffectual, who delays taking action against a usurper without a clear or intelligent rationalization for his delay. Capable of purer sentiments than the world deserves, hypersensitive to the claims of the ideal, Philaster is always on the verge of tears and of self-destruction. Now if *The Knight of the Burning Pestle* did not reveal Beaumont's ability to satirize his own romanticism, we might assume that we are responding improperly when we are amused by Philaster. But surely there is high comedy in Arethusa's complaint that the Country Fellow who tries to protect her from Philaster is intruding on their "private sports" and "recreations." Surely we are supposed to smile when Philaster later wonders if he was justified in stabbing a woman *who would not strike at him*. Consider the denouement of the play, in which Bellario, the cause of dark sexual jealousies, is revealed as a maiden in disguise. Confessing her holy love for Philaster and her vow never to marry, she begs to be allowed to serve Philaster and his wife. The divine Arethusa, freed from earthly suspicions, welcomes Bellario to live with them after their marriage. Here is a cosy domestic arrangement that passeth understanding—a Neoplatonic sublimation of desire carried to a conclusion that seems fantastic even in the context of the play. Lest we should miss this incredible marriage of sexual and spiritual satisfactions, Philaster immediately turns our attention to Megra and Pharamond, whose carnality provided a consistent foil to Arethusa's, Philaster's, and Bellario's platonic devotions. Megra and Pharamond are, to be sure, banished and their lustfulness artistically exorcised. Yet if their licentiousness were not an accustomed part of the court, Arethusa's virtue would not have been so easily maligned, and distrusted by her own father and lover. Beaumont does not satirically suggest that Arethusa is the ideal and Megra the reality of courtly love. He is concerned with literary postures, not with social realities. He is content with the subtle comedy of incongruity that results when literary convention brushes against the facts of life.

We can only conclude that plays like *Philaster* and *The Maid's*

Tragedy are constructed in the manner of optical illusions. They quite literally change shape when viewed from different perspectives and distances. They were supremely successful in their time because they appealed to the sophisticated and unsophisticated alike, to those for whom the theater was a literary experience and to those who demanded only casual entertainment. As works of the theater they do not demand close attention but they reward it with dazzling displays of wit. The superficial playgoer finds a world of enchantment, of never-ending surprises and breath-taking suspense, of noble sentiment and thrilling action. The perceptive reader finds beneath the surface enchantment outlines of grotesque or amusing farce, and underworlds of ironic inversions and pathologies calculated to elicit a "metaphysical" shudder.

The Changeling

Whether under different circumstances Beaumont might have been a more serious artist one cannot say. He must have had some awareness that he was devoting very considerable talents to unworthy ends. He must have known that his opportunism was as much a betrayal of his own genius as it was a betrayal of the nobler traditions of tragedy. Nevertheless he brought to a stage which had nearly expended its creative energies a new concept of tragic irony, which after lying dormant for nearly a decade flowered in the far greater art of Middleton. The indebtedness of *The Changeling* to *The Maid's Tragedy* is specific enough, I think, to indicate that Middleton fulfilled his genius in tragedy as much through collaboration with Beaumont as with Rowley. There are also ironic inversions of Petrarchanism in *Women Beware Women*, but their meaning becomes evident only after a study of the "romanticism" of *The Changeling*. Thus we will begin with *The Changeling*, though it was probably the slightly later play, and use its crystalline brilliance to illuminate the more obscure intention of *Women Beware Women*.

The Changeling imitates the form, not the substance of *The Maid's Tragedy*—its ironic techniques, not its verse or characters. De Flores, kneeling before Beatrice and begging for the service of murder, recreates (with a difference) Amintor's gesture of Petrarchan service to his cruel fair, Evadne. Later De Flores and Beatrice invert the closet scene between Melantius and Evadne; where Melantius had to convince his sister of her vileness as a whore in order to make her his willing assassin, De Flores must convince Beatrice of her sin as a murderess to make her his whore. At the close of *The Maid's Tragedy* Evadne comes bloody-handed to Amintor to receive her reward for her murder of the King; so too at the close of *The Changeling* Beatrice would be loved by Alsemero for her murder of Alonzo.

The subplot of *The Changeling* mirrors in burlesque the Petrarchan conceits of the main plot. Even as De Flores accepts the service of murder to win Beatrice, so also Franciscus and Antonio place themselves in Isabella's "daunger" by assuming the roles of madman and fool. Their adventure for her favors embodies with a comic literalness the blindness and madness of love and provides a burlesque antimasque to the more chilling inversions of courtly love in the main plot. When Lollio (like De Flores) discovers his mistress' incipient frailty, he too would nibble at the feast of her wantonness. But she silences him with the threat to use her Petrarchan powers:

> Sirrah, no more! I see you have discover'd
> This love's knight errant, who hath made adventure
> For purchase of my love; be silent, mute,
> Mute as a statue, or his injunction
> For me enjoying, shall be to cut thy throat.
>   (III. iii. 251–55)

Perhaps these Petrarchan parallels, added to the thematic and verbal links between plot and subplot noted by Miss Bradbrook,[8] convince us that the madhouse scenes are not wholly extraneous and irrelevant. But they do not convince us that plot and subplot form an organic unity or that the subplot makes a significant enough contribution to the meaning of the play to justify its repeated interruption of the main plot. To understand the necessity of the subplot, however, we need only try to imagine *The Changeling* without it. Then we realize how narrow is Middleton's tragic focus and how thin is the texture of the main plot. As in *Romeo and Juliet*, the secret passion of the heroine is the vortex into which are drawn the lives of the minor characters: Alonzo, Tomaso, Diaphanta, and Vermandero. But the minor characters of *The Changeling* have hardly the richness or fullness of Mercutio, the Nurse, Capulet, Benvolio, and the Friar, nor have they the same kind of psychological and moral reality with which Beatrice and De Flores are endowed.

When the narrative impulse reigned in the drama—when the emphasis lay in the acting out of a story—the stage was usually crowded with peripheral characters somehow or other involved in a tragic fable or used to create the setting in which the action occurs. Though the stress may have fallen (as in *Romeo and Juliet*) on a few great dramatic arias, there were transitional scenes enough to provide a narrative recitative. In *The Changeling*, however, Middleton eliminates transitions or is content to use the archaic device of the dumb show (at the beginning of Act IV) to provide narrative information. Where an earlier dramatist might have used several scenes to trace Beatrice's growing intimacy with De Flores, Middleton leaps from Beatrice's submission to De Flores to her meeting with him on her wedding night, and subtly intimates the evolution of their relationship by the nature of their new entente. Interested only in crucial moments of psychological and moral tension, he allows Rowley to provide a discrete comic recitative between his superb arias. Indeed, he can flatten out peripheral characters and reduce setting to impressionistic vagueness only because Rowley thickens the single strand of the main action (Beatrice's tragic relation to De Flores) with a comic subplot similar to those which Ford, for similar reasons, interweaves with his tragic actions.

In addition to the subplot, Rowley, it is assumed, wrote the first and last scenes of *The Changeling*, which seem relatively colorless and uninspired and yet are perfectly attuned to their dramatic functions. The romanticism of the opening scene is, I think, deliberately conventional and deliberately embroidered with literary artifice. "Our Ladies Church" of Reynolds' tale, where Alsemero first meets and falls passionately in love with Beatrice, is changed in the first line of the play to a "temple," the better to invoke memories of Troilus and Leander. His first encounter with Beatrice is a Petrarchan love duel, an exchange of hearts comparable to Romeo and Juliet's impromptu sonneteering. How very different are these romantic overtones from the "literary" artificiality of *The Maid's Tragedy*. Middleton[9] (or Rowley) does not attempt to fashion a dramatic universe in which the

Petrarchan code is the natural law of behavior; indeed, we can hardly imagine De Flores and Beatrice taking the King and Evadne's mutual vow of fidelity in lust. Compared to Beaumont, Middleton is a realist who studies literary illusions as a part of human experience and who knows that they inhere in codes of honor and in youthful dreams of romantic fulfillment.

The opening scene of *The Changeling* is devoid of the grim ironic foreshadowing which we come to expect in Jacobean tragedy, because the romantic mood must predominate; there will be time enough later in the play to intimate that Beatrice's passion for Alsemero will be consummated in a "marriage" to De Flores. Still we can find subtle and prophetic dissonances beneath the romantic harmonies of Alsemero and Beatrice's love duets. Although they sing sweetly in tune, Alsemero's colorless platitudes and complacent assurance of the holiness of his love do not quite jibe with Beatrice's bolder affection or with her determination to have him regardless of the circumstances to which he is ready to bow. When she instinctively shudders at the sight of De Flores, Alsemero soothes her fears with the commonplaces of an unimaginative and impercipient mind. She does not yet appreciate De Flores' qualities, but the audience may well suspect that he is more her mate in passion and in will than Alsemero.

When Beatrice again appears she has already committed herself to the thrilling adventure of forbidden love—to the secret meetings and clandestine plans that are to erase romantically the obstacles between desire and fulfillment. Her childish delight in her cleverness is already apparent in the self-congratulatory mood of her soliloquy at the beginning of Act II:

> Methinks I love now with the eyes of judgement,
> And see the way to merit, clearly see it.
> A true deserver like a diamond sparkles;
> In darkness you may see him, that's in absence,
> Which is the greatest darkness falls on love,
> Yet is he best discern'd then
> With intellectual eyesight.
>   (II. i. 13–19)

But when Alonzo appears not long after, it is hard to see any difference between his colorless, blind devotion and that of Alsemero.

Moreover, the lurking De Flores provides an apt commentary on her platonic musings. By a curious coincidence their thoughts are exactly parallel. As she reflects on intellectual love, he enters meditating obscenely on the foul faces which have "plucked" sweets without restraint. She voices the romantic ideal; he turns it seamy side out by translating it into realistic sexual terms. Undaunted by the abuse of his cruel fair, De Flores witnesses, though he does not overhear, the first clandestine meeting of Alsemero and Beatrice. It is a latter-day balcony scene, adorned with romantic sighs and mutual pledges of religious devotion; but where Juliet casuistically sought to obliterate family names, Beatrice more pointedly longs that "there were none such name as Piracquo." Alsemero, so like Beatrice in "expression," interprets the wish and makes an immediate chivalric gesture: he will murder Alonzo "honorably" in a duel. At the very moment, however, that he bodies her unspoken thought, their marriage of true minds disintegrates. She instinctively knows that this Petrarchan service requires a different kind of man; she knows that she needs De Flores even though she loves Alsemero. The vehemence with which she rejects Alsemero's gesture, and the cold-bloodedness with which she fastens on De Flores as a fit murderer, underline the disparity between Alsemero's storybook romanticism and her equally naïve but ruthless calculation. She is the stronger, the dominating figure. His vain attempts to break in upon her private, racing thoughts are nearly comic. And once again the spying De Flores sets the Petrarchan tableau in cynical perspective. To Alsemero Beatrice's infidelity to Alonzo is proof of her devotion to him. To De Flores it is evidence of an inherent frailty which a calculating man might turn to sensual profit.

Beatrice's choice of De Flores confirms her "intellectual eyesight." A touch of her hand, an interest in his complexion, and a heavy sigh are all that is needed to make him beg to serve her in murder. The ironies of this Petrarchan situation are less macabre than those of Amintor's wedding night but more complex. For when the innocent girl seduces the amoral sensualist, illusion compounds illusion; an eternal bargain is struck by two self-absorbed minds, seemingly ignorant of each other's motives, and completely mistaking their mutual accord. Deriving an almost orgiastic pleasure from Beatrice's touch, De Flores is nevertheless realist enough to note the suddeness of her admiration for his pimpled face. His cynical assumptions about the nature of women lead him, however, to accept the crude masquerade of her courtship. Convinced that she is, or can be, a whore in her affections, he believes that on this "blest" occasion he has caught her still warm from Alsemero. Moreover, because he has no romantic dreams of fidelity in love, he does not assume that Beatrice's overtures mean she no longer desires Alsemero. They merely indicate to him that she will sensibly divide her favors to gain the man she loves, an arrangement which is perfectly agreeable to him. Thus while he cynically miscalculates her motive, he has no illusions about the true locus of her desire.

Inexperienced in passion, Beatrice has no idea of the fierceness of the sexual appetite she plays upon, any more than she understands the meaning of the crime she casually arranges. But while she can consciously blot out of her mind the nature of the temptation she offers De Flores, the way she accosts him indicates clearly that instinctively she knows he hungers for her. When he begs to serve her, she tells herself that he must be greedy for money, yet he has not spoken a word of gold and she has led him to this point by appealing to his passion rather than his pocketbook. Though she must deceive herself in order to deceive him, they understand each other better than words can tell. Or if they do mistake each other's nature, they nevertheless complement each other superbly: his ruthlessness matches her need, his passion her longing. Side by side, they hasten towards a communion of blood in flawless stychomythia:

> *Beat.* Then take him to thy fury!
> *De F.* I thirst for him.
> *Beat.* Alonzo de Piracquo.
> *De F.* [*rising*] His end's upon him;
> He shall be seen no more.
>
> (II. ii. 134–36)

"How lovely now," Beatrice responds, "Dost thou appear to me!"

Beaumont, to give the devil his due, also builds individual scenes to masterful crescendos of passion or violence; but each of his tense dramatic situations is like a coiled spring that expands by exhausting its potential energy and then must be wound again. Thus nothing is inevitable in *The Maid's Tragedy* except the unexpected turn of events that re-engages the characters in newly suspenseful variations of their previous relationships. In contrast Middleton builds the drama of Beatrice's compact with De Flores to a climax that is doubly harrowing because it is so clearly anticipated in the first seduction scene. We know in advance that she will await De Flores' news of murder with smug expectancy, congratulating herself on her cunning arrangement of life, her mind enraptured with the "virtue" of her love for Alsemero. De Flores will arrive warm in Alonzo's blood, panting in anticipation of the feast that lies before him. Then will follow the mutual undeception, the bargaining, the blackmail, and the final reckoning in which he, more reckless and absolute in his passion, must prevail. Whereas Evadne's submission to Melantius is a conventional repentance given a macabre and melodramatic twist, De Flores' confrontation of Beatrice captures so purely the drama of desire and loathing, of self and moral discovery, that much of earlier tragedy seems by comparison embroidered and rhetorical. As comprehension dawns, Beatrice retreats in terror from De Flores' rude advances and from his inexorable dialectic, clinging desperately to her "ignorance" of his desires and to the poor shreds of her "innocence" and "honor"; with the world crashing around her, she clings to proprieties and reminds De Flores of the social barriers between them. Like the speaker in Marvell's poem, De Flores has neither world enough nor time to indulge his "Lady's" fancy. The Petrarchan dream has ended; she must read her character in the mirror which he thrusts before her: the deed's creature, the woman dipped in blood, the whore in her affection.

Mr. Eliot remarks that Beatrice's tragedy is that of "the unmoral nature, suddenly trapped in the inexorable toils of morality—of morality not made by man but by Nature—and forced to take the consequences of an act which it had planned lightheartedly. Beatrice is not a moral creature; she becomes moral only by becoming damned."[10] Yet Beatrice does not achieve through damnation the redeeming moral awareness which comes too late to Marlowe's Faustus. Her "moral" awareness actually leads to viler degradation because it does not include remorse. She is appalled by the consequence of her sin, not by the sin itself. She is revolted by the price she must now pay, but not by the criminal act she has already committed. Even after De Flores has anatomized her nature, her obtuseness is revealed in her pathetic plea, "Let me go poor unto my bed with *honour*."[11]

De Flores' triumph over Beatrice is a ruthless imposition of his cynically amoral view of moral realities. His contempt for her—the contempt of the realist for the dreamer—is genuine enough and indeed makes the more compelling his dying claim that he loved her "in spite of her heart." There is perhaps some of Bosola's punctilio in his angry refusal to be rewarded with gold, but he has no perverted sense of honor. Although he needs and will take the gold she offers, he will not take it in lieu of her body because he always placed "wealth after the heels of pleasure." Only in the savoring of her virginity is his sexual appetite in any way sophisticated. He does not mind sharing her with Alsemero; neither his ego nor his "honor" demand her fidelity. He would not, however, be satisfied with his reward were he not convinced of her maidenhood. How comic in contrast is Alsemero's honorable care for Beatrice's virginity and his romantic machinery of philtres and potions which declare her above suspicion.

By now Beatrice has entered a labyrinth in which, as in a nightmare, every motion towards Alsemero draws her closer to De Flores, and every turn brings her back to the starting place, so that she must commit again the crimes that wed her to De Flores. Like Evadne she is caught in shifting Petrarchan triangles which dissolve only with death. First she is publicly betrothed to Alonzo (her Paris) but secretly belongs to Alsemero (her Romeo). She hires De Flores to erase the triangle but instead he becomes a part of it. After Alonzo's murder, Alsemero becomes the publicly accepted lover (her Paris) while De Flores assumes Alsemero's role of clandestine "husband" (her Romeo). Just as she pleaded modesty to escape Alonzo's wedding bed, so she must plead modesty to escape Alsemero's. (Like Alonzo, Alsemero is warned of Beatrice's infidelity, but like Alonzo, he can see only "modesty's shrine" in her forehead.) Having once bribed a servant so that she can enjoy Alsemero's love, she must bribe a servant to accept the fruits of her earlier crime. And once again she discovers that anarchic sexual passion will not submit to a literary chicane like the bed trick; once again she learns that life is not quite like a romantic *novella*. Again she *needs* De Flores though she *loves* Alsemero; and ultimately, of course, need and love are one. Her wedding night consummates her marriage to De Flores, not her marriage to Alsemero: her only love is born of her only hate.

More clearly than before, his courage and ruthlessness match her anxious needs; his immediate thought of murder elicits her instinctive assent. Though his face still repels her, she has climbed to the top of the platonic ladder and can love with intellectual eyesight and judgment. Her admiration for this wondrous necessary man and her cool skill in obtaining a reward for his service confirm the growing suspicion that they were planned for each other. Now we know that she was not poisoned by De Flores' touch because she contained his poison already within her. She instinctively feared in him that which was latent in her. He was her "fate," her destiny, because he realized the potentialities of her nature, and because only through him could she satisfy that craving for romantic experience which is fulfilled in the breathless adventure of murder and adultery. Like Middleton's other heroines, Beatrice must be betrayed to be true to herself. She must know De Flores in order to know herself, for only he can free her from the chains of convention and of family duty. He *is* her Petrarchan lover; his single-minded, reckless, consuming sexual hunger is the closest approximation she will find to the literary dream of absolute passion.

After the intense drama of the wedding night, the final scenes of *The Changeling* are undoubtedly anticlimactic. Alsemero's confrontation of Beatrice is a pale imitation of the earlier magnificent "closet scene," and the off-stage catastrophe of De Flores' revenge upon Beatrice seems an unfortunate waste of dramatic possibilities. Textual scholarship allows us to blame Rowley as inadequate to the task of writing the final scene and to blame Middleton for entrusting the conclusion of his masterpiece to an inferior talent. But in truth the last scene contains some very powerful writing, and the fault would seem to lie not in its execution but in its conception, or rather in its fidelity to the total conception of the main plot. Another dramatist might have given Beatrice and De Flores a more heroic death scene. Middleton adheres, at the expense of theatricality, to his idea of the sordidness and vulgarity of their relationship. Like trapped animals they turn on one another; their dark deeds are darkly answered. Up to the very moment of her death, when shame overwhelms her, Beatrice brazens out the lie of her fidelity to Alsemero, refusing to admit her relationship with De Flores, much less her admiration for his accomplished criminality. Even in her dying confession she insists that her "honor fell with" De Flores; i.e., before he robbed her of her virginity, she had been (like Othello) an "honorable murderer."

De Flores is more admirable because he does not attempt to cling to any moral illusions about himself. When Beatrice babbles of honor, he more candidly speaks of "safety" and "pleasure." Unlike earlier malcontents he is not consumed with hatred for a society in which he has lost status, nor does he lay bare its vices and follies. His mind is so filled with desire for Beatrice that his "choric" commentary is limited to cynical meditations on the psychology of sexual attraction. Yet his strength, candor, and resourcefulness are an oblique commentary on the polite society from which he is excluded. Those who belong—the men of "judgment" like Alsemero, Vermandero, Alonzo, and Tomaso —are like Beatrice absorbed in charades of honor. Their impercipience and ineffectuality provide the foil in which De Flores' uncanting will to action glitters. On the other hand, Middleton will not allow us to forget that De Flores' will to action is a disgusting prurience. If De Flores is more true to himself than is Beatrice, he never rises above the sheer animality of his sexual appetite. He dies a complacent lecher, still somewhat contemptuous of Beatrice yet cynically licking his lips over the sweetness of her virginal surrender.

Taking a larger view of the final scene, one sees that its weakness is the price which Middleton must pay for the intensely focused drama of the preceding scenes. Although Beatrice's "marriage" to De Flores is sealed on her wedding night, the drama of their relationship is not then exhausted. She is still caught between admiration and loathing, affinity and repulsion; indeed, she is still caught between one kind of love for De Flores and another for Alsemero. But as the play draws to a close Middleton can no longer concentrate on the relationship of Beatrice and De Flores to the exclusion of all else. He must widen the dramatic focus and create at least the illusion of unity by finally involving the peripheral characters in the tragic action.

To be sure, Middleton makes no genuine effort to weight Tomaso with tragic significance. Although he is *the* revenger, or more correctly, the *would-be* revenger of the play, that role seems to Middleton no less a literary imposture than the Petrarchan dream. Wandering aimlessly through the play, muttering darkly of vengeance in the melancholy accents of Hamlet, Tomaso is not so much a character as a literary ghost. More persuasive as a revenger is Alsemero, a cuckolded Hamlet who turns with belated fury on the woman he loved to anatomize her deformity. Urged by Jasperino to search soundly the ulcer of Beatrice's whoredom, he confronts her with Hamlet's question to Ophelia: "Are you honest?" But these Shakespearean echoes (if indeed they are such) can only emphasize that Alsemero is "not Prince Hamlet nor was meant to be." He is so insensitive to hypocrisy that he must twice be told by Jasperino of Beatrice's infidelity and he must actually spy on her meetings with De Flores before he can believe her guilty. Unlike Reynolds' Alsemero, who suspects the truth of Alonzo's disappearance, Middleton's Alsemero suspects nothing even though he understood Beatrice's wish that Alonzo be eliminated and volunteered to perform the service. Since he is not clear-sighted himself, he fails wretchedly at De Flores' role of moral tutor. Despite his fever of self-righteousness, she is still the stronger personality and now shares some of De Flores' cunning and resourcefulness. She admits that she had Alonzo murdered but she will not admit that she is De Flores' mistress. Moreover she actually usurps De Flores' role in this closet scene, because now she demands Alsemero's love as her reward for the Petrarchan service of murder. Alsemero is plainly intimidated. He will not admit complicity in Alonzo's murder, but he is shaken by her demand and by her lie of fidelity. Once again De Flores is required to translate Alsemero's gesture—this time his gesture of vengeance—into effective action.

At the end of *The Changeling*, as at the end of *Romeo and Juliet*, the divided worlds of the play come together when those who were ignorant of the secret lovers gather about their fallen bodies. Middleton might have used the startled onlookers as a tragic chorus to define the pity and terror of Beatrice's fate. Yet once again he preserves the integrity of his tragic idea at the expense of dramatic effect. Those who stare at the dead criminals are the shallow innocents, who in a lame and mechanical peroration marvel at their own experiences. Incapable of deep emotion and concerned primarily with their "honor," they cannot pity the fallen Beatrice nor in any measure understand her. Their mood is complacence, not compassion. Alsemero does not mention the lash of his cuckoldry, but the imagery of an earlier speech sheds light on his moral indignation. When he sends De Flores in to Beatrice, he relishes the meeting in his imagination:

> I'll be your pander now; rehearse again
> Your scene of lust, that you may be perfect
> When you shall come to act it to the black audience,
> Where howls and gnashings shall be music to you:
> Clip your adulteress freely, 'tis the pilot
> Will guide you to the *mare mortuum*,
> Where you shall sink to fathoms bottomless.
>   (V. iii. 115–21)

Vermandero is more shaken, not by the loss of a daughter, but by the blot on his reputation:

> O, my name's enter'd now in that record
> Where till this fatal hour 'twas never read.
>   (V. iii. 183–84)

But in losing a daughter he has gained a son in Alsemero, who is ready at all times with sage and comforting advice:

> Let it be blotted out; let your heart lose it,
> And it can never look you in the face,
> Nor tell a tale behind the back of life
> To your dishonour. . . .
>   (V. iii. 185–88)

In the end all are "satisfied" with the possible exception of Beatrice, whose dying plea for forgiveness is totally ignored.

Women Beware Women

Although it is possible that the rambling *Women Beware Women* was actually written after *The Changeling*,[12] it seems to me a less mature play, the work of a dramatist well skilled (perhaps too well skilled) in the techniques of comedy but not yet aware of the need for economy and intensity of tragic effect. In *The Changeling* Middleton is ruthless in his concentration upon the psychological drama of De Flores and Beatrice. In *Women Beware Women* his interests in character are so catholic and democratic that it is difficult to say which are the major figures. *We* may recognize Bianca as the most tragic character in the play, but Middleton makes little effort to set off her *Liebestod* from the jumbled homicides of the masque. Moreover he allots nearly as much time to Leantio as to Bianca and spends as many tedious pages on Sordido and the Ward as on Isabella and Livia. Even if we grant that Sordido and the Ward add to the ironic effect of certain scenes, we cannot see the overwhelming necessity for their dreary indecencies. There is enough "comic relief" and enough ironic laughter without their presence; when the plot grows tense we long for the release of tears, not for the release of vulgar humor. More difficult still to understand is the collapse of tone, plotting, and characterization in the last act, when Middleton regresses to a sensationalism more naïve than the archetypal murderous masque of *The Spanish Tragedy*.

Unless we assume that Middleton's audience insisted upon a hackneyed and trite denouement to tragedy, we cannot say that dramatic convention forced him to a tawdry sensationalism. Only if we could be sure that the Jacobean dramatists had a perfect knowledge of their limitations, could we argue that what they did badly they did unwillingly. The fact is that a mere lack of humor did not prevent Ford from writing "comedy," and, if we may judge from *Hengist* as well as *Women Beware Women*, his lack of genuine instinct for the sensational did not prevent Middleton from attempting melodrama. We might even say that regardless of the tastes of his audiences, Middleton required a wild and bloody denouement in *Women Beware Women*, for having denied a genuine capacity for tragic emotion to his characters he had at last to submerge their personalities in melodrama to make them seem like tragic figures. Because they were not born to play tragic roles, he had to slaughter them wholesale to create a superficial impression of tragic doom.

Though less enigmatic than the title of *The Changeling*, the title of *Women Beware Women* is more misleading because it points to a central theme more appropriate to the broadside balladeer than the tragic poet. We might characterize the play as a study of moral disintegration, but this label hardly distinguishes it from *The Changeling* or from any other Jacobean tragedy. Like *The Changeling* it is a drama of reaction rather than action. Like *The Changeling* it is concerned not so much with the consequence of immoral decision as with the psychological nature of the decision itself. And like *The Change-ling* it rings ironic variations on romantic themes. It opens with a fairy tale elopement, a love that defies social conventions and admits no impediments. It closes with a *Liebestod* reminiscent of *Romeo and Juliet:* when Bianca's attempt to poison the Cardinal recoils on the Duke, she drinks from the poisoned cup to join her lover in death. The central irony of *Women Beware Women* does not lie, however, in the juxtaposition of romantic illusion and cynical lust. It lies instead in the conflict between reckless romantic ardor and the sensible com-promises with passion advocated by a society which envies the luxuries and imitates the sophisticated codes of the court.

Even though *Women Beware Women* is set in Italy, its char-acters are London citizens, blood brothers to the *personae* of Middle-ton's city comedies. It is in fact the kind of realistic bourgeois tragedy that Jonson might have created out of the vision of greed and lechery that takes a comic shape in *The Alchemist* and *Bartholemew Fair.* Where Jonson's dialogue creates vivid sensuous impressions of the sights, sounds, and stenches of London life, Middleton's richly meta-phorical verse delineates the minds of his characters and creates a cumulative portrait of the habits and mores, vanities and vices of the social world to which they belong. In this world respectability and vice walk arm in arm; there is no place for the fantastic depravities that haunt Tourneur's imagination. Like Jonson's, Middleton's sinners are confidence men rather than cutthroats. They are honorable lechers who sin discreetly and who calculate their enormities with a due regard for propriety. If they rob a woman's virtue, they will murder her husband to make her an honest woman again. If they commit incest they nevertheless abhor the vulgarity of "daylight" lechery. They are moved by sermons, and they are fond of their brothers, sisters, and nieces; forever prudent, they keep a watchful eye on the futures of those they love. The animalistic feeding imagery with which De Flores describes his lust is not appropriate to their more genteel appetite to enjoy the sweets of life. Their thematic images of feasting are imbued with a spirit of reasonable compromise and informed by the knowledge that banquets do not come every day.[13]

At the center of this world is Livia, the witty prime mover, who epitomizes its wisdom and folly. Her cynicism is good-natured and her intrigues are until the final scenes devoid of any malice. Although she is too experienced and too frank in her own satisfactions to believe in another woman's virtue, she is, nevertheless, a good companion—especially of men, who admire her unsentimental shrewdness and candor. Indeed, her pleasure in being treated as their equal helps to explain the callousness with which she betrays her own sex. She is a masterly seducer because she knows her victims far better than they know themselves. And her cynical insight makes plausible and comprehensible the startling metamorphoses of Isabella and Bianca into glistering whores.

At the beginning of the play Isabella appears a virtuous and forlorn maiden who, like Ford's Penthea, incarnates the misery of enforced marriage. As the action progresses she becomes an increasingly sympathetic and pitiable figure. First she is betrayed by her father into a vicious marriage contract. Next she is betrayed by the uncle she loves, who hungers for her incestuously. And when, after repulsing him, she is more lonely and vulnerable, she is betrayed by Livia, the only other person whom she thinks she can trust and who pretends to love and pity her.

Or does Livia betray her niece? She does not encourage her to love incestuously. She does not even mention Hippolito's name except in passing. Since the wretched Isabella longs for freedom, Livia merely offers her the compassionate lie that Fabricio is not her father and therefore need not be obeyed. It is not Livia's fault that her niece eagerly embraces incest thinking that it is only adultery—that she freely prefers an illicit liaison to a chaste rebellion against her father's authority. By the time Isabella reaches her immoral decision it should be as inevitable to us as it is to Livia, for we cannot expect a girl who is supinely obedient to a foolish father to cut herself off from family and society by proclaiming her illicit ancestry. She is a true child of her time, brazen enough to have a "friend" but too weak to defy social conventions. And she has before her the admirable example of her mother, who, according to Livia, enjoyed both love *and* marriage and died with a spotless reputation. The calm with which Isabella learns of her mother's liaison confirms the impression of disillusioned worldliness created by her earlier aside about marriage (I. ii. 162–86). Even then it was clear that she did not really hope for happiness in marriage, which is customarily a mercenary and inequitable arrangement in her society. How shallow, moreover, is her scruple concerning incest; the very thought of it horrifies her, but she is not horrified by the thought of submitting to a man who is consumed with incestuous lust. Her only regret is that she was so bitter to Hippolito, the "poor gentleman," who deserved her love, not her reproach. Must we not agree with Isabella that Livia's "virtuous pity" has given her the means to know herself?

Bianca's acceptance of her whoredom presents a more difficult problem of interpretation because we feel that her innocence is far more genuine and profound than Isabella's, and because she has already shown that she is not enslaved by the crass conventions and values of her society. Her futile pleas to the Duke emphasize the callousness of his violation of her body and her spirit, for he assumes that her resistance is an appetizing spice of coyness. Meanwhile Livia waxes witty at the chess table and Guardiano congratulates himself on a job of pandering well done. The double action on the gallery and at the chess table further deepens the horror of the seduction by associating the unspeakable and the familiar in such a way as to suggest that the unspeakable is all too familiar to Livia and Guardiano.

Bianca's return from the gallery might have provided Ford with a moment of exquisite pathos. But instead of the weeping, shame-ridden girl we expect, Bianca enters calm, ironic, more than reconciled to her status as the Duke's mistress. The dewy innocent has returned a calculating strumpet, who curses her "poisoners" and yet finds the poison delicious. Her chaste devotion to Leantio was genuine enough, but now her fairy tale idyll is ended. As Miss Ellis-Fermor suggests, the shock of betrayal has "dislocated" Bianca's nature.[14] Her overwhelming agony of shame on the gallery has bred an indifference to future defilement. Her contemptuous aside to Guardiano reveals that she has already assumed the Duke's superior position to this pandering slave. And she can now enter into the sardonic mood of Livia's *double-entendres*:

> Now bless me from a blasting! I saw that now,
> Fearful for any woman's eye to look on;
> Infectious mists and mildews hang at's eyes,

The weather of a doomsday dwells upon him:
Yet since mine honour's leprous, why should I
Preserve that fair that caus'd the leprosy?
Come, poison all at once.

.   .   .   .

                    I'm made bold now,
I thank thy treachery; sin and I'm acquainted,
No couple greater; and I'm like that great one,
Who, making politic use of a base villain,
He likes the treason well, but hates the traitor;
So I hate thee, slave!

(II. ii. 425–48)

Awakened by the prince's kiss from her romantic dream, Bianca has been carried back to the society from which Leantio stole her—a society in which the vileness of others is the excuse for one's own immorality, in which chastity is a merely physical fact and honor is synonymous with reputation. Since Bianca's honor is leprous (since it is known that she has submitted to the Duke) then there is no longer any point in fidelity to Leantio. Her honeymoon over, she now sees her poor estate through the practical eyes of Leantio's mother and the Duke; and the remembrance of things past floods back in nagging demands for the luxuries and courtly pleasures to which she was born. When she displays her smutty sophisticated wit in the banquet scene, we sense that she has not been thrust into an alien experience but returned to a familiar reality. Soon recovered from her qualm of honor she moves like Beatrice from a superficial and immature romantic attachment to a deeper passion for the man who seduced her—a passion so intense that it drives her to murder.

With Bianca's enthronement as the Duke's mistress and Isabella's marriage to the Ward, the action of *Women Beware Women* nears its logical conclusion. Nothing remains for Middleton but to unravel the threads of plot wound about Livia's machinations. Since the unravelling will be in the comic mode—a discovery of deceptions foisted by a witty intriguer—the instrument of truth is appropriately the serio-comic Leantio. In the midst of casual carnalities, his platitudinous mind keeps alive the ideal of marriage, though his pain at losing Bianca is more erotic than moral. Too gauche to accept gracefully the not uncompensated role of cuckold, he will be revenged on his faithless wife. But how? Livia's love-at-first-sight (a bawd's desire vicariously aroused by Leantio's longing for Bianca) provides the means. Accepting Livia's sudden passion as "the flattery of some dream,"[15] he takes revenge by indulging in an even more sordid adultery than his wife's. Draped in a stallion's finery, he struts and frets before Bianca in a comic closet scene that leads only to his murder.

His death brings to Livia, Hippolito, Isabella, and Guardiano a moment of half-truth, but since they are incapable of genuine suffering they cannot acquire the wisdom that suffering may bring. Bewildered, confused, incapable of self-knowledge, they turn on one another with hatred and recrimination and finally with murderous intrigue. Forgetting the joy with which she entered into adultery, Isabella exclaims:

> Was ever maid so cruelly beguil'd,
> To the confusion of life, soul, and honour,
> All of one woman's murdering!
>
> (IV. ii. 130–32)

Hippolito is even more plaintive in his obliquity. He cannot understand how Livia could repay his "care/ Of reputation and a sister's fortune" by telling Isabella the truth about their love. A perfect amoralist in his life, he becomes at death's door a perfect moral chorus; still we feel it only an accident that he is given the memorable lines about lust and forgetfulness, because nothing in his preceding speeches suggests a capacity for moral illumination. He does not grow beyond his previous moral stature; he merely loses his identity as a character in the machinery of the masque.

Bianca's swan song, which harmonizes unrepentant passion and sincere remorse, is truer to her dramatic personality. For she has already demonstrated an ability to reflect upon her experiences and to profit from them. At the beginning of Act IV, for example, she muses over the strange pattern of her life and concludes that poor parental discipline has made her what she is at present:

> . . . 'tis not good, in sadness,
> To keep a maid so strict in her young days;
> Restraint
> Breeds wandering thoughts, as many fasting days
> A great desire to see flesh stirring again:

I'll ne'er use any girl of mine so strictly;
Howe'er they're kept, their fortunes find 'em out;
I see't in me. . . .

(IV. i. 30–37)

Who would not accept whoredom to acquire such a sensible philosophy of raising children?

Despite the artistic inadequacy of the catastrophe of *Women
Beware Women*, it is fitting that Bianca should fall in the indiscrimi-
nate slaughter of the last scene, because she has no individual destiny
that sets her apart from the other characters in the play. Like Isabella,
Livia, Hippolito, and Guardiano, she is doomed by Middleton's dramatic thesis, not by her own passionate will. Her fate exemplifies the
way of a world which would provide a better subject for dark ironic
comedy than for tragedy. Significantly enough, there is room in
Women Beware Women for the Cardinal but not for a figure like
De Flores. There is a place for a moral chorus but not for a character
who can bring immoralists face to face with moral reality. The
Cardinal's sententious sermons merely provoke Bianca to mockery of
religious ideals and to murderous thoughts. The Duke is more deeply
touched by his brother's exhortations. He vows (though it is hard)
not to lie with Bianca again until he can possess her "lawfully," without "sin and horror"; that is, until his plan to have Leantio killed has
borne fruit.

The pitiless precision of the portraits of the Duke, Bianca, Livia,
Isabella, and Hippolito explain why Middleton is one of the few Jacobean tragedians who are not accused of obliquity. Yet one would
hardly call Middleton a moralist in art. Although he does not senti-
mentalize vice, he does not particularly dignify virtue or convince us
that ethical ideals have a vital bearing on human conduct. He does not,
like Webster in *The White Devil*, lend a heroic magnificence to
adultery; but neither does he offer a saving remnant of virtue in figures
like Giovanni and his mother, Cornelia, and Marcello. He shows us the
facile degradation of the respectable which Jonson depicts in *Volpone*,
but he does not include a Celia and Bonario to balance the portrait and
to suggest that in addition to a norm of avarice and lust there is also a
norm of decency as well. The only figure in *Women Beware Women*
whose scruples are not suspect is the Cardinal, and his belated ineffec-

tual entry into the plot actually intensifies the impression of universal immorality by providing a traditional standard with which to measure it. Moreover he does not belong to Livia's world as Celia belongs to Corvino's; he is an alien who speaks a language which none of the other characters really understand. His commonplace moralism startles us because it suddenly recalls the ethical values to which Livia's society does not even pay lip service.

Of course moral affirmation in art does not require a sane and balanced portrait of life; even while he draws a sordid portrait a dramatist may convince us of the beauty and truth of moral precept. And we cannot assume without evidence that every dramatic world is intended as a microcosm of reality, especially when the playwright's subject is a singularly unattractive group of sinners. But neither can we ignore the panoramic effect deliberately created in *Women Beware Women* by the doubling and even tripling of the incidents which illustrate the corruptibility of innocence. The consistent dramatic pattern of greed and lust, which is linked metaphorically with a mundane fabric of social customs, creates the impression that the behavior of Middleton's characters is, in fact, a social norm rather than an antisocial aberration. (Even Leantio's mother, for example, ignores the implication of the Duke's invitation in her greediness to participate in Livia's banquet.) The wholesale slaughter of the last scene is purgative, but it does not convince us that the opportunity now exists to sweep away amoral attitudes engrained in the fiber of daily life.

I do not wish to imply that *Women Beware Women* is a deeply cynical play. The impression of an underlying cynical thesis is, I think, the result of Middleton's unsuccessful attempt to create tragedy out of the materials and conventions of satiric comedy. His bourgeois setting, his plotting, and especially his characterization of Livia, whose intrigues are more in the tradition of Brainworm than of Iago—all these point backward to the realistic comedy of the first Jacobean decade, which is based on fundamentally cynical premises. The comic dramatists assume that cuckoldry is as ludicrous as it is universal. In their social myth, marriage is a convenient arrangement for merchant's wife and rakish gallant; respectability is the art of publicly reprehending the private itch. But the cynicism of realistic comedy is in the end transmuted if not annihilated by a quasi-sentimental or romantic denouement. We can smile at the prospect of enforced marriage because we are confident that the bride-to-be will be abducted from the simple heir by a debauched yet more suitably gallant lover. We can laugh at cuckoldry because we know that the jealous husband will be eventually reconciled to his fate if not to his wife. In *Women Beware Women*, however, the cynical *données* of realistic comedy are neither transmuted nor annihilated; instead they are extended to their logical antiromantic conclusions. The wretched bride-to-be does not wish to be rescued from her enforced marriage when she can have both simple heir and gallant lover. The jealous cuckold is not reconciled to his fate; he finds instead a "revenge" appropriate to his vulgar breeding. The moral impression of *The Changeling* is quite different because it leaves no doubt that the "innocence" of Alsemero and Vermandero is the norm of polite society, whose decorums, if somewhat shabby, nevertheless limit the range of sensual appetite.

Whether Middleton's tragedies are more objective or less critical of life than those of Jonson, Tourneur, and Webster is not an easy question to answer. It seems to me that Middleton is unique among the tragedians not so much for his "clinical detachment" as for his total indifference to the ideal in human nature. If he actually portrayed the destruction of innocence without stirring any pity or compassion in his readers, his plays would strike us as perversely deficient in moral sensibility. We do not object to his pitilessness because he convinces us that ultimately his characters deserve no pity, that their virtue is easily debased because it is superficial or counterfeit to begin with, and that there is no trace of the spirit in their carnal passions. Thus even when his plays blaze like diamonds they are cold to the touch. Yet coming after the speciosity of Fletcher, Middleton's irony has an astringent virtue. After the frivolity of tragicomedy, his dissection of literary illusions and honorable shams brings back to the stage a long absent integrity and seriousness of purpose. If the nobility of Penthea was far beyond his ken, his investigations of social morality may well have suggested to Ford the line of artistic inquiry which culminated in the memorable affirmations of the spirit in *The Broken Heart*.

CHAPTER VIII

John Ford

O F THE TRAGEDIES written between 1622 and the close of the
theaters, only Ford's rank beside the masterpieces of the
first decade. Blessed with the virtues of a constitutional monarch—
sobriety, sincerity, and conventionality—Massinger had to be content in tragedy with unsubstantial regal gestures; he could not command the imagination as did the earlier Jacobeans. Shirley's dramatic
authority was even more limited; at his best (in *The Cardinal*) he
proves himself a skillful manager of plot. Because Ford had the courage
and the will to break new dramatic ground, he was a less consistent
and "correct" playwright than they. Yet even when his reach exceeds
his grasp, he is indisputably the last of the Jacobeans—the last dramatist to make an original and significant contribution to early seventeenth-century tragedy.

Far more clearly than Middleton's, Ford's tragedies are an aristocratic rather than popular entertainment. His portraits of "noblesse"
have a dignity and integrity that are lacking in Beaumont and Fletcher's
posturing heroes. His ideals of love, as the date of *The Peers' Challenge*
(1606) indicates, derive from Elizabethan Neoplatonism, not from the

witty Petrarchanism of *The Maid's Tragedy* or *The Changeling*. Indeed, where Middleton ironically dissects the shams of honor, Ford attempts to recapture its meaning as a guide to the conduct of life. Informed by a courtly (though not always refined) sensibility, his plays are more remote from the actualities and exigencies of Jacobean life than any play we have studied so far. He is interested in the ethical problems that arise when the reality of marriage travesties the ideal, but he is not interested in the immediate social problem of enforced marriages. His plays do not teem with the references to contemporary manners and mores which "English" the Italian tragedies of Tourneur, Webster, and Middleton. He projects the aristocratic values of his age into a storied or aesthetically distanced past, where Friars deliver medieval sermons and brokenhearted lovers express the timeless pathos of willow pattern figures.

How distant Ford's art is from that of the earlier Jacobeans can be measured paradoxically by the extent to which he plagiarizes Shakespeare, a dramatist remote enough from Caroline audiences to provide a source of fresh and original situations.[1] Ford's drama is to Shakespeare's and Marlowe's as Euripides' is to Aeschylus' and Sophocles'. His tragic arena is bounded by the conventions of society; his tragic subject is the mystery of the heart. That his drama is more "psychological" than Middleton's, Webster's, Beaumont's, or Shakespeare's is not, however, beyond all dispute. If *The Broken Heart* seems to lack plot, it is because Ford is more interested in creating a tragic rhythm of lyric feeling than in psychological explorations. Like Aeschylus in the *Agamemnon* he develops a tragic situation, not a tragic sequence of events; he dramatizes the mounting, unendurable pressure of remembered wrongs that explodes at last in a spasm of violence. In Ford's "Oresteia" (which is set, interestingly enough, in ancient Sparta) familial crime—the sacrifice of a sister to a brother's ambition—is also treacherously revenged and the stain of murder expunged by ritual, through the ceremonious deaths of Orgilus and Calantha. All in all, Ford's psychological interests are as dramatic as Middleton's, and they lead to scenes of confrontation in *Love's Sacrifice* that are as theatrical as any in *The Changeling*. If we must blame psychology let it be for the tedious, vulgar subplots which Ford requires to flesh out the narrowly focused emotional dramas of *'Tis Pity* and *Love's Sacrifice*. Or let us say that in *Love's Sacrifice* Ford, like Middleton, loses interest in his characters before their destinies are consummated because he is concerned only with the psychological drama of their relationships and not with their ability to confront death.

Though Ford departs from the dramatic techniques of the earlier Jacobeans, he also builds upon their achievements. When he attempts to imitate earlier melodrama, his passion is strained and meretricious. When he is content to suggest through stylized utterance the deep-rooted passions which previous dramatists had unforgettably depicted, he achieves a unique artistic perfection. It is not accidental that many of the terms applied to Ford's drama are usually reserved for criticism of the plastic or pictorial arts, for in his finest plays the sound and fury of melodramatic conflict give way to the relative stasis of ceremonial gesture. Moments of intense feeling are recorded; sensationalism and violence intrude. But the total impression is of a tranquility and delicacy far removed from Webster and Tourneur. The aim in such plays as *The Broken Heart* and *The Lady's Trial* is not to hold a mirror up to nature but to capture an ultimate "ritual" expression of love and aristocratic "noblesse." The protagonists of earlier tragedies were noble in their individuality—in their refusal to bow before circumstances. Ford's most admirable characters, however, seem to lose their individuality at climactic moments. Their nobility in the face of death springs not so much from depth of character as from an aristocratic awareness of the role which they must play—of the need to subordinate all personal feeling. They seem to realize that dying well (like living well) requires art and knowledge. They become, so to speak, artists within a work of art crystallizing through studied attitude the aristocratic values of their society; they make the aesthetic expression of virtue a virtue in itself.

To recognize Ford's method of stylization is perhaps to understand why his attempts at comedy are unsuccessful as well as indecent. His Elizabethan and Jacobean predecessors used clownish simplicity as a ground burden to the sophisticated "divisions" of courtly love. They contrasted the artificial posturings of romantic heroes and heroines against the more realistic (if somewhat burlesqued) affections of maids and servants. Ford's comic characters are also coarser-grained than his heroes, but they are not realistic or satiric social types. They do not bring the sounds and smells of workaday London into the perfumed corridors of Veronese palaces. Instead they are caricatures—at times grotesque ones—of his romantic protagonists. It is as if Ford, knowing the true proportions of his delicate lovers, deliberately distorts them for comic and moral contrasts, to create lewd antimasques to romantic tragedy. The vulgarity of the gutter candidly reported (as in Marston) has at least a natural and earthy vitality. The vulgarity of the boudoir, burlesqued by a writer who had no comic talent, is more often than not simply disgusting.

Earlier dramatists were more uneven in their artistic achievement than Ford, but he alone wrote plays like *Love's Sacrifice* that are both delicate and gross, finely wrought and carelessly patched together. Only in *The Broken Heart* does one feel that he perfectly executed his artistic intention. In *'Tis Pity* his reach exceeded his grasp; his techniques were not refined enough for the moral and aesthetic complexity of his subject. Although the chronology of Ford's plays remains problemmatical, *'Tis Pity* seems to me the earliest of the tragedies.[2] Far more successful artistically than *Love's Sacrifice*, it is notwithstanding less mature in its characterizations and less sophisticated in its themes than the other tragedies. It lacks the concern with aristocratic codes of behavior that marks Ford's later plays and it is the only one which pretends to an ideological significance in the manner of earlier Jacobean plays.

Ford's treatment of incest is the most daring in Jacobean drama, but it is not as unique as critics have made it appear. The debate over nature and moral law in the opening scene of *'Tis Pity* recalls similar dialectical moments in the plays of Marston, Tourneur, and Fletcher. In the first speech of the play, the Friar warns his student, Giovanni, against the intellectual subtlety and curiosity that lead men away from God:

> Dispute no more in this, for know (young man)
> These are no Schoole-points; nice Philosophy
> May tolerate unlikely arguments,
> But Heaven admits no jest; wits that presum'd
> On wit too much, by striving how to prove
> There was no God; with foolish grounds of Art,
> Discover'd first the neerest way to Hell;

And fild the world with develish Atheisme:
Such questions youth are fond; for better 'tis,
To blesse the Sunne, then reason why it shines;
Yet hee thou talk'st of, is above the Sun.[3] (I. i)

Echoing the quietism of Renaissance apologists, the Friar seems to recall Tourneur's assertion that God is above nature (or the sun). Like D'Amville's, Giovanni's naturalistic atheism has its libertine corollary; and like D'Amville he defends the naturalness of incest against the "customary forme" of moral law:

Shall a peevish sound,
A customary forme, from man to man,
Of brother and of sister, be a barre
Twixt my perpetuall happinesse and mee?
Say that we had one father, say one wombe,
(Curse to my ioyes) gave both us life, and birth;
Are wee not therefore each to other bound
So much the more by Nature; by the links
Of blood, of reason; Nay if you will hav't,
Even of Religion, to be ever one,
One soule, one flesh, one love, one heart, one *All?* (I. i)

The Friar counsels mortification of the flesh and self-abasement, but like earlier Jacobean heroes Giovanni finds that prayers and counsel are futile, that supposed remedies against passion are "but dreames and old mens tales/ To fright unsteedy youth." Convinced that he is fated to love and perish, he dares to reveal his passion to Annabella. When she objects, "You are my brother, *Giovanni*," he answers:

I know this:
And could afford you instance why to love
So much the more for this; to which intent
Wise Nature first in your Creation ment
To make you mine: else't had beene sinne and foule,
To share one beauty to a double soule.
Neerenesse in birth or blood, doth but perswade
A neerer neerenesse in affection.
I have askt Counsell of the holy Church,
Who tells mee I may love you, and 'tis iust,
That since I may, I should; and will, yes will. (I. iii)

Up to this point the moral pattern of *'Tis Pity* seems almost predictable. The only question would seem to be whether Giovanni will (like Malheureux) renounce his naturalism in time, or (like D'Amville) acknowledge God too late. The deliberate equivocation about the "Counsell of the holy Church" signals a new emphasis in characterization, however—a turning away from ideology to psychology. Intimating the shallowness of Giovanni's atheistic convictions, it prepares us for the casuistry with which he later rationalizes his seduction of Annabella. When the horrified Friar warns of catastrophe, Giovanni replies:

> Father, in this you are uncharitable;
> What I have done, I'le prove both fit and good.
> It is a principall (which you have taught
> When I was yet your Scholler) that the Frame
> And Composition of the *Minde* doth follow
> The Frame and Composition of *Body:*
> So where the *Bodies* furniture is *Beauty,*
> The *Mindes* must needs be *Vertue:* which allowed,
> *Vertue* it selfe is *Reason but refin'd,*
> And *Love* the Quintesence of that, this proves
> My Sisters *Beauty* being rarely *Faire,*
> Is rarely *Vertuous;* chiefely in her love,
> And chiefely in that *Love, her love to me.*
> If *hers to me,* then so is *mine to her;*
> Since in like Causes are effects alike. (II. v)

There is no more intellectual seriousness in this "unlikely argument" than in Giovanni's plea to Annabella, only now his improvisation is mocking and exultant. This is high-spirited casuistry for casuistry's sake, an egotistic display of shallow wit. The brilliant young scholar does not really attempt to persuade his teacher; he demonstrates again the jesting arrogance which the Friar earlier condemned by sophisticating Neoplatonic ideas. The horrified Friar does not respond in kind:

> O ignorance in knowledge; long agoe,
> How often have I warn'd thee this before?
> Indeede if we were sure there were no *Deity,*
> Nor *Heaven* nor *Hell,* then to be lead alone,
> By Natures light (as were Philosophers
> Of elder times) might instance some defence.
> But 'tis not so; then Madman, thou wilt finde,
> That *Nature* is in Heavens positions blind. (II. v)

Strangely enough, the Friar does not attack Giovanni's specious syllogisms. Instead he implies that philosophy and "natural law" support rather than refute Giovanni's arguments. Though an uncompromising defender of religion, the Friar admits what had never before been admitted on the Jacobean stage: namely, that incestuous desire *is* natural, though forbidden by divine law.

The Friar's reply is of course characteristic of his fideistic viewpoint. It also has a larger significance in relation to Jacobean debate over nature and moral law. The recurrent link between libertine naturalism and incest in Jacobean drama was not fortuitous, because a justification of incest was implicit in the libertine argument for unconfined love and is in fact wittily explicit in Donne's "Elegie XVII." One footnote to the Friar's speech is provided by François Garasse, who attacks the libertine Vanini for associating with a man who excused some forms of incest:

> Le mal-heureux Lucilio Vanino, Atheiste tres-envenimé, tesmoigne en ses Dialogues qu'il a recogneu dans Geneve un Ministre Flamand qui se moquoit de tout ce qu'on appelle scrupule, nommément en matiere de vilainies, & dogmatisoit publiquement dans cette Bethauen, que les incestes en premier & second degré, ne sont pas plus grand peché que les actions iournalieres de boire & manger: Et rendoit une raison du tout horrible, pour laquelle il s'imaginoit que les Loix humaines seulement, & non pas les Ordonnances divines eussent defendu les incestes.[4]

To Garasse's orthodox mind any defense of incest was a manifest sign of depravity. To more liberal minds, however, the naturalness or unnaturalness of incestuous desire was a more complex matter. Charron, for example, is not convinced that incest is unnatural. Indeed, he cites the prohibition against incest as evidence of the power of *custom* over *natural* desire:

> But who would beleeve how great and imperious the authoritie of custome is? He that said it was another nature, did not sufficientlie expresse it, for it doth more than nature, it conquereth nature: for hence it is that the most beautiful daughters of men draw not unto love their naturall parents, nor brethren, though excellent in beautie, winne not the love of their sisters. This kind of chastitie is not properly of nature, but of the use of lawes and customes, which forbid them, and make of incest a great sinne. . . . And it is the law of *Moses*

which forbad it in these first degrees; but it hath also sometimes dispensed therewith. . . .[5]

In 1625 Hugo Grotius, the famed authority on ethics, came to a somewhat similar conclusion about incest. Although he refutes moral relativism and presupposes the universality of moral law, he insists upon carefully defining the sanctions for moral precepts. He warns against rashly accounting "among things forbidden by nature, those things which are not manifestly so, and which are forbidden rather by Divine Law: in which rank haply you may put copulations without marriage, and some reputed incests, and usury."[6]

The late Renaissance acknowledgment of the naturalness of sexual desire makes comprehensible the Friar's "retreat" to a fideistic position. In his speeches, as in *The Atheist's Tragedy*, there is a partial acceptance of a naturalistic view of man and the universe. If there were no power superior to nature and no goal in life higher than that of satisfying natural impulses, the Friar concedes, the naturalist's position would be in some respects defensible. But like Tourneur (and like the moral philosophers of the late Renaissance) the Friar insists that a wholly naturalistic view of the universe is incomplete, that nature in "Heavens positions" (i.e., as law-giver) is blind.

The significance of the Friar's answer to Giovanni, then, is not its apparent surrender to libertine sophistry but its calm, assured dismissal of "ignorance in knowledge." The debate over nature is ended, the naturalistic casuistry which had provoked so many learned and lengthy confutations is now summarily rejected. In fact compared to D'Amville, Giovanni is hardly a dangerous opponent of morality. If nature really is his goddess, she receives scant acknowledgment in his speeches; and although he has a facile wit, he has no ideology that would substitute for traditional ethics. Because his atheism is lacking in conviction he is easily terrified by the Friar's threats of damnation. When he despairs of gaining Annabella he is a frightened child; when his love is fulfilled, he jokes about heaven or hell. All in all, his rebellion is more emotional than intellectual. The once mighty naturalist is now impersonated by an unsteady youth, who scarcely takes his own arguments seriously.

It requires a peculiar insensitivity to the nuances of characterization and verse in *'Tis Pity* to treat Giovanni as Ford's spokesman. But

it is no less an error to turn Ford into a champion of orthodoxy by identifying him with the Friar, who is, despite his choric role, a somewhat
muddled moralist. Unless we understand the Friar's place in Ford's
moral design, he must seem an ambiguous character: on the one hand,
kind, earnest, and sincere; on the other hand, politic, insensitive, and
unscrupulous. The contradictions disappear, however, when we realize
that the Friar represents not traditional morality as such but a peculiarly legalistic, authoritarian religious ethic. Preaching sin and
damnation, the Friar upholds a moral "ideal" that abases man before
the divine will and negates his rational humanistic participation in
divine government. When Giovanni first confesses his incestuous desires, the Friar counsels him to

> fall downe
> On both thy knees, and grovell on the ground:
> Cry to thy heart, wash every word thou utter'st
> In teares, (and if't bee possible) of blood:
> Begge Heaven to cleanse the leprosie of Lust
> That rots thy Soule, acknowledge what thou art,
> A wretch, a worme, a nothing: weepe, sigh, pray
> Three times a day, and three times every night:
> For seven dayes space doe this. . . . (I. i)

The suggestion of superstitious, "magical" exorcism is not inappropriate, for the Friar's idea of morality does not rise far above a primitive fear of punishment. His later sermon to Annabella is an exercise in
terror:

> . . . there is *a place*
> (List daughter) in a blacke and hollow Vault,
> Where day is never seene; there shines no Sunne,
> But flaming horrour of consuming Fires;
> A lightlesse Suphure, choakt with smoaky foggs
> Of an infected darknesse; in *this place*
> Dwell many thousand, thousand sundry sorts
> Of never dying deaths; there damned soules
> Roare without pitty, there are Gluttons fedd
> With Toades and Addars; there is burning Oyle
> Powr'd downe the Drunkards throate, the Usurer
> Is forc't to supp whole draughts of molten Gold;
> There is the Murtherer for-ever stab'd,
> Yet can he never dye; there lies the wanton

On Racks of burning steele, whiles in his soule
Hee feeles the torment of his raging lust. (III. vi)

The Friar's worldly "realism" does not clash with his other-
worldly piety; it is instead a direct consequence of it. His literalistic
mind views morality wholly in terms of crime and punishment; he
regards sin with the mentality of a criminal lawyer. Deeply attached
to Giovanni and Annabella, he would have them, if possible, avoid sin
altogether. But if prayers, fasting, and self-mortification are unavailing,
then he would have them commit the smallest possible crime and incur
the lightest punishment. "Looke through the world," he advises Gio-
vani,

And thou shalt see a thousand faces shine
More glorious, then this Idoll thou ador'st:
Leave her, and take thy choyce, 'tis much lesse sinne,
Though in such games as those, they lose that winne. (I. i)

He is even more politic when he preaches comfort to the remorseful
Annabella, who carries Giovanni's child:

. . . despaire not; Heaven is mercifull,
And offers grace even now; 'tis thus agreed,
First, for your Honours safety that you marry
The Lord *Soranzo*, next, to save your soule,
Leave off this life, and henceforth live to him. (III. vi)

The Friar's idea of precedence is disturbing and his conception of
heavenly grace ironic, for the deceitful marriage which he advises is
neither an effective nor a moral solution. Nevertheless his legalistic
mind is working here at full pressure. He does not consider that Annabella's marriage will be unjust to Soranzo and a travesty of the sacrament of wedlock. All that matters to him is that it will construct another legal and moral barrier between the sinning lovers. It succeeds,
however, only in dragging Giovanni and Annabella into deeper spiritual and moral degradation.

The opposition between Giovanni and the Friar, then, is not a
simple antithesis of sin and piety, darkness and light. Both are insensitive to the ideal claims of morality. The Friar forces Annabella into
marriage to save her "honour"; Giovanni murders her to save her
"name." Giovanni rejects morality as "customary forme"; the Friar

substitutes the empty "customary forme" of marriage for its true meaning. Giovanni exalts anarchic desire, the immediate sensuous response to beauty that denies all but the present ecstasy. The Friar stands for an ethical code that seems no more than a dread coercion. With the Friar we reject Giovanni's specious rationalizations, but we respond more sympathetically to his lovely description of Annabella.

> View well her face, and in that little round,
> You may observe a world of variety;
> For Colour, lips, for sweet perfumes, her breath;
> For Iewels, eyes; for threds of purest gold,
> Hayre; for delicious choyce of Flowers, cheekes;
> Wonder in every portion of that Throne:
> Heare her but speake, and you will sweare the Sphaeres
> Make Musicke to the Cittizens in Heaven. (II. v)

Sweetness and affection hover in these lines; the worn Petrarchan conceits take on fresh beauty and meaning. Here is a love of the flesh that touches the spiritual, an ardor that is unsullied by the courtly sensual wit of Suckling and Carew.

If Ford endows Giovanni (particularly at the beginning of the play) with his own poetic sensibility, he does not apologize for his illicit passion any more than Shakespeare apologizes for Hotspur's rebellion by giving him the most memorable lines in *Henry IV*. Like Shakespeare in *Antony and Cleopatra*, Ford dares to find beauty, tenderness, and devotion in a forbidden love. Without confusing moral values, he explores the commonplace truth that there are crimes and *crimes*. There is a difference between Annabella's selfless love, Hippolita's vicious passion, and the disgusting animalism of Putana, who applauds Annabella's submission:

> Why now I commend thee (*Chardge*) feare nothing, (sweete-heart) what though hee be your Brother; your Brother's a man I hope, and I say still, if a young Wench feele the fitt upon her, let her take any body, Father or Brother, all is one. (II. i)

If it is true, as some critics claim, that Ford believed in an amoral deterministic psychology,[7] then it is strange that he should state his "philosophy" in such revolting terms and through so despicable a mouthpiece. While he does not bow to the conventionally moralistic opinion that all illicit desire is sordid, he upholds the more profound

truth that submission to illicit passion degrades. In his tragedies he
pities lovers who are trapped by circumstances not of their own making—by the accident of their births or of loveless marriages; yet he
recognizes full well that it is circumstances that try men's characters
and lives. To Ford the romantic defiance of circumstances has a Marlovian beauty, but it is also a symptom of weakness, of an inability to
endure misfortune and calamity. Even when Giovanni's affection is
relatively innocent, it is incipiently corrupt. He lies to win Annabella,
and his love is increasingly warped by the fear and jealousy that shadows its first ecstatic consummation. Because (as he realizes) there can
be no lasting fulfillment of their love in marriage, their passion can
only defile them as they grow accustomed to the stealthy satisfaction
of incestuous and adulterous desire. Before the play ends Annabella
is a helpless pawn in the struggle between a jealous lover and a jealous
husband, both infatuated with revenge. Soranzo cannot bear the sting
of cuckoldry although he seduced Richardetto's wife; Giovanni cannot bear the thought of another man possessing Annabella. Tormented
by jealousy and coarsened by stealth, Giovanni's love changes from
breathless adoration to insane possessiveness. In the final throes of despairing egoism he comes to believe that Annabella's life literally belongs to him. When their relationship is discovered, he murders her as
part of his "revenge" on Soranzo.

Still loving her brother, Annabella feels before she dies the agony
of their hopeless existence. And though he remains a defiant atheist,
Giovanni eventually admits that the moral law which condemns his
love is not simply a "customary forme":

> . . . if ever after times should heare
> Of our fast-knit affections, though perhaps
> The Lawes of *Conscience* and of *Civill use*
> May iustly blame us, yet when they but know
> Our loves, *That love* will wipe away that rigour,
> Which would in other *Incests* bee abhorr'd. (V. v)

But the moral order which he at last recognizes is far different from
the Friar's, for having found damnation on earth, Giovanni does not
fear another judgment. Urged by the Cardinal to "thinke on thy life
and end, and call for mercy," he replies: "*Mercy?* why I have found
it in this *Iustice*." Death comes to Giovanni as a "guest long look't

for"; justice is merciful when it ends an intolerable existence. Thus despite its bloody finale, *'Tis Pity* is not haunted by the earlier Jacobean preoccupation with death. It is, like *The Broken Heart*, a tragedy of spiritual disintegration, of heroes and heroines trapped in a living death which only death can end.

Unlike earlier dramatists Ford does not ponder universal questions. Certain that moral values are constantly reaffirmed by man's experience, he presents the rare individual instance that proves conventional moral generalizations. It is not surprising, however, that some critics have interpreted *'Tis Pity* as a decadent apotheosis of passion,[8] because Ford does not completely translate his moral vision into effective artifice. His judgment of Giovanni would seem clearer, for example, if there were another moral chorus than the Friar, whose vision remains narrow and prosaic and whose speeches do not impress the imagination as do Giovanni's. Because there does not seem to be any alternative to the Friar's and Giovanni's irreconcilable and unacceptable positions, moral knowledge and poetic intuition do not melt into a single humane, ethical perception. And because Giovanni grows more insensitive to ethical values as the play proceeds, his belated admission of guilt seems almost an afterthought, a sop to Nemesis rather than a final illumination.

It should be Annabella who positively affirms the humanity of moral law and who weds ethical judgment and poetic insight. Possessing a moral sensitivity which Giovanni lacks, she feels the loathsomeness of their sins while he knows only the torments of jealousy. Unfortunately, however, Annabella plays too ambiguous a role in the moral action to serve as an ethical touchstone. At one moment she seems to have risen above carnality; at another moment she seems like Giovanni corrupted by incest and adultery. Now she plays the repentant sinner, now the wanton who brazenly boasts of her lover to her husband. Even when she is conscience-stricken, Giovanni fills her mind. Her nobility lies in the generosity of her love for him, not in a victory over desire.

But the fact that we cannot erase all the ambiguities of *'Tis Pity* should not lead us to exaggerate its failings. When we consider the daring of Ford's intention and the difficult problems of moral discrimination which his subject posed, we must admire his achievement. Indeed his boldness should offend only those who are dogmatic in their ethics and who can picture only stereotypes of virtue and vice. If Ford imperfectly executes the moral design of *'Tis Pity*, he does not completely obscure it, and we need only turn to *The Broken Heart* to grasp the ethical viewpoint that does not completely and lucidly emerge from the earlier play.

The Broken Heart

In contrast to the glowing life and passion of *'Tis Pity*, *The Broken Heart* seems somewhat pale. The violence that erupts in the last act does not so much quicken the dramatic action as add to the hidden soul-destroying burden of silent griefs. An Elizabethan dramatist, one imagines, would have cast *The Broken Heart* in the romantic mold of *Romeo and Juliet*. He would have set upon the stage another tale of star-crossed lovers ruined by hostile circumstances. Ford is more interested, however, in emotional reaction than in romantic action. His play begins after the most dramatic incidents of the fable have occurred. He studies, as it were, the aftermath of romantic tragedy, the cumulative shock of misery and frustration on the lives of Penthea, Orgilus, and those who share their unhappy fates.

The tragedy of Penthea is to be betrayed by the three men who love her: her brother, Ithocles, who for ambition forces her into a loathsome marriage; her evil-minded "humorous" husband, Bassanes, who imprisons her to possess her entirely; and her former lover, Orgilus, who tries to seduce her from her marriage vows. To Ithocles and Bassanes, Penthea's misery brings a redeeming awareness of the sins of ambition and jealousy. Orgilus' spiritual fate is more uncertain. Although Penthea's death seals his decision to murder Ithocles, his revenge is motivated as much by self-pity and envy as by love; there is, in fact, a touch of Giovanni's crazed vanity in his thought and actions. On the other hand, his misfortune demands our sympathy and he achieves in the acceptance of death a dignity lacking in his struggle against the circumstances of his life. His revenge is certainly immoral, but his claim to Penthea's love is not explicitly refuted except by Penthea, whose feelings are ambivalent if not contradictory.

By conventional standards Orgilus' love for another man's wife

is adulterous, even though Penthea's marriage was tyrannically enforced and is a shameful travesty of the wedding vow. Before Ithocles
interfered, Penthea and Orgilus shared a chaste and "approved" affection. Indeed, according to Elizabethan custom, they were "married"
by plighting their troth even though an official ceremony had not yet
been performed. When Orgilus confronts Penthea he does not place
the rights of love above the bond of marriage. He claims a wife, not a
courtly mistress: "I would possesse my wife, the equity/ Of very
reason bids me" (II. iii). More than anyone else, Penthea is aware of
the immorality of her marriage; she feels violated, defiled, and even
prostituted by her loveless servitude. In effect she admits Orgilus'
prior claim when she later says to Ithocles:

> . . . she that's wife to *Orgilus*, and lives
> In knowne Adultery with *Bassanes*,
> Is at the best a whore. (III. ii)

And yet when Orgilus presses his claim she denies it:

> How (*Orgilus*) by promise I was thine,
> The heavens doe witnesse; they can witnesse too
> A rape done on my truth: how I doe love thee
> Yet *Orgilus*, and yet, must best appeare
> In tendering thy freedome; for I find
> The constant preservation of thy merit,
> By thy not daring to attempt my fame
> With iniury of any loose conceit,
> Which might give deeper wounds to discontents. (II. iii)

When he continues to plead for her love, she turns on him angrily:

> Uncivill Sir, forbeare,
> Or I can turne affection into vengeance;
> Your reputation (if you value any)
> Lyes bleeding at my feet. Unworthy man,
> If ever henceforth thou appeare in language,
> Message, or letter to betray my frailty,
> I'le call thy former protestations lust,
> And curse my Starres for forfeit of my iudgement.
> Goe thou, fit onely for disguise and walkes,
> To hide thy shame: this once I spare thy life. (II. iii)

We may admire Penthea's strength of will and still question her
wisdom. We may wonder what value resides in an utterly meaningless

dedication, or what purpose is served by fidelity to a marriage that exists in name only. By spurning Orgilus she condemns him as well as herself to a living death and ensures catastrophe. Perhaps in this instance Ford suggests that it would have been wiser to challenge circumstances than to submit passively. Perhaps it would have been more moral for Penthea to find happiness with Orgilus than to observe the "customary forme" of marriage.

How easy it is to falsify the central issue in *The Broken Heart* by reducing it to a simple conflict of values—the "promptings of the heart" versus "conventional morality."[9] Actually Ford's presentation of character leaves no doubt that Penthea is wiser as well as stronger than Orgilus, who advances the claim of love as an absolute that negates circumstances and time itself. Penthea does not deny that she was once promised to Orgilus, but she will not confuse the past with the present. Admitting the vileness of her marriage, she nevertheless accepts it as one of the irremediable accidents that distort the shape of men's lives. The opportunity for happiness which she and Orgilus once possessed no longer exists because they have themselves changed. Like Giovanni (indeed, like most of Ford's heroes), Orgilus is weaker than the woman he loves and crushed by a far lighter burden than she bears. The misery that makes her compassionate and generous makes him selfish and self-pitying. Although he attacks Ithocles' tyranny, he insists on the privilege of authorizing his own sister's marriage and enjoys the power even if he does not abuse it. Embittered, wretchedly frustrate, he enters into a labyrinth of deceptions and disguises that ends in murder and self-destruction.

Far more realistic than Orgilus, Penthea recognizes the true nature of the alternatives that face her. If she flees with Orgilus it must be outside society and law, without hope of the joyous fulfillment of marriage. If she refuses, Orgilus may yet find happiness and she will preserve intact the citadel of her mind. Her thoughts are pure even though her body is defiled; the shame of her "adultery" rests upon Ithocles. Thus while Orgilus' claim to Penthea is in the abstract just, he demonstrates his unworthiness of her by pressing it. She spurns him pityingly, aware of the gulf that has sprung between them, recognizing that he is "fit only for disguise" and a ruin of his former self. There is obviously more frustrate desire than selfless devotion in his plea. He speaks of Neoplatonic devotion but his imagery reveals the hunger of sensual appetite:

> All pleasures are but meere imagination,
> Feeding the hungry appetite with steame,
> And sight of banquet, whilst the body pines,
> Not relishing the reall tast of food. . . . (II. iii)

For Penthea, then, the choice is between an evil-minded husband who feverishly schemes to inter her alive and an embittered lover who feverishly schemes to steal her away. Both are ungenerous, both are wildly possessive. The gentle Penthea, who had almost attained the strength to endure her life with Bassanes, is crushed by the shock of Orgilus' betrayal.

For from exalting the claim of individual desire over the bond of matrimony, *The Broken Heart*, like Ford's other tragedies, depicts the warping of love that cannot grow and mature. It is quite true that Giovanni and Orgilus express Ford's romantic idealism—his poetic worship of love—but they also betray that idealism by their jealousy and by their desire to possess rather than serve beauty. Indeed, the highest expression of love in Ford's drama is not the reckless ardor of Giovanni and Orgilus but the generous devotion of Annabella and Penthea.[10] And though Tecnicus is the official "philosopher" of *The Broken Heart*, it is Penthea who, expressing in the beauty of her own life the correspondence of poetic vision and moral knowledge, re-affirms the essential humanity of ethical ideals. If the portrayal of Penthea leaves any doubts about Ford's attitude towards marriage, those doubts are erased by the solemn beauty of Euphranea's betrothal and Calantha's wedding to Ithocles in death.

Love's Sacrifice

I have withheld discussion of *Love's Sacrifice* until now, not because I assume that it was Ford's last tragedy but because we can scarcely understand Ford's intention (or failure) in this bewildering play except by reference to *'Tis Pity* and *The Broken Heart*. Miss Sargeaunt and Professor Harbage place *Love's Sacrifice* before *The Broken Heart*; G. E. Bentley and H. J. Oliver place it after.[11] I would argue only that *Love's Sacrifice* is not a shaky piece of apprentice work by an inexperienced tragedian. If anything it is a careless, per-haps hasty, composition by a very skilled dramatist who was too con-fident of his ability to camouflage a splintered plot with the trappings of melodrama.

To begin with, the moral confusion that surrounds the heroine of *Love's Sacrifice* is quite different from the contradictions in the portrait of Annabella. Ford is not uncertain about Bianca's nature, nor is there any inconsistency in his development of her character. She does not abruptly change in the last act; instead Ford abruptly shifts his standard of judgment (his moral point of view) in order to as-similate the last act within his tragic design. One notes, moreover, that when *Love's Sacrifice* staggers into obliquity it is because Ford de-liberately abdicates artistic responsibility. Instead of resolving im-aginatively the tragic situation developed in the first two acts, he patches together a conclusion out of the First Folio. There are also imitations of Shakespeare in *'Tis Pity:* lines from *Othello,* a recollec-tion of Laertes' poisoned rapier, and remembrances of *Romeo and Juliet* in the roles of the Friar and Florio and in the enforced marriage. But these echoes are relatively unobtrusive and seem unconscious trib-utes to a dramatist whose art had become an integral part of Ford's poetic experience. The imitations of *Othello* in *Love's Sacrifice* are an entirely different matter; they constitute a gross and uninspired pla-giarism of scenes and situations, characterizations and dialogue. One can easily believe that Ford wrote the latter half of the play (espe-cially scenes III. iii and IV.i & ii) with a copy of *Othello* before him, taking care only to drag what is marvelous in Shakespeare down to a pedestrian level. This kind of imitation would be inconceivable in a young dramatist making his first bid for the laurel of tragedy; it would be more understandable in a writer who had already enjoyed success as an independent playwright and was secure in or indifferent to his reputation.

Despite the inanities of the last act, we can, I think, infer from it Ford's original intention. He set out, it would seem, to write a more ironic and richly plotted version of *Othello,* in which Iago (D'avolos) exaggerates but does not completely fabricate the unfaithfulness of Othello's (Caraffa's) wife. In Ford's version, the trusted young friend does betray the husband's confidence. In Caraffa's absence Fernando repeatedly importunes Bianca, who, unlike Desdemona, does not actually love her aging husband although she is grateful to him and is determined to be a loyal wife. Innately gracious and dignified, she does not invite Fernando's illicit courtship and she falls in love with him against her will. For three acts, she is Ford's most subtle psychological portrait, a woman who fights a silent and losing battle against her ambivalent feelings. Though she angrily rejects Fernando's pleas, she allows them to continue, even providing an opportunity for him to speak when they are alone. When she protests too well her indignation (which is unfeigned if impure), and Fernando pledges to end his courtship, she comes to his bed and offers herself to him with the threat that she will kill herself if he takes her.

Here is the familiar Fletcherian boudoir scene with a moral difference. Despite the latent eroticism of the situation, it has a rare psychological delicacy. Hungering for Fernando's affection and too weak to resist his passionate demands, Bianca thrusts the burden of restraint on his shoulders. At first skeptical, Fernando is at last convinced of Bianca's integrity; through a daring gamble she is now able to accept his devotion without fear of guilty consequences.

If Ford had left Fernando and Bianca's relationship as it is at the end of the second act, his play might seem more coherent. The murder of Bianca would then be deeply ironic because she would have preserved her innocence only to be "punished" by the horn-mad Caraffa. But Ford knew the human heart too well to portray Bianca's "victory" as a genuine solution to her emotional conflict. At the very moment that she disarms Fernando, she lowers her own defenses; indeed, her triumph over passion is built on the sands of her weakness. Because she spends her total moral capital in refusing Fernando's adulterous advances she cannot endure in her resolve; too confident of *his* restraint, she feels free to enjoy his love in every way short of adultery. As their "harmless" dalliance grows more brazen, adherence to her marriage vow changes from a positive article of faith to a meaningless bar to her desires. And finally she joins the libertines in attacking the chains of custom:

> Why shouldst thou [Fernando] not be mine? why should the laws
> The Iron lawes of Ceremony, barre
> Mutuall embraces? what's a vow? a vow?

Can there be sinne in unity? Could I
As well dispense with Conscience, as renounce
The out-side of my titles, the poore stile
Of *Dutchesse;* I had rather change my life
With any waiting-woman in the land,
To purchase one nights rest with thee *Fernando,*
Then be *Caraffa's* Spouse a thousand yeares. (V. i)

By now there is little resemblance between Bianca and Desdemona. The tragedy of martyred innocence is no longer possible; we
can only anticipate the tragic fall of a woman who attempted an impossible compromise between fidelity and passion. Since Ford's characterization of Bianca overstepped the bounds of his original intention,
he had either to alter his dramatic design or juggle his moral values.
He chose to do the latter. Returned to the court, Caraffa hears D'avolos' venomous report of Bianca's lechery. The great temptation scenes
in *Othello* are drearily rehashed; Caraffa gives Bianca fair warning of
his jealous suspicions, and when he discovers her kissing Fernando, he
murders her. Fernando is about to defend himself against Caraffa when
he learns of Bianca's death. Dropping his sword, he exclaims:

Unfortunate *Caraffa;* thou hast butcher'd
An Innocent, a wife as free from lust
As any termes of Art can Deifie.

.   .   .   .

          If ever I unshrin'd
The Altar of her purity, or tasted
More of her love, then what without controule .
Or blame, a brother from a sister might,
Racke me to Atomies. (V. ii)

While Caraffa sneers, Fernando continues:

          . . . *glorious Bianca,*
Reigne in the triumph of thy martyrdome,
Earth was unworthy of thee. (V. ii)

Impressed too late by Fernando's sincerity, Caraffa sees the "truth."
In the silliest final scene in Jacobean tragedy, Fernando, wrapped in
a winding sheet, drinks poison in Bianca's tomb. Caraffa, not to be out-
done, washes away his "sinne" in blood, his last thoughts dwelling on
his "chaste" wife and "unequall'd" friend.

It would be pleasant to believe that this last scene is deliberately ironic or even a burlesque of romantic melodrama. But if there was any joke intended in *Love's Sacrifice*, it was played on the actors and the audience. I imagine that we must take the entire last act as seriously as we can, although we do not have to agree that Bianca should be worshipped as a saint because she could not be convicted of adultery. Whereas Penthea was defiled in body but chaste in thought, Bianca has adulterous appetites and the technical chastity of a loyal wife. To keep his play together, Ford travesties the moral viewpoint of his other tragedies; as Coleridge remarked of Fletcher's plays, chastity is here valued "as a material thing—not as an act or state of being."

Perhaps some of the obliquity in *Love's Sacrifice* is the result of Fletcher's influence. The boudoir scenes are reminiscent of *The Lover's Progress*, and the retreat from a serious ethical problem through a twist of plot recalls the denouement of *A King and No King*. Still we cannot blame Fletcher for Ford's irresponsibility, for his use of cheap theatrics, and for his ranting parody of the conclusion of *Romeo and Juliet*. I suspect that Ford, having wandered into deeper water than he purposed in the first two acts of *Love's Sacrifice*, found it easier to drift along with scraps of other men's plays than to strike out for shore again. Bianca's role is the only spark of inspiration in the last act and that spark produces more smoke than fire. When Caraffa accuses her of adultery, she does not defend her technically sound "honor." Instead she attempts to shield Fernando by assuming his guilt, by playing a brazen slut so effectively that we cannot decide whether she is an innocent posing as a wanton, or a wanton posing as an innocent acting the part of a wanton.

To a reader familiar only with the tragedies, confusion and sensationalism may seem more characteristic of Ford than the refinement and sensitivity which we find in *The Broken Heart*. Those who also study *The Lover's Melancholy*, *Perkin Warbeck*, and *The Lady's Trial*, however, will have a truer sense of Ford's quality. They will know a dramatist who did not always possess the tact required for the investigation of the darker ways of passion, but whose judgments were based on a clearly defined set of values. Indeed the very nature of Ford's subjects indicates that he wrote with a far greater ethical assurance than did his predecessors. In the absence of pervading skepticism, he was free to probe beneath the surface of conventional morality and to investigate the rare individual instance that proves the moral "rule." Because he was concerned with the individual rather than the typical, Ford does not offer universal truths. Instead each of his plays, perhaps even *Love's Sacrifice*, adds another fraction to a cumulative knowledge of the human heart.

Twentieth-century criticism has insisted upon Ford's "modernity," either by praising his psychological insights or by damning his "scientific" amoral view of the passions. I imagine, however, that we need no more modern a guide to Ford's view of character than the liberal ethic of *Biathanatos*. If Ford does not arrive at Donne's conclusion that "there is no externall act naturally evill," he shares Donne's knowledge that circumstances "condition" acts and give them their moral nature. Like Donne he insists upon an ethical judgment that is individual, flexible, and humane, not rigid, dogmatic, and absolute. Like Donne he believes that moral values are shaped by the processes of life even as they in turn shape the nature of human relationships.

A modern dramatist might have viewed the tragic situation in *The Broken Heart* as an unresolvable dilemma that baffles judgment. Ford, however, challenges the reader to perceive those permanent values on which judgment rests. Although he lived in an age of warring factions, he wrote with a deeper sense of the communion between the individual and society than did Chapman or Webster. And unlike Middleton he had a clear view of the ideal in man's thought and conduct and a poignant awareness of the tragedy that befalls when the bonds of friendship, love, and devotion are warped or sundered.

CHAPTER IX

Shakespeare

LOOKING BACK upon the three decades of tragedy that ended with Ford, one sees an apparently eccentric pattern of creativity. Partly because many Jacobeans served their apprenticeship in comedy, there is no "curve" of artistic development in their tragedies —no fumbling ascent to Olympus. Their tragic genius flames into view at its apogee and consumes itself like a meteor falling in the earth's atmosphere. Their first tragedies are, generally speaking, their most brilliant; their later works have less artistic vigor but greater moral security or balance. In almost every instance the Jacobean tragic inspiration is short-lived. As the first white heat of scorn and indignation fades, the Jacobean tragic sense of life fades too if it is not actually extinguished by philosophical or religious convictions.

We cannot expect that Shakespeare's drama will conform to a pattern derived from a study of his lesser contemporaries. They abide our scholarly questions because they were absorbed in topical and peripheral issues and because they used the stage for extraliterary purposes—to confute the politician or the naturalist. Shakespeare escapes the tyranny of scholarly exegesis because he grasped always the permanent significance of contemporary problems and because his vision of life was so comprehensive that his art has never lost its relevance to the human situation. Although we must familiarize ourselves with the Petrarchan codes of the Renaissance to grasp the witty conceits of *The Maid's Tragedy* and *The Changeling*, we need only see the world feelingly to understand Troilus' narcissistic hunger for an absolute romantic dedication.

Because he sees the world feelingly, Shakespeare performs the immemorial service of the artist to society: he humanizes the categorical imperatives which the stern didacticist offers as the sum of ethical truth. If all marriages were made in heaven, then it would be just to complain that Shakespeare romanticizes adulterous love in *Antony and Cleopatra*. But since marriages among the great have been, since the beginning of civilization, political and military alliances, there is a place in Shakespeare's sympathies and in ours for Antony and Cleopatra. Although he lived in an age which frequently confused the moral and the moralistic in art, he did not preach. He must have known there was really little danger that his nut-cracking listeners would go the way of his tragic heroes; they were not Hamlets, Lears, or Macbeths, nor were they likely to murder their wives over the loss of a handkerchief. A realist even in his fairy tales, he did not make a cautionary example of Autolycus; he knew all too well that a mere fiction was not going to eradicate the purse-snatching that continued in the very shadow of Tyburn.

As we might expect, Shakespeare's relation to his Jacobean contemporaries was one-sided. His tragedies preceded most of theirs; he was quite literally their master, not their colleague. It is difficult in fact to imagine what seventeenth-century tragedy would have been like had not Shakespeare developed the tragic art of Kyd and Marlowe to a miraculous perfection. His poetry, his characterizations, and his dramatic situations are an integral part of the creative experience of the men we have studied and are assimilated in their plays. Perhaps the richness and variety of his achievement overwhelmed minor talents and inspired immature writers to self-destructive pursuits of "originality." For the major talents, however, he was a creative and liberating force, a dramatist who expanded the horizons of artistic possibility. Because he did not have a clearly defined theory of tragedy and because his view of life was deceptively neutral, his influence did not channel tragedy into as restricted a mode as that which Jonson established for seventeenth-century comedy.

It was easier, in fact, for the Jacobeans to write under the shadow of Shakespeare's genius than it is for us to place him among his contemporaries. The richness and variety of his art only accentuate the singleness of mood and subject matter and the narrowness of vision in their tragedies. How earnest and unnecessary seem Chapman's attempts to reconstruct philosophical values when the truth and beauty of moral ideals appear in Shakespeare as the bedrock reality of human experience. How superficial seem the terrors of Tourneur and Webster compared to that intuition of the horror and absurdity of life which is given to Macbeth. The compassionate ironies of *Measure for Measure* were beyond the scope of other Jacobeans, who could see only the mockery of man's fumbling attempts at justice; who could portray the twisted dedication to the "cause" of honor which dooms Othello but not the sublime charity of Cordelia's "No cause, no cause" which redeems Lear's sufferings. Because Shakespeare's was the most comprehensive mind, we cannot treat his plays as another fraction of the totality of Jacobean tragedy. His vision of life is the whole that includes and exceeds the sum of the other dramatists' partial perceptions. There is hardly a tragic theme or mood of the first decade which does not find expression in his plays, particularly those between *Hamlet* and *Macbeth*. Even in the dark comedies, as we shall see, we can trace Shakespeare's progress towards the all-embracing spiritual and moral drama of *Lear*, the only Jacobean play large enough to confront and resolve the challenge which evil presents to man's belief in himself and his universe.

Some readers will protest that Shakespeare's "solution" to the problem of evil lies not in the great tragedies but in the plays that followed. Just as Dr. Johnson found the last scenes of *Lear* too painful to contemplate, so critics refuse to accept its vision as Shakespeare's most profound dramatic intuition. *Lear* is to them a part of a spiritual journey that ended only on the mystical heights of the late romances. They look beyond the anguish of the tragic period to the autumnal grace of *The Winter's Tale* and *The Tempest*, in which innocence is rediscovered and reborn, and evil is only an appearance. It seems a

pity, however, to burden such lovely and fragile plays with a staggering weight of philosophical, allegorical, and symbolic significances.
Their charm is melancholy; their wisdom lies in a bittersweet acceptance of the maturity and sophistication that inevitably replaces the
innocence of youth and that makes possible the corrupted "artistic"
sensibility of Leontes. There is no certainty, moreover, that Miranda's
brave new world will not end in the sorrows that Prospero vividly remembers or that the romantic illusions of youth will not be shattered
by a society that breeds Antonios and Sebastians. The vision of *Lear*
is not transmuted by *The Tempest;* in different moods and modes both
plays express the ineffable goodness of life and the transcendent experience of love in a world where brother turns on brother and age
suffers painfully and long.

If Shakespeare's art were more like Chapman's, we might seek in
it the kind of intellectual and moral pilgrimage that led from *Bussy
D'Ambois* to *Caesar and Pompey*. Indeed, because Chapman's ideals
evolved throughout his artistic career, his tragedies must be studied
as a continuum. But because Shakespeare's values never altered, each
of his plays bears separate witness to the quality of his mind and art;
they are unique entities informed by common ideals and standards of
judgment. By statistical measurements, the satiric mood of *Troilus and
Cressida* is uncharacteristic of Shakespeare, but so too, by the same
standard, is the apotheosis of sensual love in *Antony and Cleopatra*
and the vision of depravity in *Lear*. The "essential" Shakespeare is in
each of the plays and in all of them, not in any particular group or
dramatic mode. At different times he was absorbed in different aspects
of life—in the gaiety and innocence of youthful courtship or in the
animality of sexual vice, in the intrinsic decorums of political authority
or in the anarchic ambition that destroys social order. Particularly at
a time when traditional values were being questioned, his imagination
dwelt upon the brutality of evil that in all ages challenges man's ideals.
But though we can say that Shakespeare's understanding of man and
society broadened and deepened throughout his career, we cannot say
that in any play he lost faith in humanity and in its ideals, or that in the
late romances he rediscovered the belief in universal harmony shattered in *Lear*. It is a reckless critic indeed who undertakes to describe
what personal metaphysical assumptions (if any) underlie the plays.

The art of Shakespeare's early plays may be imperfect and immature; but the characterizations and values are never jejune. He offers no unexamined enthusiasms, no facile or naïve optimisms. The darker side of heroic aspiration, the sacrifice of humane values in the arena of public action, and the egotism that breathes in a lover's sigh, all are as manifest in his Elizabethan as in his Jacobean plays. There is as acute a perception of political realities in *Richard III* as in *Coriolanus*, as clear-sighted a view of honor in the "Henriad" as in *Troilus and Cressida*. We must assume also that Shakespeare's capabilities as a dramatist determined, particularly in his early years, the subjects that he chose and the manner in which he treated them. Although he constantly explored the possibilities of his art and in play after play enlarged the frontiers of poetic drama, he maintained a just correspondence between aspiration and achievement; his artistic reach lengthened only as his grasp of the medium became more certain. We can if we wish condemn *Richard III* as crude and immature tragedy, but it would be more accurate to describe it as one of the most successful melodramas ever written. At each stage of his development, Shakespeare brought to their highest perfection the various genres of the Elizabethan and Jacobean stage. And because his genius was bounteous, he did not feel the necessity of repeating an earlier triumph at a later date. Had Shakespeare's genius been less fecund, the pattern of his drama might have been quite different. Hence we must be extremely wary of those critics who read his plays as a form of spiritual autobiography.

We find nothing in *Antony and Cleopatra* or *Coriolanus* which suggests that Shakespeare's view of the struggle for power changed after *Macbeth*; and despite its questionable shape *Timon of Athens* bears witness to Shakespeare's capacity for tragic emotion at the very time that he was about to embark on the late romances. I omit these later tragedies from discussion only because they seem to me quite removed from the "Jacobean" issues which link the earlier tragedies and dark comedies to the works of Shakespeare's contemporaries. They add to our knowledge of Shakespeare's mind and art, but they shed little light on the epistemological questions which lie at the heart of Jacobean tragedy. If we approach Shakespeare primarily by way of plot, we may conclude that *Othello* and *Macbeth* are the most "Jacobean" of his tragedies, because, like many of the plays of Tourneur, Webster, Middleton, and Ford, they portray the disintegration of moral will and purpose. Great soldiers who become cowardly assassins, Othello and Macbeth are infinitely closer to such hero-villains as Byron, Vindice, Brachiano, De Flores, and Giovanni than are Hamlet and Lear. But any broader view makes it apparent that *Hamlet* and *Lear* represent Shakespeare's deepest involvement in the tragic issues of the first Jacobean decade. Their larger, more philosophical actions and choric commentaries define the problem of moral decision and belief in an evil world and dramatize the tragic need of the idealizing mind to discover, accept, and relate itself to the realities of the universe. In one way or other, of course, all of Shakespeare's great tragedies are discoveries of moral and spiritual reality; all are concerned with what man knows and what he needs, with his capacity to conceive and adhere to ideals. And, not surprizingly, these tragic themes can be found in the other plays written during the same period. It has often been noted that *Troilus and Cressida* and *Measure for Measure* deal with the disparity between appearance and reality. More importantly, it seems to me, they are concerned with man's hunger for ideal values and dedications—for honor or justice, for ideal passion or purity. I discuss these plays in detail because their questionings of values and their analyses of justice, legality, and charitable love guide us to the central moral and intellectual drama of *Lear*. They are also interesting in that they anticipate the concern with societal morality which we find in Middleton and Ford. Because they present moral situations as ambiguous as those in *The Broken Heart*, they too divide the critics and demand the kind of liberal ethical response for which Donne pleads in *Biathanatos*.

Othello and *Macbeth*

As we shall see, the dark comedies fall in a line of artistic thought that runs from *Hamlet* to *Lear*. *Othello* is not so much outside that line as a tangent leading from it. More specifically, it restates the universal questions of *Hamlet* and *Lear* in the personal terms of a single intimate relationship. Although recent critics have found weighty intellectual significances in the imagery of *Othello*, it seems to me that less is at stake in its action than in the other tragedies because of the intense particularity of its characterizations. What other Shakespearean hero has Othello's carefully defined exotic past and racial background? What other villain manifests his evil as Iago does, not in the unscrupulous ambitions or acts of a Claudius or Edmund but in every utterance of a meticulously detailed and highly individualized personality: the vulgar, lewd, money-hungry, chiseling, envious, disappointed Ancient? When we ignore this particularity and attempt to make universal or symbolic figures of the characters in *Othello* we only distort them. That is to say, the jealous Moor would seem to us as fatuous as Roderigo were it not for the unique circumstances of his personality, his race, his innocence of Venetian society, and his belated discovery of a love so rare and miraculous as to be outside the ordinary realm of belief. From *Othello* as from all Shakespearean tragedy we can abstract certain profound and general truths about the world in which we live. Man's vileness, Iago demonstrates, we know; his purity of heart we only think we know. His guilt we can prove; his innocence we must believe in because it cannot be "proved." But Othello's own tragic recognition is of a much more limited sort. While sentimental critics would have us believe that all of Shakespeare's tragic heroes are "improved" or ennobled by their suffering, it is not clear that Othello gains a new or greater wisdom from murdering Desdemona. Though he recovers enough of his former stature to admit that he is an "honourable murderer," he learns only the simple truth which was obvious to the coarse Emilia, to Cassio, and even at last to the foolish Roderigo—that Desdemona was chaste. His discovery of the "truth" about marriage was itself an illusion, his moment of truth simply a reversal of the maddened and obscene judgment passed on his wife.

Like *Hamlet*, *Othello* traces the deceptive appearances of life, but its plot inverts the tragic situation of Denmark. In Cyprus the faithless woman is true to her husband and the disillusioned idealist false; the revenger's desire for "ocular proof" is an unmitigated horror and his revenge a travesty of justice. In Cyprus Iago is a debased and pathological Hamlet, an aggrieved malcontent plotting his vengeance, hypersensitive to any show of falseness, witty and theatrical in his temperament, expert in staging impromptu dramas. Where *Hamlet* celebrates the capacity of the philosophical mind to penetrate beneath illusion, *Othello* reveals the capacity and will for self-deception which ego nourishes. It reveals too the cunning irrationality of human reason and the subtlety with which man can prove to his satisfaction a truth which has no connection to fact. To be sure, Iago speaks always of fact, but he is the least empirical of Shakespeare's villains. His philosophy rests upon a continuing denial of the reality he daily perceives: the reality of Othello's "constant, loving, noble nature" and of Desdemona's "goodness" and "virtue." His specious logic, which descends syllogistically from lewd and twisted postulates, is more ancient than modern, more a perversion of Scholastic reasoning than an adumbration of a scientific or positivistic rationalism.

Middleton, one imagines, would have made *Othello* into an ironic tragedy of "honor" similar to *Women Beware Women*. There is no tinge of mockery, however, in Shakespeare's portrait of Othello, though the Moor's anguish, like Troilus', reveals the involvement of masculine ego in ideals of sexual fidelity. Shakespeare would have us pity the vulnerability of his greathearted soldier, who, used to absolute trust in himself and in those about him (his treasured Michael Cassio), requires certainty in love when there can be no certainty but the intuition of the heart. A stranger in Venetian society, instinctively feared by those who need and applaud his generalship, he has no other support than his sense of personal worth. The overwhelming sadness of his fate is that he could love Desdemona selflessly only when he had lost all sense of self, only when he had nothing left to wager on her faith.

Though the poison which Iago pours into Othello's ear has violent and at last fatal results, it is quickly purged by the antidote of Emilia's scorn and insistence upon the truth. As Othello returns to soldierly dignity, the heart aches for the innocence (his as well as Desdemona's) that has been destroyed, for the nobility that has been laid waste, and for the rare love that cankered in first blossom. With the characters on the stage we wonder at the senselessness of Iago's malice, but we are not touched by his cynicism, for its vulgar errors and distortions of life are manifest in Desdemona's radiant spirit and in Emilia's and Cassio's capacity for devotion. We cannot be intellectually persuaded by the casuistry of his "divinity of hell" because it makes no appeal to the intellect. It has finally only a reptilian logic; it seeks to hypnotize the mind by the sinuous weaving of obscene suggestion and image. *Macbeth* is a more disturbing play than *Othello* because it is embraced by the darkness which is focused in Iago's mind and because its hero falls into so deep a spiritual abyss that Othello's position is by comparison angelic. Where Othello struggles against the poison of Iago's lies, Macbeth struggles dreadfully against his own nature and wins the terrible victory of his damnation. There is nothing mean in his envy of others or in his nihilism. Crime is to him a mystical experience: he sees visions and hears voices. He knows what it is to surrender to the darkness of the soul.

It is interesting that J. W. Allen should refer to *Macbeth* when he discusses the moral fallacies of *The Prince*. Machiavelli, Mr. Allen remarks, "would have his Prince commit murder and feel like Lady Macbeth: 'A little water clears us of this deed.' He has no glimpse of the possibility that, later, the murderer may in despair be asking: 'Will these hands ne'er be clean?' The sense of the mysterious in good and evil, the sense of the poisonous nature of evil that Shakespeare felt so strongly, had no existence for his mind."[1] No less than Machiavelli is Lady Macbeth blind to the relation between acts and consequences, between what men do and what they become. Her speeches breathe contempt for those who have the "natural" will to power but not the nerve or the candor to accomplish what they will. Her exaltation of treachery—this "great business" of murder—translates into dramatic terms that admiration of heroic evil which is a recurrent aspect of Machiavelli's thought. To be sure, Lady Macbeth and her husband are fumbling politicians. The one is too weak, the other too cruel to enjoy sovereignty. They do not know how to reap the benefits of peace, order, and stability which Machiavelli thought could come from the vilest of deeds. But then who could have succeeded where they failed? Although Machiavelli could imagine that a murderer might successfully pretend to virtue, he had only the barest realization of the central moral truth of *Macbeth*—that only a murderer can play a murderer's role successfully. Those who might rule well—those who have the milk of human kindness—must shrink from the vicious act which sovereignty requires or having committed it must become the deed's creature.[2]

Far more greatly than Webster in *The Duchess of Malfi* Shakespeare explores in *Macbeth* the mystery of man's will to self-destruction—his capacity to commit the acts which violate his essential being. If Macbeth did not covet the throne, he would have no "reason" to kill Duncan; yet Shakespeare does not make us feel that he thirsts for the sweet fruition of an earthly crown in the way that Richard III and Claudius do. The most that Lady Macbeth can say in her astute analysis of her husband's nature is that he is "not without ambition." When Macbeth weighs the act before it is committed, he lamely concludes that he has "only ambition" to spur him on. If Shakespeare wished us to feel that Macbeth was driven by an insatiable lust for power, he failed miserably to achieve his purpose. But why need we demand that a tragic hero be more logical in his motives than a hero of a novel? If we applaud Dostoevski's understanding of the psychopathology of crime, must we not also applaud Shakespeare's portrait of Macbeth, who like Raskolnikov commits a crime that revolts him, who like Raskolnikov rehearses it first in hallucination, who like Raskolnikov walks towards the deed as in a trance, scarce believing that he can commit the act which fortune has cast in his way? Macbeth no more murders for ambition than Raskolnikov murders for money. Like Raskolnikov he kills for self, for "peace"—to end the restless torment of his imagination. He must prove to himself under the goading of his wife that he is a "man," even as Raskolnikov must prove to himself that he is not a louse or a bedbug like the people around him. Macbeth kills because his wife makes him admit that he wishes to kill; and because he condemns himself before he kills Duncan, the act of murder is fraught with a hatred of self which eventually and inevitably becomes a hatred of all of life.

If the murder of Duncan seems to us unmotivated, what shall we say of Macbeth's later and more gratuitous villainies? Before he kills Duncan Macbeth is harrowed by the fear of "consequences," of the chain of retribution which will return the poisoned chalice to his lips. His fears are mistaken; the great business succeeds beyond imagining. Duncan's sons flee and are accused of the crime; Macbeth is accepted as King, and Banquo, the one man who suspects his guilt, is willing to keep silent and be his chief counselor. There need be no fearful consequences for Macbeth except that the "peace" of murder has not descended; on the contrary, his self-loathing has been intensified by the need to hide his true self from the eyes of others. He tells himself that his fears in Banquo stick deep, yet quite obviously his true need is to murder Fleance. How much more "logical" would be his desire to extinguish Banquo's line if we felt that Macbeth had strong dynastic ambitions. But he has no children, only envy of all those who live at peace with themselves and with the world. For Macbeth, hell is other people.

A more conventional dramatist would have suggested that Macbeth piles murder on murder because his first act of blood brutalizes his nature. Shakespeare gives us a more terrible Macbeth who is driven to kill again and again because he cannot live with the memory of his first crime. Though the crime was perfect, neither he nor his wife was perfect in the crime. After the intoxicating rapture of murder wears off, she sinks into madness. Her diseased mind seeks to erase the horror of what she and Macbeth have done by rehearsing the murder scene over and over again in her dreams until the memory no longer tortures. Macbeth, more accustomed to killing and more capable of enduring in blood, seeks to erase horror with horror. He will re-enact the crime again and again until his nature and his role are one, until he is "perfect" in his part, and a full feast of slaughter has blunted all moral sensitivity. As the recurrent imagery of drunkenness intimates, Macbeth's craving for blood is like a drunkard's thirst for oblivion, one that can bring no release because each satisfaction merely intensifies the original need, and the only oblivion can be in beastiality itself.

No other passage in Jacobean tragedy touches the nihilism of Macbeth's final soliloquy. Only Webster could conceive of a similar horror at the lunacy of existence and a similar weariness and hopelessness of spirit. Having wasted time in the attempt to seize its promise and its offered opportunities, Macbeth is at last haunted by the deserts of vast eternity that enclose man's minuscule existence in time. If the anguish of the damned sounds musically on the ears of the saved, then there is comfort here for some; otherwise *Macbeth* is the most unpleasant of the tragedies. Though order is restored at its close, though evil is purged and Macbeth receives the gift of oblivion, there is no sense of repose or reconciliation in its final scenes. Macbeth is the only hero of mature Shakespearean tragedy who goes to his doom struggling wildly against it, clinging to the life that torments him because he cannot bear the thought that it is the be-all and end-all of sentience. His death becomes him better than the hired slaughter of Macduff's wife and children, but it is of a piece with the sequence of vile and bloody deeds which make up his life within the play. Fear, horror, blood, darkness, hallucination are merely a part of the special world of *Macbeth*, a world which breeds neither a Desdemona nor a Horatio. The dry-eyed sons of Duncan flee after his murder lest they be suspected of the crime. Banquo is equivocal in his virtue; Macduff allows his defenseless family to be slaughtered and displays a curious worldliness in his interview with Malcolm. Of course he finally passes the test which Malcolm offers, he is finally revolted by Malcolm's self-portrait of vice; yet how much, how very much of vice will Macduff accept in a sovereign before his stomach turns.

The darkness to which Macbeth surrenders is not, like the filthiness of Iago's thoughts, engendered wholly in the mind. It is as much a part of the "order" of nature as is the light of the spirit. When one part of nature sleeps, another preys. Only the codes of civilized society allow the weak and aged to lie safely beside the fierce and practiced warrior. Only because Macbeth is strong in Duncan's right, is Duncan king. Actually Macbeth casts himself out of the community of men by committing the crime that occurs to many men—to Banquo as well as Cawdor. He fails to restrain those cursed thoughts which nature gives way to in repose and which trouble the sleep of many innocents. The difference between Macbeth and Banquo is that the one would murder for the throne while the other "wouldst not play false, /And yet wouldst wrongly win": that is to say, Banquo is content to repress his suspicions of Macbeth and to collaborate in his regime because his son will profit from Macbeth's crime.

Unable to admit that he has made the world a hell, Macbeth attempts to project the horror of his life as the pattern of all existence. For if consciousness is nothing more than a cosmic joke, then the senseless fury of his acts is no worse than the peaceful lives of those who are led quietly to oblivion. Do we feel that Macbeth's hatred of life is as diseased as Iago's vision of reality? Or do we feel that within the imaginative confines of the play the values which give meaning to life—honor, obedience, love, "troops of friends"—are dwarfed by the vastness of Macbeth's intuition, that these values are final only to those who do not look into the darkness, who stay within the finite circle of light which the candle of society casts upon the infinite darkness of time and space? I do not mean that Shakespeare uses Macbeth to express a personal sense of the absurdity of existence. I mean only that we must turn to the other tragedies to feel the infinite worth of those human qualities which outshine the darkness.

Hamlet

The impression of vastness in *Macbeth* is created almost entirely by poetic suggestion. The play lacks the intellectual dimension and richness of thought which make *Hamlet* seem to the critics the most philosophical of Shakespeare's plays. Honor, revenge, justice, political order, Stoicism, friendship, familial piety—how many Renaissance ideas and ideals come under scrutiny in the halls of Elsinore. And yet how little is there in the lines of *Hamlet* which testifies to Shakespeare's intellectual or philosophical powers. Subjected to philosophical analysis the great speeches in *Hamlet* yield commonplaces. We treasure them for their incomparable poetry, not for their depth and originality of thought—for their revelation of Hamlet's soul, not for their discovery of the human condition. Many questions are raised in the play but few are answered. The question of action in an evil society, one might say, is resolved by an expedient dear to Victorian novelists: a change of air, a sea voyage from which the hero returns calm if not resolute, buoyed by a vaguely optimistic fatalism that is half-Christian, half-Stoic.

My point is not that Shakespeare tricks us into accepting a sham or meretricious resolution in *Hamlet*, but that we do not find in Shakespearean drama the intellectual schemes of Chapman's tragedies. Even when Shakespeare seems to dramatize a thesis, he does not debate philosophical positions. He is not interested in abstract thought but in characters who think, who have intellectual as well as emotional needs, and who, like Pirandello's characters, cry aloud the reason of their suffering. The "problem" of *Hamlet* is not an intellectual puzzle. It arises because the play creates so marvelous a sense of the actual improvisation of life that we can find no simple logic in its sprawling action. Unable to comprehend or accept the totality of Shakespeare's many-sided hero, we search for a more logical, more consistent, or more pleasant Hamlet than the play affords. We try to arrive at Shakespeare's moral ideas by reading Elizabethan treatises of psychology and moral philosophy, when it is only by studying the total artifice of *Hamlet* that we can understand why its hero seems to us the most noble, pure-minded, and blameless of Shakespeare's tragic protagonists. What is not near Hamlet's conscience is not near our own because he is our moral interpreter. He is the voice of ethical sensibility in a sophisticated, courtly milieu; his bitter asides, which penetrate Claudius' facade of kingly virtue and propriety, initiate, so to speak, the moral action of the play. And throughout the play our identification with Hamlet's moral vision is such that we hate what he hates, admire what he admires. As centuries of Shakespeare criticism reveal, we accuse Hamlet primarily of what he accuses himself: namely, his slowness to revenge.

Our moral impression of Hamlet's character derives primarily from what he says rather than what he does. It is an almost intuitive awareness of the beauty, depth, and refinement of his moral nature, upon which is thrust a savage burden of revenge and of disillusion. If Shakespeare's characters are illusions created by dramatic artifice, then what we love in Hamlet is an illusion within an illusion: i.e., the suggestion of Hamlet's former self, the Hamlet whom Ophelia remembers and who poignantly reappears in the conversations with Horatio, particularly before the catastrophe. Through his consummate artistry Shakespeare creates within us a sympathy with Hamlet which becomes almost an act of faith—a confidence in the untouched and untouchable core of his spiritual nature. This act of faith, renewed by the great speeches throughout the play, allows us to accept Hamlet's brutality towards Ophelia, his reaction to Polonius' death, his savage refusal to kill Claudius at prayer, and his Machiavellian delight in disposing of Rosencrantz and Guildenstern. Without the memory of the great soliloquies which preceded it, our impression of the closet scene would be vastly different. And, in fact, to attempt to define Hamlet's character by weighing his motives and actions against any system of Renaissance thought is to stage *Hamlet* morally without the Prince of Denmark, i.e., without the felt impression of Hamlet's moral nature which is created by poetic nuance.

Life is mysterious and unpredictable in *Hamlet*. Appearances are deceptive, little is what it seems to be, and no man can foresee the consequence of his acts. Yet we are not left with the sense that Shakespeare's characters move through the mist which envelops Webster's tragic universe. We see with a perfect clarity that the pattern of catastrophe emerges inexorably as the consequence of Claudius' hidden guilt and from his need for deviousness and secrecy. If the ambiguities and the mysteries of *Hamlet* irritate us, it is because we expect an omniscient view of character in drama; we are not used to seeing a play almost entirely from the point of view of a single character. We do not realize that our identification with Hamlet is as complete as with a first-person narrator of a novel. We see little more than he sees; we know little more about the other characters—about Gertrude's crimes or Rosencrantz and Guildenstern's treachery—than he finally knows. If we had to examine objectively the facts of the play to decide whether Hamlet should have had Rosencrantz and Guildenstern executed, then their innocence or guilt would be a crucial matter; but since like Hamlet we identify Rosencrantz and Guildenstern with Claudius' cause, what they knew or did not know of Claudius' plans "does not matter."

It is Hamlet (not the Romantic critics) who creates the problem of his delay in revenge. Were it not for the self-lacerating soliloquies in which he accuses himself of the grossness and insensitivity which he despises in his mother, the thought that he delays would not occur to us. During a performance of the play we do not feel that Hamlet procrastinates or puts off action. From his first appearance, he is engaged in a secret struggle with the shrewd and suspicious Claudius; there is scarcely a moment when he is not fending off one of the King's spies or dupes. In the study a critic can be quite bloodthirsty about Hamlet's failure to dispatch Claudius. In the theater, however, one does not feel that Hamlet should have skewered Claudius at prayer or should have been more interested in Claudius' damnation than his mother's salvation. Nor does one feel that the Hamlet who says, "The interim is mine" is "delaying."

This is not to say that Shakespeare posed an artificial problem in Hamlet's soliloquies in order to make mad the critics and appall the scholars. The problem of action in an evil world is as real in *Hamlet* as in many of the revenge plays of the period. True to his father's command, Hamlet engages in fierce struggle against the world without tainting his mind. False to himself and to his father's advice, Laertes is corrupted and debased by the hunger for vengeance. Although Hamlet commits rash and bloody deeds and comes to take a sardonic delight in flanking policy with policy, he does not, like Vindice, become unfit for life. On the contrary, we feel that he dies just when he is ready to embrace life, when his cloud of melancholy has lifted and he stands before us the very quintessence of dust—beautiful in mind and spirit, noble in thought and feeling, alert, high-spirited, superior to the accidents and passions which corrupt lesser men. We do not feel that Hamlet must die because he has sinned. The inevitability of his death is an aesthetic, not moral, expectation created by the insistent imagery of death, by the mood of the graveyard scene, by Hamlet's premonitions, and by the finality of Claudius' triple-stopped treachery. The calm of the graveyard scene, coming after the feverish action that preceded Hamlet's departure for England, seems a false recovery before death, that brief moment of detachment and lucidity which is often granted dying men. Enhancing this poignant impression are the very simple, quiet responses of Horatio, who attends the final hours of his Prince.

The problem of action in *Hamlet* is posed immediately and ultimately by Death, the philosophical tutor who forces man to consider the value of existence. Because the death of his father has made life meaningless, Hamlet wishes for the release of suicide, which is by traditional standards a cowardly evasion and negation of life. Yet, paradoxically, the willingness and eagerness of Fortinbras' army to die seems to give meaning to a cause that would be otherwise contemptible and valueless. And whether one takes arms against a sea of troubles (an apparently hopeless undertaking) or suffers the arrows and slings of outrageous fortune, there is only one possible conclusion to the action of life, the stillness of the grave. *Hamlet* begins with terrified sentries awaiting the return of the dead. It closes with the solemn march of soldiers bearing Hamlet's body "to the stage." Throughout the play Hamlet faces the most ancient and abiding philosophical problem: he must "learn how to die," i.e., how to live with the fact and thought of death. When he first appears, he seems overwhelmed by his first intimate experience of mortality—the sudden, unexpected loss of his father. Claudius may first address the court on affairs of state and then grant Laertes his "fair hour," but eventually he must deal with the gross insult of Hamlet's ostentatious mourning. In his most suave manner he offers his stepson the consolation of philosophy; he refers to the immemorial fact of mortality and grief, to the common-ness and naturalness of death, to the need for the living to dedicate themselves to life. For Hamlet these platitudes have no meaning. He does not mourn because *man* dies; nor is he tormented only by the loss of a father. When he exposes his inner feelings in the first soliloquy we realize that Claudius has completely missed the point. Hamlet's problem is not to accept his father's death but to accept a world in which death has lost its meaning and its message for the living—a world in which only the visitation of a Ghost restores some sense of the mystery and awe of the grave. In his disgust for Gertrude's frailty, Hamlet broods over the debt that the living owe to the dead, the wife to the husband and the son to the father. Gertrude advises her son not to seek his father in the dust, but the Ghost brings the shattering command that the living owe the dead the obligation of vengeance, of taking arms against a world which destroys virtue. Though anguished that the time is out of joint, Hamlet embraces revenge as a dedication which is to give meaning to an otherwise empty existence. And justly or not he accuses himself again and again of failure to carry out his obligation to the dead.

When he returns to Denmark from his sea voyage, however, he is no longer tormented by guilt; his self-laceration and disgust with life have given way to a stoic calm that obliterates the need for immediate action. He has not formulated a new philosophy or come to intel-lectual terms with life. He has the fatalistic composure possible only to those who have achieved an intimate communion with death—who have killed and have narrowly escaped a mortal stroke. Having passed through a lifetime of experience in a brief span, he seems to share Montaigne's knowledge that men do not require philosophy to know how to die, because life provides all the requisite information and no man has yet failed to pass the test of his mortality. Our life, the action of *Hamlet* reveals, is a process of dying and all roads end where the gravedigger's work begins.

A mind that can trace Alexander's dust to a bunghole can no longer envy the heroic dedication of a Fortinbras. Although still intending to call Claudius to account, Hamlet is no longer obsessed by an obligation to the dead; he speaks mainly now of punitive justice and of his personal conflict with the King. Ironically enough, experience has taught him the sageness of Claudius' platitudes. The young mourner who cried out against the commonness of death now finds solace in its vast equality and anonymity. Counseled before not to seek his father in the dust, he now recoils from the skull of Yorick, who played with him as a father with a child. Compared to the stink of putrefaction, the sins of the flesh seem now more amusing than revolting to Hamlet. Once he hugged death as an escape from the burden of living; now the too too solid flesh melting from the bone no longer seems a consummation devoutly to be wished for. We see in his detached meditations on death a new dedication to life, for he is amused not by the vanity of existence but by the absurd ways in which men waste their precious hours of sentience. What do the living owe to the dead? The coarse familiarity of the gravediggers with the remains of the departed suggests a final answer.

Like all men Hamlet can triumph only over the impersonal fact of death. When he learns that the grave is for Ophelia, his jesting detachment vanishes. As the funeral procession enters the stage, the wheel comes full circle; the play begins again with another mourner in Hamlet's role. Now it is the youthful Laertes who protests with hyperbolic and theatrical gestures of grief the dishonor of his family that is symbolized by the "maimed rites" of death. His emotional extravagance elicits Hamlet's last moment of theatricality: the struggle in the grave that again strips dignity from the ceremony of death.

In the breathing space before the fencing scene there is a haunting moment of repose, of youthful communion, of laughter at Osric's absurdity; there is a poignant sense of recovery and stability. Is there also a more positive religious note? Are we to assume from Hamlet's references to heaven, divinity, and providence that he is now convinced of the great moral design of creation? Or do we see a Hamlet bowing before a universe which defies man's intellectual attempts at comprehension? The sequence of accidents that saved his life appears in retrospect providential, but it provides no guide to future action, no counsel, no direction. Although his restlessness at sea seemed a touch of grace, he shrugs off his misgivings about the fencing match. For to ascribe every premonition to heavenly guidance is to reduce belief to superstition. And Hamlet defies "augury." How much more deeply religious is his surrender to the mystery of his fate than Laertes' concern with the niceties of ceremony. Whether Ophelia deserves Christian burial is a question fit for the mocking and subtle casuistry of the gravediggers. Indeed, if the form of her burial is to determine her ultimate destiny, then she must be eternally grateful to Claudius, who forced the Church to inter her in hallowed ground. Although some modern critics argue like Laertes over the fine theological issues of the play, the perceptive reader understands that the form of Ophelia's burial matters more to the living than to the dead.

More clearly in *Hamlet* than in *The Spanish Tragedy* or *Tamburlaine* one can see the inner direction which great tragedy takes at the close of the Elizabethan age. For Shakespeare as for Kyd and Marlowe the fact of man's mortality is not the essential pathos of tragedy. That pathos lies in their heroes' anguished discovery of a universe more vast, more terrible, and more inscrutable than is dreamt of in philosophy. In *Hamlet* and Jacobean tragedy man suffers to be wise, and, indeed, his knowledge of reality is a more intense form of suffering than the illustrators of *De casibus* tales could imagine.

Troilus and Cressida

After the melancholy deeps of *Hamlet*, *Troilus and Cressida* and *Measure for Measure* seem strange interludes of mockery and denigration, retreats from the tragedy of evil to the comedy of vice. They are problems if not problem plays, "un-Shakespearean" in temper and viewpoint, ambiguous in characterization. They seem to turn ideals of chivalry, justice, and mercy seamy side out. The lecher leers over the virgin's shoulder; the romantic idealist falls in love with a whore; one touch of nature in the loins makes the whole world kin. But they are not so much comical satires as dialectical dramas in the manner of *Byron's Conspiracy;* like Chapman's play they approach the issues of tragedy ironically and analytically, and thus engage the intellect more than the imagination. If by comparison to the *Iliad* and the medieval gestes of Troy, *Troilus* seems a mockery of heroism, it is not contemptuous of the virtues which men sacrifice at the altar of war. Behind the joke of Achilles' cowardice and Pandarus' aching bones lies a serious study of man's aspiration towards the ideal in love and war.

In *Troilus* Shakespeare explores the paradoxical truth that war and lechery—the most primitive human activities—have from the dawn of civilization excited man's highest poetic faculties. The heroic legend immortalizes the conflicting dualities of man's nature and poses the central problem of his quest for ideal values. Chained to the earth by animal desires, condemned by mortality to the tyranny of time, man nevertheless hungers for a dedication that will give permanent significance to his life. Even in the savagery of war he learns some final truth about his humanity; even in untimely death he satisfies a hunger for experience that might otherwise be unfulfilled. Religion and philosophy escape the oppression of time by postulating eternal metaphysical values. The chivalric ideal challenges time with an appropriate recklessness by exalting the transitory qualities of youth, beauty, and strength and by placing its absolutes within the realm of mortality. By sophisticating primitive impulses with ceremonial ritual, it heightens and glorifies the sensation of life that flames in the brief orgiastic pleasures of love and war. It finds its eternity in the ecstatic moments of sexual possession and military conquest, the ancient complementary proofs of manhood and virility.

The Homeric myth tells of a decade of slaughter for the possession of a beautiful woman; the analytic intellect seeks a more realistic and complex motive for human sacrifice. It cannot believe that men died for the sake of a faithless woman, especially after years of futile, senseless struggle. Logic insists that ultimately both sides must have despised Helen. And thus Diomedes speaks for the Greeks:

> She's bitter to her country. Hear me, Paris:
> For every false drop in her bawdy veins
> A Grecian's life hath sunk; for every scruple
> Of her contaminated carrion weight
> A Troyan hath been slain. Since she could speak,
> She hath not given so many good words breath
> As for her Greeks and Troyans suff'red death.[3] (IV. i. 68–74)

Hector expresses the same thought with greater courtesy when he pleads:

> Let Helen go.
> Since the first sword was drawn about this question,
> Every tithe soul 'mongst many thousand dismes
> Hath been as dear as Helen. I mean, of ours.
> If we have lost so many tenths of ours
> To guard a thing not ours nor worth to us
> (Had it our name) the value of one ten,
> What merit's in that reason which denies
> The yielding of her up? (II. ii. 17–25)

Here is the wearisome condition of warring mankind: two great civilizations locked in mortal combat for the sake of a woman whom neither side desires, corrupted and enervated by seven years of futile struggle but still unwilling to sacrifice the principle of honor for which the war is being fought.

The conflict between Trojan and Greek has many analogues in Shakespeare's drama. It is foreshadowed by the opposition between Richard and Bolingbroke and Hotspur and Hal, and it is recalled by the dichotomy of Egypt and Rome in *Antony and Cleopatra*. On one side is a decaying world of chivalry, courtly and romantic, softened by feminine influence and refined in sensibility. On the other side is a purely masculine, realistic world of soldiery and empire, pragmatic in its values, uncritical of its goals, concerned only with the attainment of power. The character of Troilus expresses the doomed, tainted nobility of a highly sophisticated yet immature civilization. He unites the impetuous valor of Hotspur and the romantic ardor of the inexperienced Romeo; he is the hero of medieval saga and the lover of the Renaissance sonnet cycles. His restless spirit protests the dullness of life; he shares Hotspur's contempt for wariness and for niggling calculations of profit and loss—for the *quid pro quo* by which reason determines the value of things. Like Chapman's early heroes, he would subjugate the material world to his poetic imagination. He speaks for the individual will against the restrictions and decorums of society.

The result of Troilus' romanticism is philosophical anarchy, but his ideal of honor is consistent in its premises. He has no illusions about the value of Helen; indeed, he actually exults in her soilure because it bears witness to the ideality of Troy's chivalric adventure. If the possession of a faithless drab were the goal of battle, then the cause would be worthless; but Helen is merely a symbol of the real issue. The Greeks do not want her; they seek to impose their will on Troy, and honor demands that the chivalric will be free and unconquered. Moreover the real enemy is not the Greek soldier but stagnation, the rusting of unused strength and vitality. Even if Helen is not worth the spilling of a single drop of blood, she is nevertheless

> a theme of honour and renown,
> A spur to valiant and magnanimous deeds,
> Whose present courage may beat down our foes,
> And fame in time to come canonize us. (II. ii. 199–202)

To the romantic ego, man is the measurer of all things; nothing has value except as he treasures it. Against the realist's credo that the value of an object is its selling price (what other men will pay for it), Troilus sets forth the romantic ideal that the only significant values are those intangibles which a man will not sell at the price of his own life.

Hector protests the complete subjectivity of Troilus' idealism. He pleads for objective criteria of judgment, for a recognition of the absolute, "natural" values which reason determines and which inhere in the customs of society. Whereas Troilus sweeps aside moral considerations as irrelevant, Hector argues the immorality of keeping Helen:

> Nature craves
> All dues be rend'red to their owners. Now
> What nearer debt in all humanity
> Than wife is to the husband? If this law
> Of nature be corrupted through affection,
> And that great minds, of partial indulgence
> To their benumbed wills, resist the same,
> There is a law in each well-ord'red nation
> To curb those raging appetites that are
> Most disobedient and refractory.
> If Helen then be wife to Sparta's king
> (As it is known she is), these moral laws
> Of nature and of nations speak aloud
> To have her back return'd. Thus to persist
> In doing wrong extenuates not wrong,
> But makes it much more heavy. (II. ii. 173–88)

Here is the voice of sanity and reason but not necessarily of objective judgment. If value does not dwell in the "particular will," then it does not dwell either in general opinion. The mere accumulation of subjective judgments does not, as Montaigne noted, create objective values, nor does the stamp of custom approve what is "natural." Once the question of values is raised, it is legitimate to ask, "What is reason but as 'tis valu'd?" Actually Hector is more of a romanticist than Troilus; he would be the Red Cross Knight, the chivalric defender of rational ideals. Troilus sees more realistically that honor and reason lead in opposite directions:

> Nay, if we talk of reason,
> Let's shut our gates and sleep. Manhood and honour
> Should have hare hearts, would they but fat their thoughts
> With this cramm'd reason. Reason and respect
> Make livers pale and lustihood deject. (II. ii. 46–50)

If it is "mad idolatry/ To make the service greater than the god," it is the only idolatry appropriate to the god of war. For how many military causes were worth the waste and misery which they entailed? There is rarely a "reason" for war except for the loathsome truth which honor hides, that men want to fight.

It is a measure of Troy's corruption that the *débat* between Hector and Troilus is purely theoretical, a courtly charade that ends with Hector's announcement that he has sent his personal challenge to the Greeks. The Trojan heroes not only hold their honors dearer than their lives but dearer also than the lives of thousands of defenseless countrymen. Because there is no "cause" for battle, their dedication to honor is in fact a dedication to personal vanity. And yet there is a terrible innocence in Troilus' self-deception. By making theoretical abstractions out of his egoistic desires, he assumes that he has elevated them above the materialism of life and turned the "performance of his heaving spleen" into a metaphysical value. He is scornful of ordinary getting and spending but he chaffers for honor on the battlefield by selling other men's lives. Exalting the individual judgment over vulgar opinion, he nevertheless takes as his absolute the "immortal" reputation that rests on the giddy props of other men's memories. By refusing to calculate the cost of the war because honor is at stake, he discards as worthless the very Trojan lives his valor protects. Actually he is not an intellectual anarchist because he recognizes as valid only his own subjective conclusions.

Troilus is Shakespeare's most subtle study of narcissistic infatuation. The defense of a slut and the worship of a wanton suffice as mirrors to reflect his image as a chivalric lover. He is not gulled by Cressida's pose of modesty, nor is she a hypocrite. She is a daughter of the game which men would have her play and for which they despise her. She sees beneath the ceremonies of courtly love the commerce of desire in which all selling prices are artificial and the pleasure of possession unequal to the thrill of anticipation. More realist than sensualist, more wary and weary than wanton, she is alone in Troy and defenseless among the Greeks. Like Troilus she believes that women are as they are valued, but she is too experienced to place a value on her affections that is different from her worth in men's eyes. To Troilus she is the Lesbia of the sonnets, but the rest of Troy assesses her at a lower rate. And she sees from her treatment by Diomedes and the other Greeks that her price has fallen still further. Having lost Troilus except for the nightly "visitations" which will satisfy his appetite, she sells when she can—she is not for all markets.

To view Cressida's infidelity as a cynical traducement of the ideal of courtly love is to miss the larger commentary which Shakespeare makes upon the masculine ego. The brutal casualness with which Diomedes "wins" his lady satisfies more frankly and grossly the same impulse that lies behind Troilus' romanticism. The worshipping of a courtly mistress and the moaning anguish of an unrequited lover are poses that enhance the value of sexual possession. They afford an opportunity for self-dramatization; they enable the "refined" sensibility to prolong by anticipation the transient ecstasy of sexual union. What are women but as they are valued *by men?* Troy would not sell Helen, its theme of honor, for the price of survival, but it barters Cressida for a single prisoner. The noble Hector uses Andromache's beauty and chastity as the subject of his martial brag but when she begs him to avoid the fatal battle, he rudely thrusts her away and orders her into the palace. When his honor is at pawn, he owes a higher obligation to his enemy than to his wife.

Even as Troilus intellectualizes the chivalric code of Troy,

Ulysses exemplifies the pragmatic realism of the Greeks. Astute, ruthless, cunning, he is Shakespeare's ultimate characterization of the politician, whose art is the manipulation of other men's ambitions and desires. Like the Trojans, the Greek leaders hold a council of state, but they are not concerned with the value of the war, only with a strategy that will bring it to a swift and successful conclusion. Seven years of futile bloodletting have eroded the Grecian spirit. Dissension, envy, and discontent have destroyed martial discipline and sapped the will to victory. Achilles lies in his tent, enamored of a Trojan woman, jeering at his leaders. The pompous Agamemnon lacks the qualities of leadership, and Menelaus, the cuckold, is universally despised. Although superior in force of arms, the Greek army is impotent and incapable of storming the gates of Troy.

Ulysses assesses the situation shrewdly. This is no time to probe the ulcer of a worthless cause. The demoralized Greeks must be distracted from the sordid circumstances of the war by a contemplation of metaphysical harmonies; the illusion of common counsel must be obtained by reference to abstract assumptions on which all men agree. Although Ulysses requires no soaring lecture on order and degree to diagnose the disease which rots the Grecian spirit, we detect no trace of irony or hypocrisy in his magnificent and oft-quoted speech. After all, this is the kind of abstract idealism which does not commit the realist to any particular course or code of action, and which comfortably reaffirms Ulysses' position in the Greek hierarchy against Thersites' cynicism and Achilles' rebellious pride. Because his idealism lies outside the realm of political action, he can at one time describe the universal order of nature and at another time remind Achilles that one touch of nature makes the whole world kin in frailty and giddiness. He can speak of the correspondence between the microcosm of the state and the macrocosm of the universe and then remark that honor, degree, and high estate in the little world of man rest upon ephemeral opinion.

We expect from the experienced and clear-sighted Ulysses a truly objective assessment of value. We find, however, that Ulysses has no opinions of his own on the worth of glory, honor, war, and love. He is an expert critic of other men's opinions; his most penetrating observations are on the vagaries of mob psychology:

                    Let not virtue seek
Remuneration for the thing it was!
For beauty, wit,
High birth, vigour of bone, desert in service,
Love, friendship, charity, are subjects all
To envious and calumniating Time.
One touch of nature makes the whole world kin,
That all with one consent praise new-born gauds,
Though they are made and moulded of things past,
And give to dust that is a little gilt
More laud than gilt o'erdusted. (III. iii. 169–79)

Without illusion, the realist is a connoisseur of other men's illusions; indeed, their illusions are the only realities with which he is actively concerned, the only ones on which he bases his calculations. If there are permanent and intrinsic values, they do not enter into or influence the course of political maneuver. Trapped in the same circumstances that corrupt Achilles and Troilus, Ulysses maintains his intellectual clarity by withholding all judgment except on the practical issues of war and state. Thus in a way his poised rational objectivity is more subversive of values than Troilus' impetuous romanticism. He is the Shakespearean analogue of Warwick in *St. Joan:* the urbane, civilized statesman, free from dangerous enthusiasms or prejudices, who is capable of instigating atrocities because he recognizes only political necessities.

    Ulysses' policy brings Troy to its appointed doom. As in the "Henriad" and in *Antony and Cleopatra,* the realist defeats the romanticist, the politician vanquishes the chevalier, the masculine world of ambition and empire subjugates the more feminine world of courtly ceremony. In *Troilus,* however, the pattern of events seems too overtly dialectical; intellectual analysis robs the heroic fable of its inherent pathos. The waste of beauty, youth, and valor does not achieve personal and poignant significance in the fates of Hector and Troilus because they exist as characters only to exemplify a thesis. They are actors in an intellectual drama whose meaning they never comprehend; they are doomed by circumstances and by the tainted values of the civilization which they lead to destruction. Because the burden of redeeming a worthless cause rests on their shoulders, they grow more and more infatuated with honor, until the pursuit of a "goodly armour" leads Hector into the cowardly ambush by which Achilles regains his "reputation." The Greeks are equally driven by "necessity." Although Ulysses correctly diagnoses the disease of pride and emulation that infects Agamemnon's army, he dares not cure the disease because there is no other incentive to heroic action than the thirst for reputation. Universal law may demand that pride be checked, but political necessity demands that arrogance, envy, and stupidity be intensified and exploited. Sold like merchandise, the bartered Cressida becomes a Grecian drab because the difference between a courtly mistress and a common stale lies not in what men desire of her but how they treat her. The most exquisite courtesan of the *ancien régime* would have become the local trollop in an obscure army camp; for while an aristocratic courtier will pay with words, vows, and deeds for the faith of his mistress, the less refined soldier will pay a smaller price for a more temporary gratification.

Troilus' romantic ideal demands that Cressida be faithful; his self-esteem demands that she be true to *him*. As he watches her submit too easily and coyly to Diomedes, his ego is more deeply wounded than his heart; he suffers without illumination:

> This she? No, this is Diomed's Cressida!
> If beauty have a soul, this is not she;
> If souls guide vows, if vows be sanctimonies,
> If sanctimony be the gods' delight,
> If there be rule in unity itself—
> This is not she. O madness of discourse,
> That cause sets up with and against itself!
> Bifold authority! where reason can revolt
> Without perdition, and loss assume all reason
> Without revolt: this is, and is not, Cressid!
> Within my soul there doth conduce a fight
> Of this strange nature, that a thing inseparate
> Divides more wider than the sky and earth;
> And yet the spacious breadth of this division
> Admits no orifex for a point as subtle
> As Ariachne's broken woof to enter.
> Instance, O instance! strong as Pluto's gates:
> Cressid is mine, tied with the bonds of heaven.
> Instance, O instance! strong as heaven itself:
> The bonds of heaven are slipp'd, dissolv'd, and loos'd. (V. ii. 137–56)

Troilus is not disillusioned; he projects his inner confusion into a law of universal chaos and would have us believe that because *his* vanity is stricken the bonds of heaven are slipped. If he were a more consistent philosopher, he would realize that he has no reason to complain, for if the individual mind sets the value of all things, then Diomedes is entitled to his estimate of Cressida's worth and she to her estimate of Troilus' affections.

Out of the sordidness of Cressida's infidelity, however, a new romantic cause is born. Another soiled woman becomes the theme of chivalric honor and the cause for senseless struggle. Now Troilus rages after Diomedes; now Diomedes assumes a courtly pose and dedicates Troilus' horse to his whore. The tables turn, the charade of chivalry approaches burlesque, but one touch of nature still makes the world kin. When Hector dies the charade ends: the appetite for glory reverts to a primitive bloodlust, for chivalry is a luxury which only the winner can afford. Refusing to calculate the cost of Hector's death lest it destroy the Trojan will to combat, Troilus has no reason to fight except for the savage impulse to kill. And after he and Ulysses have commented on the frailty of affection, it is only fitting that Pandarus should have his chance to speak. Naturally Pandarus is disappointed with Troilus' ingratitude. Even a bawd has feelings, and though he derived a vicarious pleasure from trading in flesh, his negotiations for Troilus were more selfless and "innocent" than the heroic idealism that doomed Troy.

The comic complaints of a syphilitic bawd end the play on a note of derision that seems to vindicate Thersites' scabrous cynicism. Yet the total impression of *Troilus* is hardly nihilistic. It is a depressing play, not because it establishes the futility of man's search for ideal values but because it is a sociological and psychological analysis of decadent values. Like Ulysses, Shakespeare is concerned here only with the nature of man's illusions, not with the essential worth of his ideals. The gestes of Troy do not mock the selfless dedication of Cordelia and Kent; however, they provide an ironic gloss for the chivalric gesture that costs Edmund his victory and his life.

Measure for Measure

It would seem a vast journey from the gates of Troy to the streets of Vienna, from the grand passions of legendary heroes to the petty sexual vices which absorb the attention of Angelo and Elbow. And yet *Measure for Measure* and *Troilus* are complementary plays, dual studies of the relationship between a society and its ideals. Troy falls in a purposeless chivalric adventure. Vienna survives because its citizens are wise enough to adjust their ideals of law to the needs of common humanity. Within its walls bureaucrat and bawd, priest, novice, judge, and jailer take their customary places, creating and solving the mundane problems of society. Passion and compassion temporarily submerge the orderly processes of municipal government but legality triumphs in the city magistrate's office and in the city jail. Tragedy threatens insignificant lives and sacred honors but is averted by the politic stratagems and unheroic compromises that sustain communal life.

Although *Measure for Measure* is concerned with a familiar norm of crime and punishment, it invites hyperboles of criticism and divides its interpreters into polar factions. On one extreme are those who, seeing only Morality theme and structure, interpret the play as an allegory of divine love and mercy. On the opposite extreme are those who, seeing only sordidness and deviousness—an innuendo in every passage—read the play as a scornful exposure of hypocritical pieties, as the nadir of Jacobean cynicism. In the center are the "uncommitted," who cannot wholly reject or reconcile the extreme views and who therefore conclude that the play is artistically flawed, that it mixes genres and modes, confuses romance and satire, *novella* chicanery and moral dilemma. I would suggest, however, that we can undogmatically "recapture" the integrity of *Measure for Measure* by recognizing that Shakespeare, writing in the late Renaissance, uses a Morality framework to distinguish rather than identify the human and the divine. His subject is not the drama of the soul but man's tragicomic attempts to live up to his ideals.

One can find almost anything in Vienna except greatness, for it is a comic world of little men dwarfed by the minor catastrophes their weaknesses create. It is the *critics* who ponder the moral dilemmas in *Measure for Measure*. The characters in the play do not wrestle with problems of moral choice because they do not recognize them. Assured of certain certainties, they hurry down unfamiliar pathways, pausing but a moment at each blind turning. Unaccustomed to examining their own actions, they do not reveal in soliloquy unexpected depths of conviction or perplexity. The Duke offers only one formal, semichoric comment on the responsibilities of office. Isabella pauses before and after her visit to Claudio simply to confirm her instinctive, inevitable decision. Angelo three times approaches the edge of self-knowledge only to retreat, first into incredulous dismay, next into despairing but facile cynicism, and last into craven fear. Because they place themselves at the center of their moral universes (as ruler, virgin, and judge), they never gain that complete awareness of self which redeems the coarser-grained Claudio. Indeed, like most respectable people, they are better at deceiving themselves than at deceiving others. Lacking the brilliance of Edmund or Iago, they try their amateur hands at bribery, extortion, and perjury without notable success. Angelo, the villain of the piece, is so cowardly and inept that we can only despise him. He engages in vicious projects but is thwarted at every move. He schemes feverishly to hide his lechery but it is a general subject of conversation on the stage. Like most of the people around him, he is a dissembler by expediency rather than by nature. Possessing the mentality of a smug, efficient bureaucrat, he fears great responsibilities but carries out, with utter assurance, the specific assignment given him by the Duke.

Measure for Measure, then, does not cast off all human "lendings" to lay bare the soul of depravity or saintliness. Rather it sheds new light on human "lendings"—on the forms, observances, and values which normalize civic relationships. It dramatizes the "social mode" of morality, the counterfeited expression of divine law and judgment, mercy and love in ordinary life. Its thematic image is, in fact, the counterfeit coin, the debased marker of worldly value which passes undetected until weighed against an uncorrupted standard of worth. Counterfeitings and substitutions are everywhere in the play. First Angelo substitutes for the Duke and the Duke counterfeits a friar. Later Angelo proposes that Isabella substitute her body for Claudio's life. But Mariana's body counterfeits Isabella's, and still later Ragozine's head counterfeits Claudio's. In the denouement the intricate pattern of substitutions reverses itself until all identities are restored and revealed, and Vienna returns to its customary habits and businesses.

Behind the politic maneuverings of Viennese justice, however, rises the "uncorrupted standard" of the Morality, evoked in metaphor and dramatic debate, reminding the audience (if not the actors) of the angelic compassion and impartiality that is rarely found in human pleadings. In Vienna, Justice is first represented by a ruler who admittedly did not punish offenders, and next by his Deputy, a heartless legalist who commits worse crimes than those he condemns. Mercy (Isabella) is cold in her plea; too willing to accept the harsh sentence of the law, she must be prompted by the evil-tongued, evil-minded Lucio. Actually, she plays the role of Mercy only by an accident of blood. Her motive is not a selfless redeeming love of humanity but the selfish love of sister for brother. Committed to a religious ideal of chastity, she has no pity for Claudio's frailty. She cannot (as Mercy should) forgive him his sin, but she would not have him suffer for it.

Isabella walks into Angelo's office armed with a cloistered virtue. Her pleas lack conviction because she naïvely believes that severity is an inherent attribute of justice; she is as rigid a moralist as the "prenzie Angelo" and as disdainful of other people's weaknesses. Strict in her own ethic, she divides humanity into two categories: those who never sin and those eternally damned for even a single trespass. Thus she does not plead the obvious extenuating circumstances of her brother's crime—his youthfulness, his true affection, and his intention to marry —for these are irrelevant considerations opposed to the irreparable breach of "all-building law." But equating Angelo's role with that of a Divine Justicer, she eloquently pleads that he perform the Godlike office of mercy.

Isabella's pleas fall on deaf ears, not because Angelo is cruel, but because he is a realistic administrator who distinguishes between the divine and human offices which she confuses. He never claims to have judged Claudio with divine omniscience. "Be you content, fair maid," he advises; "It is the law, not I, condemn your brother." Unable to grasp this distinction Isabella pursues her contradictory argument to its illogical conclusion. At one moment she demands that Angelo be

Godlike in his decisions; at the next, she questions whether Angelo can judge Claudio at all because he shares Claudio's human weaknesses. Angelo, however, has the perfect answer for those who doubt one man's ability to judge another:

> 'Tis one thing to be tempted, Escalus,
> Another thing to fall. I not deny
> The jury, passing on the prisoner's life,
> May in the sworn twelve have a thief or two
> Guiltier than him they try. What's open made to justice,
> That justice seizes. What knows the law
> That thieves do pass on thieves? 'Tis very pregnant,
> The jewel that we find, we stoop and take't,
> Because we see it; but what we do not see
> We tread upon and never think of it. (II. i. 17–26)

That is to say, in an imperfect world perfection is an absurd criterion of justice. Although divine law and the nature of God are inseparable because one springs from and exemplifies the other, civil law is distinct from, and superior to (by its ideality), the nature of any one man. Thus while God could not justly punish man for vices which He shared, a human judge can rightly condemn those weaknesses of the flesh which no man wholly escapes. And though God, who sees all, cannot justly punish one sinner while a thousand escape, a human judge, who cannot see all, may rightly punish those criminals who are caught.

Angelo's conception of the law may seem too expedient, too ready to compromise with the inequitable accidents of life. But it is completely untouched by Pompey's cynicism. When Escalus asks,

> How would you live, Pompey? By being a bawd? What do you think of the trade, Pompey? Is it a lawful trade? (II. i. 236–38)

Pompey answers, "If the law would allow it, sir." Pompey would have us believe that morality is changeable opinion codified in varying laws. Angelo, in contrast, insists that though enforcement of a law may languish, the moral imperative behind the law remains constant. He carefully distinguishes, however, between moral imperative and law. When Isabella pleads,

> I have a brother is condemn'd to die.

> I do beseech you, let it be his fault,
> And not my brother,

Angelo answers in amazement:

> Condemn the fault, and not the actor of it?
> Why every fault's condemn'd ere it be done.
> Mine were the very cipher of a function,
> To fine the faults whose fine stands in record,
> And let go by the actor. (II. ii. 34–41)

Moral law sets the standard of behavior, civil law maintains the standard; the former condemns, the latter punishes. "Judge not that ye be not judged" may be the highest ideal of *individual* relationships, but as a legal principle it can only subvert society.

The heartless Angelo infuriates us with his smugness; yet he speaks a partial truth which the Morality framework clarifies rather than contradicts. The Divine Arraignment of the Morality is supremely detached from mundane social problems. It is concerned only with the uniquely precious and individual soul. Judgment in Vienna, however, has utilitarian social ends. The law's purpose (as Angelo, Lucio, and the Duke agree) is to restrain man's potential wickedness, to "fear the birds of prey" and prevent "future evils." Utility is, in fact, the chief justification of punitive law, without which it would simply presume God's judgment. And even with this justification, punitive law remains one of civilization's ugliest necessities, incapable by nature of rising above a *lex talionis*. The hangman is a very necessary servant of society, but as we see in *Measure for Measure*, he is generally despised, or rather (as his name suggests) abhorred. In Vienna punitive law renders justice not so much to the condemned criminal as to the rest of society, which protects itself against anarchic lawlessness by harsh examples. Claudio may not, strictly speaking, deserve to die, but concupiscence must be checked; and what better example to the Lucios of the world can the law set than the hanging of an almost innocent man?

Angelo sees clearly the social function of law but he cannot see beyond it. He worships legality in the name of justice because he has, after all, the viewpoint of a bureaucrat who is supposed to enforce statutes, not interpret them. A consummate prig, he congratulates himself on impersonal administration of justice because he does not realize that only in the flawless Arraignment of the Morality are legality and justice one. Like Isabella he sees good and evil as categorical antitheses, but his moral universe does not extend beyond the city limits of Vienna, in which mercy cannot be freely given.

Far more humane in his view of crime and punishment is the Duke, who understands the ideal as well as the utility of civil law. He is a kindly, intelligent ruler, concerned with his people's happiness, who dislikes public ceremony and would have preferred, it seems, a quiet private life among his subjects or in a study. Worse still, he is too compassionate to impose directly the severity which the Viennese situation requires. The bawds and brothels are prospering, and more innocent indulgences go unreproved. A reform is needed; a young, vigorous, "precise" public prosecutor—an Angelo—must be engaged to clean up the stews and curb sensuality. Were it not for his gentle nature, the Duke would have undertaken this reform, but as he tells the Friar, for fourteen years he has allowed the statutes to languish and he would not now "tyrannically" punish sins he had so long countenanced. To the audience it seems as tyrannical to commission severity as to employ it personally, and cowardly to "leave town" allowing a Deputy to absorb public resentment. As the play proceeds, however, we suspect that the Duke appoints Angelo, not to escape unpopularity, but because he knows himself to be incapable of harshness. Though accepting the necessity of punitive law, he prefers, as he demonstrates, to rehabilitate rather than to sentence. And having no illusions about his Deputy, he remains in Vienna in disguise while the reform proceeds.

Critics who fail to see the Duke's personal motive for deputizing Angelo speak cheerfully of him as a "scientist" whose laboratory is the world and who empirically tests Angelo's integrity by placing him in high office. But surely no intelligent ruler tests his subordinates by giving them power of life and death when he knows beforehand their lack of simple humanity. Nor does a man as moral as the Duke experiment with human beings simply to discover what they will do. The Duke abdicates authority for very practical civic purposes and when his calculated risk becomes a social calamity, he intervenes immediately in Isabella's behalf. He pities Claudio condemned by an "angry law," yet he cannot question the severity he personally commissioned. If he simply reveals himself and denounces Angelo, Claudio must still be "justly" hanged or the reform campaign will disintegrate. He recoils, moreover, from Angelo's idea that justice is served when a lecher hangs a lecher. Reversing Isabella's demand, he would have Angelo judge *himself* as he judges others—a patent impossibility. Thus a higher justice than Vienna's demands that Claudio be set free.

To obtain this higher justice, the Duke must circumvent the forms of civil law. He must apply "craft against vice" and "pay with falsehood false exacting." Lest Mariana shrink from her ignoble role in the deception of Angelo, Vincentio assures her:

> . . . fear you not at all.
> He is your husband on a precontract.
> To bring you thus together 'tis no sin,
> Sith that the justice of your title to him
> Doth flourish the deceit. (IV. i. 71–75)

These are strange words for one seeking to transcend legal forms. Even worse, they disturbingly echo Claudio's extenuation that his "true contract" lacked but the "formality of outward order." What kind of morality condemns a sinning lover yet countenances a politic trick involving lechery, deceit, and bribery? Actually, the Duke realizes the hollowness of his "comfortable words." Though he tells Mariana " 'tis no sin," he later admits that Claudio's pardon is to be "purchased by such sin/ For which the pardoner himself is in."

Once again the Duke's clever plan goes awry. Afraid to let Claudio live, Angelo reneges on the illicit bargain, leaving Vincentio no other choice than to halt the execution and to render open justice by returning to Vienna. Even now, though, he hopes to raise the fallen Angelo. Keeping secret the fact that Claudio lives, he pits Isabella against his Deputy in an open scene of judgment. Again transcending the forms of civil law, he allows Angelo to hear his own case—to wrap himself in the public shame and ignominy that bring sudden, complete repentance.

When the Duke sheds his friar's costume, *Measure for Measure* closes with a second debate of Mercy and Justice, a second moral masque on the exalted theme of sin and redemption. This time Justice (the Duke) is incorruptible and Mercy (Isabella) truly speaks with disinterested tongue, indeed, against all promptings of hatred and revenge. And still the Duke's masque remains an elaborately contrived sham, a woefully imperfect substitute for a divine judgment. When he sentences Angelo for his crimes, Vincentio asks Isabella to forgive (for Mariana's sake) Angelo's aborted attempt on her honor:

> . . . But as he adjudg'd your brother—
> Being criminal, in double violation
> Of sacred chastity, and of promise-breach
> Thereon dependent for your brother's life—
> The very mercy of the law cries out
> Most audible, even from his proper tongue,
> 'An Angelo for Claudio! death for death!' (V. i. 408–14)

Vincentio's indictment is so stern, so just, so pregnant with moral outrage, and so precisely legal that many readers are confounded by the leniency of Angelo's sentence. They fail to see that Vincentio never intended to punish his Deputy—indeed, his impressive bill of particulars, like his masque of judgment, is merely counterfeit. In the first place, Claudio was not executed. In the second place, Angelo was not legally guilty of unchastity because his meeting with Mariana was (according to the Duke) a lawful joining of husband and wife. In the third place, Angelo was not more guilty of violating his illicit bargain than was Isabella. That is to say, the Duke could not justly punish Angelo for the crimes listed without also punishing Mariana for fornication, Isabella for breach of promise, and himself for false accusation. Moreover, the Duke, by his own high moral principles, cannot judge Angelo more severely than he judges himself—an organizer of a sordid conspiracy to purchase the life of a justly sentenced criminal. As a matter of fact, the Duke omits from his indictment the one grave offense which Angelo did commit and for which he could be legally punished: namely, the criminal abuse of high office. But then the power which corrupted Angelo was thrust upon him, against his will and entreaties, by Vincentio. To force a man to perform a duty for which he is not adequately prepared and then condemn him for his failures would smack too much of tyranny.

The Duke's pose of Justice, then, is a majestic bit of play-acting dedicated to several utilitarian ends. Angelo is shocked into complete, open repentance. Isabella, though her grace is not freely given, triumphs over vindictiveness. Her victory, however, is one of mind rather than heart. She speaks not of divine forgiveness but of the doubtful legality of the Duke's case:

> Let him not die. My brother had but justice,
> In that he did the thing for which he died.
> For Angelo,
> His act did not o'ertake his bad intent,
> And must be buried but as an intent
> That perish'd by the way. Thoughts are no subjects,
> Intents but merely thoughts. (V. i. 453–59)

Here is a clarity of legal perception which the precise Angelo might well admire. (Indeed, is not his failure to make these points himself proof of his regeneration?) Isabella's education in the world is nearly complete. Whereas before she confused them, now she nicely distinguishes between the high idealism of the Christian ethic and the practical realism of civil codes. Through her eyes we see that the ending of *Measure for Measure* is not patched together artistically or morally. The Duke does not improbably and arbitrarily reverse a tragic sequence of events. On the contrary, through his early intervention he diverted a potential tragedy towards a comic resolution by thwarting Angelo's criminal intentions and rehabilitating his moral character. Thus for once the claims of mercy and justice accord in a final scene of repentance, reconciliation, and promised joy.

This does not mean that the many readers who find the ending of *Measure for Measure* unsatisfactory are insensitive or mistaken. The ending of the play is unsatisfactory in that it disappoints our longing for a more perfect justice than the world affords and because it avoids the very moral problems which lend reality and meaning to a contrived *novella* fable. The conflict between divine commandment and human frailty, between the high ethic of the Gospel and the necessity of punitive law, is brushed aside, not resolved. To the final scene Angelo's legalistic conception of justice remains valid in the eyes of his fellow citizens and even triumphs in Isabella's "mercy." Civil law, however imperfectly it counterfeits divine judgment, must still pass current in the little, sublunary world of Vienna.

Of course, *Measure for Measure* is not simply a calculated imitation of the muddled compromises of life; by the denouement the comic design of the play is unmistakable. Across Shakespeare's stage move people who try to escape their human limitations or obligations but who discover that one touch of nature makes the whole world kin, that the cheerful cynicism of bawds mingles with their high arguments of justice and mercy, that they cannot shrug off the Lucios of this world or eradicate the breed of Pompey. Isabella would have practiced an ideal morality in a nunnery, but she is engaged, through Lucio's kind offices, in excusing the carnality she abhors. She tries to escape Angelo's lechery by appealing to Claudio's better nature, but she stumbles against the young man's (Everyman's) horror of death. She dedicates herself to a spiritual ideal, but she never frees herself from society's legalistic morality. Like many another embattled virgin she becomes less concerned with ethical ideals than with her own well-defended honor, which she must, nevertheless, publicly besmirch at the Duke's bidding. By the end of the play, however, she understands the world well enough to forgive Angelo and take her place by the Duke's side.

Angelo's education is similar but more radical. At first he moves in the solitary splendor of matchless rectitude. Next he discovers the terrible isolation of criminality. At last (or so we hope) he learns to live humbly with himself and other erring mortals. The Duke, wishing to shun temporarily the cares of office, merely embroils himself in graver responsibilities. Seeking to transcend the customary forms of civil law, he is driven to such fantastic tricks as would perhaps make angels weep. And although he dislikes the vulgar display of authority he finds that to re-establish justice he must stage his office in public view.

One finishes *Measure for Measure* with mixed feelings of amusement, pity, and scorn. Isabella and Angelo, Montaigne would say, "seek for other conditions" because they understand not their own. They take the moral measure of all things before they even know themselves. Yet when all has been said and done on stage, decency and common sense have triumphed over a fanatic attempt to stamp the insignia of an "ideal" morality on intractable human materials. With a little suffering has come a little more wisdom and understanding of man's precarious, tragicomic situation. We need not assume, therefore, that the echoes of parables and Moralities mock man's fumbling attempts at justice or mercy. Instead they whisper of an exalted ethic which man scarcely comprehends but which, on occasion (as even Angelo can testify), illumines his life with a touch of grace beyond the reach of human arts.

King Lear

The ambiguous characterizations of the dark comedies seem to emphasize the universality of frailty and illusion that qualifies moral judgment. One almost feels in *Measure for Measure* a shrugging, tolerant acceptance of the ignorance of self that brings petty virtue to the edge of great sin. But if to understand all is to forgive, then Shakespeare does not understand *all*. In *Lear* particularly his stark Morality-like characterizations define, with an almost exaggerated clarity, the elemental good and evil in man.

We do not require an extensive knowledge of Renaissance thought to recognize that *Lear* is deeply concerned with the nature of man and his universe. From a close textual study of the play, conducted with slight reference to Renaissance philosophy, Professor R. B. Heilman reports that its patterns of imagery constitute "a series of implied questions: What is man's nature? What is nature? What in the nature of things may man depend upon? From considerations of what is natural and unnatural it is only a step to the problem of justice, to which the play returns repeatedly. . . ."[4] On the one hand, the ageless contemporaneity of *Lear* rebukes the vanity of those investigators who believe that scholarly research affords a unique revelation of Shakespeare's intention and meaning. On the other hand, the complexity of theme and structure in *Lear* proves the value of historical research as a guide to what is central in Shakespeare's thought and art. At the same time that recent critics (R. B. Heilman, John F. Danby,[5] and Hiram Haydn[6]) have interpreted *Lear* as an inquiry into the nature of man, they have, to varying degrees, falsified its philosophical and dramatic structure. They read *Lear* as a dramatization of an ideological dichotomy; they classify the characters by their adherence to conflicting philosophies of nature. In one group supposedly are the "idealists," who believe in the classical-Christian concept of natural law: Cordelia, Kent, Edgar, Gloucester, and Lear. Ranged against them are the

Machiavellian (or Hobbesian) "realists," who see in nature only amoral physical energy and who view the world as a jungle in which the fittest (i.e., the most ruthless) survive.[7]

While there are undoubted references to the destruction of the feudal ethos in *Lear*, the above interpretation seems at once an oversimplification and oversubtilization of Shakespeare's intention. It construes *Lear* as an analogue of *The Atheist's Tragedy*, more profound in its view of life but puzzling in its dialectic. Despite a crudely literal moral design, Tourneur's play brings its ideological conflict to an unequivocal resolution: D'Amville admits before he dies the error of his philosophy of nature. At the end of *Lear* there is no philosophical conclusion about the nature of the universe on which all agree. Each character interprets the tragic events by the light of his own experience. The dying Edmund admits only that the wheel has come full circle. Goneril and Regan die at each other's throats without philosophical meditation. Edgar and Albany exclaim at the justice of the gods but Lear questions why anything on earth should live when Cordelia must die, and Kent sees that it is the stars that rule men's fates. Surely the deaths of Goneril, Regan, and Edmund do not prove their philosophy invalid when Cordelia, Gloucester, and Lear die with them. In a Morality the conflict between good and evil is implicitly of philosophical importance because it reaffirms the supremacy of God in His universe—a reaffirmation that does not come in the cheerless, dark, and deadly close of *Lear*. Moreover, if Edmund and the evil sisters represent a "modern" order of rationality or individualism, then we must accuse Shakespeare of sentimentally tampering with history in allowing the "wave of the future" to recede before the resurrected traditional idealism of Albany and Edgar.

It is extremely difficult also to think of Goneril and Regan as "rationalists." Cold-bloodedness may be a form of rationality but they are not even cold-blooded. They have the kingdom legitimately in their possession; they own the total reality of power which the Machiavel seeks. But they are not realists enough to tolerate their father's illusions of royalty; they must make him see himself as they see him: aged, weak, defenseless, and dependent on their whim. One imagines that the author of *The Prince* would have smiled at the "Machiavellianism" of those who risk secure power to satisfy a purely vicious, irrational impulse. For behind the coldly calculated plan to humiliate Lear lies the feverish desire to subjugate which also expresses itself in almost masculine sexual lusts. To be sure, Goneril and Regan have an air of aggrieved reasonableness but then so do Octavius Caesar, Claudius, and Richard III. (Almost all of Shakespeare's villains are experts at sanctimony.) Their rationalizations are logical, but then all immoralists have a terrifying unspoken logic of their own. They see life more clearly and simply than the rest of humanity. We may, somewhat incorrectly, call Goneril and Regan "Machiavellian" if we remember that Machiavellianism is as old as politics itself and that the *Realpolitik* began with Satan's revolt in heaven. The order which Goneril and Regan represent began with Cain. If it seems modern it is because ideals of virtue become old-fashioned and disappear while the face of evil is changeless, eternally familiar and "modern."

Edmund, disturbingly enough, is a rationalist. His scheming intellect seems always in control; his reason apparently never gives way to impulse or passion until he is touched by remorse at his death. But we need not assume that perversion of intellect is a peculiarly "modern" sin, or that it was regarded as such by the Renaissance. We find in Donne's sermons a detailed anatomy of Edmund's cynicism that is ageless in its application to human nature:

> But when we come to sin, upon reason, and upon discourse, upon Meditation, and upon plot, This is *Humanum,* to become the Man of Sin, to surrender that, which is the Form, and Essence of man, Reason, and understanding, to the service of sin. When we come to sin wisely and learnedly, to sin logically, by a *Quia,* and an *Ergo,* that, Because God does thus, we may do as we do, we shall come to sin through all the Arts, and all our knowledge . . . when we come to employ upon sin, that which is the essence of man, Reason, and discourse, we will also employ upon it, those which are the properties of man onely, which are, To speak, and to laugh; we will come to speak, and talk, and to boast of our sins, and at last, to laugh and jest at our sins; and as we have made sin a Recreation, so we will make a jest of our condemnation.[8]

Emancipated from the moral superstitions that enslave his naïve brother and father, Edmund finds in libertine naturalism a perfect rationalization for his intended villainy. His first soliloquy immediately defines, by ironic contrast to Lear's invocations of nature, his lawless rebellion against society:

> Thou, Nature, art my goddess; to thy law
> My services are bound. Wherefore should I
> Stand in the plague of custom, and permit
> The curiosity of nations to deprive me,
> For that I am some twelve or fourteen moonshines
> Lag of a brother? Why bastard? wherefore base?
> When my dimensions are as well compact,
> My mind as generous, and my shape as true,
> As honest madam's issue? Why brand they us
> With base? with baseness? bastardy? base, base?
> Who, in the lusty stealth of nature, take
> More composition and fierce quality
> Than doth, within a dull, stale, tired bed,
> Go to th' creating a whole tribe of fops
> Got 'tween asleep and wake? Well then,
> Legitimate Edgar, I must have your land.
> Our father's love is to the bastard Edmund
> As to th' legitimate. Fine word—'legitimate'!
> Well, my legitimate, if this letter speed,
> And my invention thrive, Edmund the base
> Shall top th' legitimate. I grow; I prosper.
> Now, gods, stand up for bastards! (I. ii. 1–22)

We should not, however, take Edmund's mock-heroic manifesto more seriously than he does. This is no impassioned cry of self-assertion against meaningless convention. His high-spirited wit suggests that he is not so pained by the degradation of his birth as he is contemptuous of the moral code that brands him. He is not so sensitive about his illegitimacy as he is enthusiastic about his plot against Edgar. If Edmund did not have his bastardy, he would no doubt have had to invent it. And his nature philosophy, like his bastardy, seems more a symbol than an explanation of his villainy. Apart from this soliloquy he never mentions his goddess again. Like Richard III, he is a gambler and accepts his defeat as a turn of the wheel, not as proof of intellectual error.[9]

There is, however, an irony in this soliloquy of which Edmund is unaware. A master of casualness, he would have us believe that his bastardy has not touched him at all. And yet he feels the need to empty the terms *base* and *bastard* of meaning by juggling them on his tongue. His true feelings about his birth and his "philosophy" are unmasked only when he is challenged by the disguised Edgar. "In wisdom" he should ask the challenger's name. "By rule of knighthood," he could delay the combat, and by "law of arms" he was not "bound to answer/ An unknown opposite." But victory has made him careless. What he won by superior intellect he wagers on chivalric ability, concerned only that his opponent seems aristocratic and speaks with *breeding!* Having played the role of noble brother, son, and liegeman with contemptuous hypocrisy, he now admits, as it were, the fascination that the part held. The man who joked about his bastardy hungered for "honour." He sacrificed his humanity in pursuit of the "nobility" which his reason and his "philosophy" dismissed as absurd.

The naturalism to which Edmund makes passing reference is not significant in *Lear*, and the attempt to define Goneril, Regan, and Edmund ideologically merely diverts attention from the true philosophical drama of the play, which is focused in Lear's mind. If we read the play as a conflict between philosophies of nature then Lear becomes a lay figure, a *casus belli* between warring intellectual factions, or at best a choric voice for Shakespeare's commentary on life. Some critics, I suspect, would like to ignore Lear altogether because they discuss his character with ill-concealed impatience. They acknowledge his greatness of soul and majesty of utterance, the depths and grandeur of his passion. However they find him puerile in intellect, childishly vain and self-deluded, and even criminally stupid. And when they have catalogued all his failings, they still find it impossible to explain his incredible ignorance of the world around him.

Some of the accusations against Lear are unjust. It is customary, for example, to measure his folly against political commonplaces of the Renaissance and to compare his mistake in dividing his kingdom with Gorboduc's. Actually Lear does not commit Gorboduc's unpardonable political sin of destroying the natural succession to the realm. His division of the kingdom among three daughters to "prevent future strife" seems eminently sensible and has disastrous consequences only because two of his daughters are Goneril and Regan. More often than not Lear's assumptions have the weight of theoretical authority behind them. He would no doubt have found good counsel in Erasmus and Elyot, but he needed even more the political realism of Machiavelli.

Part of the misunderstanding of Lear's character stems also from a failure to appreciate the ceremonial quality of the testing scene. Lear walks on stage an absolute monarch whose prerogative is unquestioned and who expects complete obedience. He does not ask his daughters to declare their love; he commands them. When Cordelia refuses to flatter him, he orders her to reconsider. When she refuses again, he banishes her with the outspoken Kent, who dares to intercede, and who would have Lear break a kingly vow. Here is arrogance personified, autocracy, even despotism. Yet Lear does not have the despot's greediness for power or the tyrant's fear of relinquishing authority. We are told directly that the purpose of the testing game is to enable Lear to shrug off peacefully the burden of ruling. He will give up all control of the kingdom, all sway, all instruments of royal authority. He will reserve for himself only the name of king, the respect which it elicits, and a princely retinue of a hundred followers. Before long he learns the fundamental fact of monarchy: that the title of royalty is meaningless without the homage that power demands or that love brings forth unasked.

The opening dialogue between Gloucester and Kent imparts the crucial information that the kingdom has already been equitably divided among Lear's daughters. The testing of their love is purely ritualistic, a last enjoyment of the sway which Lear intends to renounce. It is in fact a tripartite ceremony in which a vain and aging monarch plays the central role. He is, first of all, king, image of authority in the state; he is also father, corresponding ruler in the microcosm of the family; and last but equally important, he is a judge, bearer of the sacred sword of heaven. In all three symbolic roles Lear carries himself with assurance. Is he not the good king, who by dividing power while he lives, will prevent civil war? Is he not the generous father, who, for a small declaration of love (which is in any case his natural due) is prepared to give away a kingdom—to give away "all"? And is he not the perfect judge, who proposes strict, impartial measure for measure: a third of a realm for an appropriate declaration of affection? Of course, the judgment is to be purely symbolic because although Lear knows that Cordelia loves him best, he is quite certain that all his daughters will declare their undying affection—that they are (as they should be) natural children.

In itself Lear's ritual division of the kingdom is no more absurd or potentially tragic than the comparable ritual of marriage. Both ceremonies demand rehearsed answers that are perhaps greatly at variance with the participants' feelings. It would be more honest for those before an altar to state the true nature of their affections, but any declaration other than the customary avowal of eternal devotion would be as shocking as Cordelia's answer is to Lear. It is not Cordelia's "pride" or "tragic reticence" that makes the innocent ritual disastrous in consequence; it is Lear's delight in setting off his daughters against each other and his insulting insinuation that they must buy their inheritance with hyperbole. Even then all might have been well except for the precedent set by Goneril's fulsome flatteries. When Cordelia's turn comes, her plain reply is precisely the answer that Goneril and Lear deserve but it is not the answer which the occasion demands. A less fine nature might have temporized, but Cordelia's revulsion is an almost physical nausea: she cannot heave her heart into her mouth.

Lear loved Cordelia best. He "saves" her for last and turns to her with joy to accept the words of love which would in this instance come from the heart. Her measured answer makes his masque of kingly and paternal virtue seen amateurish and ill-rehearsed. Shocked, humiliated, "betrayed," he rashly disowns her, convinced at the moment that she is unnatural and ungrateful. And up to the moment when he learns the true nature of ingratitude from Goneril and Regan, he is haunted by Cordelia's unkindness. Here is a man who very slenderly knows himself and his world in which he has so long and apparently securely lived. He cannot in a crucial instance distinguish between the appearance and the reality of love because his rigid mind cannot adapt to the specific circumstance. He does not know Goneril and Regan, but he knows the natural obligation of love which they owe him; he measures the naturalness of their filial affections by the correspondence of their statements to an ideal which his mind conceives. In a sense Lear is Shakespeare's most paradoxical hero—a man who acts unjustly yet believes implicitly that justice is the rule of the universe, a king and father who acts unnaturally and yet is convinced of the existence of rational, natural order. I do not suggest that Shakespeare uses Lear to represent Elizabethan idealism, for Lear's view of nature is narrow, legalistic, egocentric, and supremely naïve; his responses are emotional rather than intellectual. On the other hand, Lear's belief in natural order is, as the play reveals, the deepest certainty of his existence. It is as necessary to him as sanity itself. Professor Hardin Craig has said that the mind of the Renaissance "moved habitually on a conceptual rather than a rational level," that it "inherited or adopted generalized simplifications, formulae, for the applications of its ethical, religious, and scientific systems. It could not consider, or at least was not in the habit of considering, observed data apart from these generalizations."[10] Such a mind, enthralled by ego, is Lear's. Small wonder that it crumbles when faced with the most terrible of realities.

Lear's education in political and moral realities is begun by three schoolmasters, the Fool, Goneril, and Regan, who, for different reasons, would have him come to terms with his folly. For the weak, dependent Fool, loyalty to Lear is a completely irrational luxury. The banished Kent returns in disguise to serve Lear because he sees, as he always will, authority in Lear's countenance. But the Fool knows that kingdoms do not rest on such rare acts of devotion, and that it is impolitic to follow a king who is king in name only. When Goneril deliberately insults Lear's drooping majesty, the Fool draws the moral:

> Thou wast a pretty fellow when thou hadst no need to care for her frowning. Now thou art an O without a figure. I am better than thou art now: I am a fool, thou art nothing. (I. iv. 210–14)

Lear is hardly an apt pupil. He is stunned by Goneril's ingratitude and by his inability to punish her except with hideous curses, yet "the marks of sovereignty/ Knowledge and reason" still support his faith in nature and in his kingly place. If Goneril is the monstrous deviation from the norm, then Regan must be "kind and comfortable." When Lear finds Kent in the stocks and sees that Regan is Goneril's twin, he cannot admit it. She has "reason" to love him. She knows "the offices of nature," and "the bond of childhood." Regan is not inclined to humor her distracted father. When he continues to play the king, she advises him to face his own situation, to seem as old and weak as he actually is.

Lear, we might say, refuses to accept reality, but this would be too simple an explanation. Before man can accept realities, he must first recognize them; and he has always clung to the belief—written large in the whole of metaphysics—that there is a more stable and enduring reality than the flux of daily experience. His daughters' evil and ingratitude tear at Lear's belief in natural order but do not destroy it. Conceived by reason, that belief can be betrayed only by reason, as it is when Goneril and Regan argue calmly, sensibly, and logically that Lear requires no retinue or outward show of kingly dignity and honor. In an ironic inversion of his quantitative measurements of love, they reduce his train from one hundred to fifty to twenty-five to nothing. The once proud Lear, who gave away "all," finally cries out:

> O, reason not the need! Our basest beggars
> Are in the poorest thing superfluous.
> Allow not nature more than nature needs,
> Man's life is cheap as beast's. (II. iv. 267–70)

In a moment of agonized illumination, Lear realizes that Goneril's and Regan's arguments are impeccable. Reason does not require such frivolities as retinue, nor can it measure a king's need for love, loyalty, and devotion. Indeed, when necessity is measured by Goneril's (or Ulysses') reason alone, man's life does become as cheap as beasts'. Reduced by his daughters to emptiness—to the Fool's "O"—Lear rushes out into the storm, maddened with rage and grief.

In one sense Lear's derangement parallels his dethronement of reason in the kingdom, his inversion of justice and family piety. At the same time his growing irrationality also mirrors the destruction of the certainties by which he had lived. After all, the first premise of sanity is that one lives in a somewhat reasonable world. To retain one's sanity one must be able to determine some logical pattern in the disorder of events. One must be able to anticipate with some degree of accuracy the result of actions taken. One must believe, pragmatically at least, in causal relationships. Lear acts "justly" towards his daughters and expects justice in return. He acts "kindly" as king and father and expects kindness in return. Reason and knowledge tell him that he is still king. And when reason and knowledge lie, Lear retreats from an insane world into madness.

Viewed against the background of Renaissance intellectual

change, Lear's madness and the chaos of the storm take on still larger significance: they symbolize the darkness of shattered faiths and the confusion of mankind wandering aimlessly and hopelessly, "having no way." Lear, Gloucester, Edgar, and Kent, symbolic figures on the barren wasteland of the heath, meet, separate, and meet again, cut off from their normal pattern of life. The heavens pour down a blind, pitiless "judgment" on the weak and the aged but mercifully allow a king the shelter of a hovel. In the cold and the rain, metaphysical formulations seem superfluous compared to the truth about human needs which the storm defines. Lear greets the half-naked, begrimed figure of Edgar as the ultimate fact of human nature, the unsophisticated one, the bare forked animal who lurks beneath the costume of civilization. Here is a starting point for a return to fundamentals, a place at which to begin an empirical distinction between natural wants and sophisticated appetites. But the half-crazed empiricism leads only to greater confusion, for if one takes from man the artifices of civilization, he becomes again an animal. His humanity, as Montaigne realized, is as much a product of custom as of nature, if indeed the two can be separated. Because his mind and emotions sophisticate his primitive wants, man rises above the animals. And because he turns the luxuries of power and wealth into "necessities," he is capable of savageries which make the animals seem, by comparison, civilized. Lear's attempt to define the nature of man empirically ends in a cynical relativism, a maddened tolerance of all depravities. Let copulation thrive! Man needs sexual release and kings need armies; nature's way is that of the wren and the gilded fly. Discarding a naïve, inadequate, optimistic rationalism, Lear arrives at the empirical "truth" of man's animality that is the cornerstone of libertine naturalism.[11]

In delirium Lear envisions a universe that travesties the orderly, hierarchical cosmos of the Renaissance moral philosophers. But his cynical commentary on hidden guilts and pretended virtue, on the corruption of justice and of family relationships, is double-edged. The bitter pleasure of universalizing his discovery of injustice is chastened by a knowledge of the follies and crimes that were hidden by his own "robes and furr'd gowns." In madness he can make admissions about himself that were before unthinkable. When he was sane he abused his absolute authority. In madness he claims (as did the Stuarts) a despotic power over all law, civil or moral, only to admit that his omnipotence is counterfeit. "No," he insists,

> they cannot touch me for coining;
> I am the King himself. (IV. vi. 83–84)

Then he adds that most ironic of observations, "Nature's above art in that respect." Unable to punish his daughters in reality, he arraigns them in his imagination, aware nevertheless that justice is not the way of the world. For a time his distraught mind enjoys the pose of monarchy, but when Cordelia's followers find him, he has grown weary of his royal pretense. "I will die bravely," he tells his captors,

> like a smug bridegroom. What!
> I will be jovial. Come, come, I am a king;
> My masters, know you that? (IV. vi. 202–4)

Fleeing from his daughters, Lear learns the facts of political life which the world has always known but which Machiavelli first candidly stated. Seeing the world too clearly he catechizes the sightless Gloucester:

> Thou hast seen a farmer's dog bark at a beggar? . . . And the creature run from the cur? There thou mightst behold the great image of authority: a dog's obey'd in office. (IV. vi. 159–63)

Gloucester, who stumbled when he saw, is "blessed" by a revelation of cosmic despair that annihilates anger and bitterness: "As flies to wanton boys are we to th' gods./ They kill us for their sport." Edgar, outlawed and proscribed, survives only by disguising himself in filth and idiocy. And on the heath, the nature of man seems no higher than that of beasts. There are but the hunters and the prey—the sophisticated ones and the bare forked animals.

Against the ruins of ancient beliefs, however, stand the unbending loyalties of Kent, Cordelia, and Edgar. Opposed to the staggering disclosure of man's inhumanity is the continuing verbal insistence that evil is a monstrous aberration, an insistence that grows more vehement as evil triumphs. Although we share Albany's horror at Goneril, we are not certain that evil is an aberration or a transient flaw in the design of creation. Who shall we say represents the norm? Cordelia or her sisters? Edgar or Edmund? Albany or Cornwall? the faithful Kent or the equally faithful Oswald? In a Morality, the inevitable triumph of

God makes a joke of satanic evil. But instead of the laughter which sounds as angels beat devils off the stage, we hear in *Lear* only the laughter of Edmund, comic interlocutor, as Edgar, Kent, Gloucester, and Lear are forced into hiding. Here is farce of a high order: the politic Edmund and Cornwall exchanging moral platitudes, faithful Kent banished for disloyalty, Cordelia and Edgar slandered and disowned as unnatural children, kindly Gloucester blinded for his "treason"— decency itself made a crime. Yet who dares say in the face of ancient and modern totalitarianisms that such inversion of values is not commonplace in society? In the totalitarian ethic, there is no higher virtue than to inform on one's own father.

The final act of *Lear* brings eventful change, a rift in impenetrable gloom, and a turn of fate that destroys ascendant evil. Still the play does not end, as does *Hamlet*, with a return to normality after a sudden, purgative spasm of violence. The return to normality in *Lear* is a brief delusory interlude between the terror of the storm and the apocalyptic agony of the last scene. For one moment all suffering seems redeemed: Edgar triumphs, the order goes out for the release of Lear and Cordelia, and joyful reunion is at hand. But just when all seems right again with the world, Lear enters with the dead Cordelia in his arms and again all's "cheerless, dark, and deadly." "Is this the promis'd end?" Is this the last judgment of the heavens? "Fall and cease!"

That some kind of justice rules the universe of *Lear* is evident, but it is at best a partial justice which metes out exact measure for measure to those who least deserve it: to Goneril, Regan, Cornwall, Edmund, and Oswald. For Cordelia, Edgar, and Kent, the innocents, and for Gloucester and Lear, more sinned against than sinning, there can be no justice. The close of *Lear*, which offended eighteenth-century moral sensibilities, is not made bearable by Albany's belated promise to reward Edgar, or by some impossible hope that the broken Kent will end his years in peace and happiness. For his immeasurable devotion to Lear, Kent seeks only the simplest and humblest satisfaction—to be recognized. This the gods will not allow. As Lear dies we do not regain our confidence in this best of all possible worlds where the torture of the rack produces such remarkable spiritual benefits, nor are we reassured of the existence of universal law. The medieval ideal of nature does not rise phoenix-like out of its ashes any more than it rose again in the scientific world of the seventeenth century. But with loss there is rediscovery; with negation, reaffirmation.

When Lear awakens in Cordelia's presence, he has been cleansed through suffering of vanity and arrogance. Almost literally born again, he is childlike in his weakness and unable to organize his thoughts. Having come to the edge of self-knowledge, he has lost the assurances which formerly made him an imposing ruler. Whereas before he took the measure of all things, now he is unable to predict Cordelia's responses; he is certain only that he is "a very foolish fond old man." When Cordelia weeps, he remembers his own tears of anger and self-pity and humbly confesses his guilt:

> Be your tears wet? Yes, faith. I pray weep not.
> If you have poison for me, I will drink it.
> I know you do not love me; for your sisters
> Have, as I do remember, done me wrong.
> You have some cause, they have not. (IV. vii. 71–75)

Cordelia's answer, "No cause, no cause" is Lear's final illumination. It is the answer of a love that reasons not the need, that does not weigh or measure duties, bonds, and obligations. In the storm Lear had clung to the idea that nature would redeem itself if he were given justice— i.e., if Goneril and Regan were cruelly punished. His unsettled mind was fascinated with legalistic machinery: with courts, arraignments, summoners, and judges. Now he no longer rages against an unjust, "unnatural" world; he no longer hungers for the name and additions to a king. Royal authority, which had seemed a ludicrous pretense in the storm, now appears a childish game of who's in, who's out. Lear needs no other certainty now than Cordelia's love.

Through the vastness of centuries, Lear takes his place beside Job as a man who was confident of the nature of the universe and who knew that measure for measure was the law of God's creation. Like Job he was driven by misery and calamity to question his own beliefs and at last the meaning of life. Like Job he receives no philosophical assurances. The Voice out of the Whirlwind does not explain why the rain falls on the just and the unjust alike. But it restores to Job that sense (close to the heart of all religious belief) of the mystery of suffering, of existence itself. The Voice reminds Job of his insignificance in the cosmic order, of his presumption in defining universal law with his limited comprehension. Lear also gains patience and humility, the stoic resignation that enables man to face the inexplicable with dignity and strength. Even more, he rediscovers the love which redeems all sorrows and without which precise, calculating virtue is brittle and corruptible. Only when he realizes the egocentrism of his ideals and the vanity of his metaphysical formulations, only when he can no longer believe that his petty legalistic conception of justice is the rule of the cosmos, does Lear (and does man) rediscover intuitively and experientially the true nature of his humanity.

Looking backward from *Lear*, we see in the pattern of Jacobean tragedy the turmoil and confusion of Shakespeare's lesser contemporaries, who concern themselves with the broken structure of Renaisance beliefs and who seek new philosophical assurances. Shakespeare alone penetrates beneath the shattered exterior, the outworn cosmology and archaic systems, to bring to light once more the indestructible certainties of the human spirit: its capacity for love, devotion, and joy; its resources of courage and compassion in the face of unimaginable terror. One can of course read *Lear* as a warning against pride, wrath, or relatives. But I suspect that like all great tragedy *Lear* actually celebrates the vulnerability of man, the sublime folly of his "needs" and aspirations, the irrationality of his demands upon the vast inscrutable universe which surrounds him.

One can sympathize with the modern nostalgia for Elizabethan belief in cosmic order and justice and with the modern desire to find a reaffirmation of that belief in Shakespearean tragedy. Living in an age swept by disorder and revolutionary change, we are oppressed by the knowledge that we can scarcely control our individual destinies, much less influence the fate of our civilization. We are not so much terrified by the infinite reaches of space as by the gigantic forces at work within the world of our daily experience. The past few decades have given us a firsthand knowledge of human savagery which beggars the Jacobean imagination. Like the characters in *Lear* we know how lightly the dress of civilization rests upon the bare forked animal we call man, and how quickly after centuries of civilized customs, laws, and institutions, man can revert to the beast. Living in the shadow of an apocalypse which threatens the continuance of life on the earth, we would like to believe that the greatest of all tragedians looked steadily into the anarchy of life and saw the immutable fact of universal law. Having deified the creative imagination, we now seek from it the kind of reassurance which religion offers to the believer.

The truth would seem to be, however, that Jacobean tragedy is reassuring only to the extent that it is not genuinely tragic, only when, as in *The Atheist's Tragedy*, religious conviction eradicates the tragic sense of life. Chapman's Stoicism is as pessimistic an optimism as one can find in literature. Jonson, Webster, Beaumont, Marston, Middleton, and Ford offer few comments and little comfort on the subject of universal order. Shakespeare allows us to agree with Edgar that the gods are just in tormenting Gloucester because he had an illegitimate child, but we do not have to turn to Edgar for such priggery; we can hear it any day over the backyard fence.

It is true that no Jacobean tragedy is an uninterrupted descent into the pit; all of the great plays end with some restoration of order or decency. We feel, particularly in Shakespeare, a vast sense of relief at the purgation of the evil that has poisoned the well-being of the characters and destroyed so much of greatness and beauty. All Jacobean tragedy suggests, moreover, that evil contains the seeds of its own destruction, that because it naturally overreaches it is sterile and self-defeating. Its vileness brings about an inevitable if belated reaction of good, for there is a limit to what even the timid and fearful will bear at the hands of oppressors. And yet how often are the forces of good ineffectual in Jacobean tragedy and how very much will the decent man accept before he endangers his security by taking sides or before he obeys his nobler instincts. It is not until the Duchess is dead that Antonio and Bosola decide to change their lives. It is not until Gloucester sees Lear hunted down like an animal that he commits himself to Lear's party, and it is not until Gloucester's second eye is threatened that the servant rebels. The noble Albany waits even longer before he sides with the right. The terrible truth that Jacobean tragedy offers is written large in the history of our world. We hope all will be well; we would have peace in our time while millions groan under slavery and the smoke of the crematoriums blackens the air.

If the only issue of Jacobean tragedy were the destruction of social order, then the return to power of decency would reconcile us to the waste of good. But even when the restoration of order is not ironic, as it is in *Sejanus,* or anticlimactic, as in *The Changeling,* we are often aware that what has been restored is not commensurate with what has been destroyed. We are not greatly cheered because tragedy suggests that only for relatively brief periods does life become so vile as to seem totally unbearable. The myth and ritual critics tell us that the tragic hero is sacrificed for the good of the community or the state and that the sacrificial pattern purges pity and fear. I wonder, though, whether we feel any differently about Hamlet's death because Fortinbras, a military adventurer, ascends the throne of Denmark. I wonder if we have any thought of the nameless, faceless, voiceless people of Lear's kingdom as the dying Lear kneels over Cordelia's body. Very rarely if ever do we feel in Jacobean tragedy the living presence of the community which is directly embodied in the Chorus of Greek tragedy. Very rarely is the ritual pattern which can be intellectually "discovered" in the action of a Jacobean tragedy an actual part of our aesthetic experience of the play.

I do not mean that the tragedians contrive moral denouements which the audience finds unconvincing or unrealistic. Supporting the moral pattern of tragedy is the pattern of history itself. Though violence may be the natural condition of humanity, civilization and the arts are possible only because the periods of wholesale human slaughter are intermittent and because the brutal reign of tyranny is not the continuing norm of life. After every fearful spasm of destructiveness —after the War of the Roses, for example—there have been moments of peace or exhaustion in which noble minds could contemplate the wearisome condition of humanity and great tragedy be written. Yet there is nothing in tragedy which assures us that this "moral pattern" will continue indefinitely, that after every period of bloodshed there will be some kind of rebirth: after every great crime, a new chance for innocence. The author of *Lear* could imagine a tragic experience so destructive of man's belief in himself and in his world as to make the future cheerless, dark, and deadly. Having seen in our time an image of "the promised atomic end," we can dread the prophecy of

Lear. We fear a cataclysm so immense that it will not matter who's in or who's out, who wins or who loses, or whether evenhanded justice is finally dispensed to friend and foe.

No less quantitative in our measurement of values than Lear, we cannot imagine that existence has meaning unless it continues perpetually. We hunger for posterity if not eternity. We stand terrified like Macbeth at the thought of the brief candle of life extinguished in the vast oblivion of time. We want to believe that the momentous adventure of the race will not be destroyed by some ignorance of motive, rigidity of thought, or meaningless arrogance as precipitates catastrophe in *Lear*. But the hope that all will be well is only an illusion in tragedy. Its great affirmations are qualitative, not quantitative. It does not calculate how many are slain or how many survive. It is not concerned with the blind suffering of the many who never rise above enslaving circumstances. It is concerned only with the suffering of the few who through suffering become truly human. To accept the affirmations of tragedy we must have the courage to cherish beauty as it is being destroyed and to rejoice in the fulfillment of human greatness no matter how indifferent to man's fulfillment or annihilation is the universe. The theologian asks us to have faith that sometime, out of time, the meaning of existence will be made known to us. Shakespeare suggests in his greatest tragedies that whatever gods may be, and whatever ultimate destiny awaits the race of man, the life greatly lived has a timeless meaning. He does not reason the need for the wearisome condition of humanity. Graced with angelic intuition, he looks into the melancholy depths of things and sees that life is good.

Other Jacobean tragedians—and I would include Tourneur and Webster—shared to some degree Shakespeare's intuition of the goodness of life, but they could not like him accept it. Yet even they bear witness against their own despair to those qualities of the human mind which reduce tragic anguish to the beauty and order of art.

Notes

Chapter I

1   In *The Elizabethan World Picture* (London, 1943), E. M. W. Till-
yard suggests that the Jacobeans were able to write great tragedies
because they had secure confidence in humanistic ideals: "Indeed all
the violence of Elizabethan drama has nothing to do with a dissolu-
tion of moral standards; on the contrary, it can afford to indulge
itself just because those standards were so powerful. Men were bitter
and thought the world was in decay largely because they expected
so much" (p. 18). No one can deny that the moral principles of the
age were high; but the question is whether the tragedians believed
that these principles did in fact govern the conduct of men or express
the reality of human conduct. I suspect, moreover, that the same kind
of negative reasoning could be used to explain away the violence that
haunts contemporary American literature.

2   See the opening chapters of *Shakespeare and the Nature of Man*,
2nd ed. (New York, 1949).

3   *Shakespearean Tragedy and the Elizabethan Compromise* (New York,
1957), Chs. I–V.

4   See Spencer's discussion of Montaigne, *Shakespeare and the Nature of
Man*, p. 49.

5 See Herschel Baker's discussion of the rise of the scientific view of nature in *The Wars of Truth* (Harvard, 1952), pp. 303 ff.

6 *A History of Philosophy*, trans. James H. Tufts (New York, 1893). p. 354.

7 In *Science and Religion in Elizabethan England* (San Marino, 1953), Paul H. Kocher traces the development of natural science as a secular study and the acceptance before Bacon of the divorce of scientific inquiry from religion (Chs. I and II). Mr. Kocher demonstrates conclusively that there was no general sense of conflict between religious and scientific truths in the late Elizabethan age.

8 See *Shakespeare and the Rival Traditions* (New York, 1952), pp. 88–89, 176–77. Actually Mr. Harbage argues that *The Revenger's Tragedy* was originally written for a private theater by Middleton.

9 Despite his attempts to be just to the "coterie" dramatists, Mr. Harbage does, I think, go out of his way to deny the high seriousness and moral intention of most of Chapman's tragedies. See for example his comments on *The Revenge of Bussy D'Ambois* (p. 153) and the Byron tragedies (pp. 283–84). He makes no reference to *Chabot* and only a passing comment on *Caesar and Pompey*. The view of Chapman that emerges is both oversimplified and distorted.

10 See *The Counter-Renaissance* (New York, 1950), pp. 380–453, *et passim*.

11 *The Enchanted Glass* (Oxford, 1950; first printed New York, 1936), pp. 188–89.

12 Una Ellis-Fermor, *The Frontiers of Drama*, 3rd ed. (London, 1948), p. 147.

13 See *The Medieval Heritage of Elizabethan Tragedy* (Oxford, 1950; first printed Berkeley, 1936), Chs. VI–X.

14 See Madeleine Doran's astute discussion of form in Elizabethan and Jacobean drama in *Endeavors of Art* (Madison, 1954), pp. 354 ff.

15 The various contemporary references to the ethic of revenge which Mr. Bowers quotes in the first chapter of *Elizabethan Revenge Tragedy* (Princeton, 1940) do not establish that it was a vital and burning issue in men's minds. Because Elizabethan moral speculations are truly encyclopedic, one could establish by a similar method of documentation that the Elizabethans were "preoccupied" with hundreds of moral questions.

16 See "Machiavelli and the Elizabethans," *Proceedings of the British Academy*, XIV (March 1928), 49–97.

17 See J. W. Allen's discussion of the Tudor "commonwealth writers" in *A History of Political Thought in the Sixteenth Century* (London, 1957; 1st ed. 1928), pp. 134 ff.

18 See Irving Ribner, "The Significance of Gentillet's *Contre-Machiavel*,"

MLQ, X (June 1949), 153–57. Mr. Ribner's argument that the English myth of the diabolical Machiavel arose spontaneously from the Elizabethan response to Machiavelli's writings is somewhat unconvincing in view of Machiavelli's notoriety throughout sixteenth-century Europe. Left to their own devices Elizabethan readers of *The Prince* and *The Discourses* might well have come to the same conclusions about Machiavelli that Gentillet did. But the striking similarities in the English, French, and Italian distortions of Machiavelli's thought suggest a common mythic tradition.

19 See Milton Waldman's fascinating study, *Elizabeth and Leicester* (London, 1945), pp. 163 ff.

20 In *Shakespeare's Doctrine of Nature* (London, 1949), John F. Danby draws a parallel between Edmund and the New Men of Elizabethan commercial enterprise. See my discussion of Danby and *King Lear* in Ch. IX.

21 The ambivalent Elizabethan response to Machiavelli is exemplified by Ralegh's *Maxims of State* and *Cabinet-Council*, collections of political precepts and observations on the art of ruling. More than once Ralegh objects to a specific Machiavellian practice, but the tenor of these works is profoundly influenced by Machiavelli's realism. Moreover Ralegh repeats many of Machiavelli's opinions (about dissimulation, for example) without criticism. See the *Works* (Oxford, 1829), VIII, 18 ff., 67–96.

22 *The Divine Right of Kings* (Cambridge, 1896), pp. 81 ff.

23 See James's statement of absolute prerogative in *The Trew Law of Free Monarchies* in *The Political Works of James I*, ed. C. H. McIlwain (Harvard, 1918), pp. 61–63; McIlwain's introduction is an excellent study of Jacobean political opinion. For the rise of absolutist theory in the sixteenth century, see Allen, *History of Political Thought*, pp. 280 ff., and 367 ff. For the medieval idea of law as the supreme authority in the state, see McIlwain, *The Growth of Political Thought in the West* (New York, 1932), pp. 188 ff., 361 ff.; also A. J. Carlyle, *Political Liberty* (Oxford, 1941), p. 19.

24 I refer to Machiavelli's attack on contemporary decadence in *The Discourses on the First Ten Books of Titus Livius* (Modern Library edition, *The Prince* and *The Discourses*), p. 273. Machiavelli's contempt for the Italian aristocracy is evident throughout *The Discourses* and particularly in Ch. LV, p. 255.

25 *A History of Modern Philosophy*, trans. B. E. Meyer (London, 1900), I, 19. We could be more charitable to Machiavelli if he had really been convinced that the means he suggested would have achieved the political end he sincerely believed in. In *The Discourses*, however, (Modern Library edition, p. 171) he admits that it would be almost

impossible to find a good Prince who would commit terrible crimes for an ultimately moral purpose or to find a ruthless adventurer who would not tyrannically exploit his princely power. After such knowledge, what forgiveness?

26 *Discourses*, p. 117.

27 *Works* (Oxford, 1850), I, 184–85.

28 See Vernon J. Bourke's discussion of Thomistic ethics in *St. Thomas and the Greek Moralists* (Milwaukee, 1947), p. 40.

29 *The Boke Named the Governour* (Everyman edition), p. 47.

30 *La Renaissance du Stoïcisme au XVIᵉ Siècle* (Paris, 1914), p. 87.

31 Pierre Charron, *Of Wisdome*, trans. Samson Lennard (London, 1608; 1st French ed. 1601), Bk. II, Ch. 5, p. 288.

32 Cf. Hardin Craig's discussion of Renaissance moral speculation in *The Enchanted Glass*, p. 199.

33 See my discussion of the development of the idea of natural law in "Donne, Montaigne, and Natural Law," *JEGP*, LV (April 1956), 213–20.

34 "The Naturalism of Donne in Relation to Some Renaissance Traditions," *JEGP*, XXII (Oct. 1923), 494–99.

35 See *Essays*, trans. John Florio (Everyman edition), II. xii. 297. All citations from Montaigne are from this edition. See *Biathanatos*, Facsimile Text Society edition (New York, 1930), p. 36. All citations from *Biathanatos* are from this edition.

36 There is almost no evidence to support modern theories that Elizabethans found in Montaigne a grave challenge to traditional Renaissance ideals of man or morality. Montaigne's skepticism and religious position were criticized by his contemporaries, but he was generally acclaimed as a moral tutor. And it is significant that François Garasse, who excoriates Charron as a freethinker, can say nothing more of Montaigne than that, like Homer, he is praised to the sky by some and damned by others (*La Doctrine Curieuse des Beaux Esprits de ce Temps ou Pretendus Tels* [Paris, 1623], p. 117). Cf. Alan M. Boase, *The Fortunes of Montaigne* (London, 1935), pp. 1–47, 164–94.

37 See the discussion of Stoicism in *The Praise of Folly*, trans. Hoyt H. Hudson (Princeton, 1941), pp. 39–40.

38 *A Table of Humane Passions*, trans. Edward Grimeston (London, 1621; 1st French ed. 1615), p. 20.

39 Jerome Cardan, *Cardanus Comforte*, trans. Thomas Bedingfield (London, 1573), sig. [Gviii] r&v.

40 Guillaume Du Vair, *A Buckler Against Adversitie or A Treatise of Constancie*, trans. Andrew Court (London, 1622; 1st French ed. 1594), p. 3.

41 *Poems and Dramas of Fulke Greville*, ed. Geoffrey Bullough (London, 1939), II, 136.

42 I refer to the massive and detailed attack on *libertins* and libertinism in *La Doctrine Curieuse*.

43 See E. A. Strathmann's excellent discussion of the confutations in *Sir Walter Ralegh: A Study in Elizabethan Skepticism* (New York, 1951), pp. 61 ff.

Chapter II

1 I follow the chronology of Chapman's drama suggested by T. M. Parrott in *The Plays and Poems of George Chapman* (London, 1910 and 1914), 2 vols. Citations from Chapman in my text are from Vol. I, *The Tragedies*.

2 See, for example, R. H. Perkinson, "Nature and the Tragic Hero in Chapman's Bussy Plays," *MLQ*, III (June 1942), 263–85; Hardin Craig, "Ethics in the Jacobean Drama: The Case of Chapman," *Essays in Dramatic Literature*, ed. H. Craig (Princeton, 1935), pp. 25–46.

3 See particularly the introductory chapter, "Chapman's Christian Humanism" and the "Conclusion" of *The Tragedies of George Chapman: Renaissance Ethics in Action* (Harvard, 1954).

4 According to Mr. Rees's thesis, the philosophy of the *Revenge* should be a Christian Stoicism (*Tragedies of Chapman*, pp. 93–94). But Mr. Rees admits that Clermont's Stoicism is a classical variety (p. 112). It would seem to follow, then, that Clermont's Stoicism is imperfect and that Clermont cannot be an ideal figure. Indeed, Mr. Rees finds in the play a Clermont torn by anxieties and uncertainties whose Stoicism is primarily a means of cheering himself up (p. 113). Most readers, however, have a totally different impression of Clermont; far from being racked by anxieties, he seems in almost every speech unbearably self-righteous and self-assured.

Mr. Rees believes that Cato's Stoic fortitude is viewed by Chapman as a Christian virtue. In his chapter on *Caesar and Pompey*, he writes: "[Cato's] suicide becomes, in Chapman's tragedy, a dramatic symbol for spiritual strength and independence, for the victory of soul over body" (p. 145). By Christian standards, however, Cato's suicide is not a spiritual victory but a cardinal sin of despair. Without directly facing this issue, Mr. Rees later apologizes for Chapman's glorification of Cato's suicide by noting that Chapman "was working within the conventions of tragedy: suicide was allowable" (p. 147). Exactly how the conventions of tragedy "allow" suicide is not clear, nor is it clear why Chapman in this crucial instance followed convention rather than Christian conscience. In any event the explanation is lame. By insisting that Cato represents a Christian virtue Mr. Rees thrusts Chapman into gross contradictions.

5 See *The Poems of George Chapman*, ed. Phyllis Bartlett (New York, 1941), pp. 221–22.

6 Note the continuing emphasis upon the conflict between reason and passion in "The Teares of Peace" (*Poems*, pp. 184, 186, 188 ff.).

7 Early in Church history, theologians had resolved the contradiction between man's submission to temporal authorities and his natural equality (in the image of God) by postulating two states of nature. Before the Fall, man was naturally free from all coercive human authorities and naturally obeyed the laws of God. After the Fall, however, coercive laws and institutions became necessary to check corrupted man's incipient wickedness. That is to say, political and social inequalities are inevitable in fallen nature and divinely sanctioned to repair the disastrous consequences of original sin (see R. W. and A. J. Carlyle, *A History of Medieval Political Theory in the West* [London, 1930], I, 12–26, 116–17, 121 ff.). We find the idea of natural equality in Erasmus' *The Education of a Christian Prince* (New York, 1936, p. 177) and elsewhere in the early Renaissance. But in the Stuart age the ideal of natural liberty becomes a major polemical weapon in the Puritan armory. Prominent in *The Tenure of Kings and Magistrates* is the affirmation that "No man who knows aught, can be so stupid to deny that all men naturally were born free, being the image and resemblance of God himself. . . ." More directly analogous to King Henry's speech, however, is Jean Bodin's secular myth of an egalitarian age of family rule which preceded the rise of civilized states. Assuming man's natural freedom, Bodin justifies political hierarchies as legitimate outgrowths of military conquests (*The Six Bookes of a Commonweale*, trans. Richard Knolles [London, 1606; 1st French ed. 1576], pp. 14, 47, 203). And, interestingly enough, in Greville's *Mustapha* (Act V. scene iii) the "old equalities of Nature" are opposed to tyrannical authorities.

8 "Of Blessed Life," *The Workes of Lucius Annaeus Seneca*, trans. Thomas Lodge (London, 1620; 1st ed. 1614), p. 617.

9 Mr. Rees finds no obliquity in the play because he regards all the praise of Bussy as deeply ironical (*Tragedies of Chapman*, p. 47). If we accept this interpretation, however, we are faced with a uniquely eccentric piece of dramaturgy—a play in which all the characters are "ironically" confused about the moral nature of the hero but the playright is clear-sighted. I fail to see what possible ironic purpose is served by the many eulogies of Bussy except to confuse the audience. In *Othello* the ironical praise of Iago's "honesty" by those whom he

dupes is artistically appropriate because deception is Iago's forte. Moreover Iago's villainy is finally unmasked within the play, while Bussy dies a hero to his enemies as well as his friends. I agree with Mr. Rees that there is a contradiction between Bussy's actions and the eulogies which he receives, but I doubt that Chapman was fully aware of, or deliberately intended, this contradiction.

10 The skepticism about customary law and vulgar opinion in *Bussy D'Ambois* has various analogues in late Renaissance thought. See Peter Ure, "A Note on 'Opinion' in Daniel, Greville, and Chapman," *MLR*, XLVI (July 1951), 331–38.

11 This choric speech and the complementary one by the Guise are crucial to our understanding of Chapman's tragic theme. Neither Mr. Rees nor James Smith, who also believes that Bussy's claim to virtue is intentionally ironic ("George Chapman ii," *Scrutiny*, IV [June 1935], 51–54, 60), can satisfactorily explain why these choric speeches exist at all. John Wieler suggests that Bussy is responsible for his tragedy because "he has been willing to engage in irrational conflict with the world" (*George Chapman: The Effect of Stoicism Upon His Tragedies* [New York, 1949], p. 50). But it seems in the play that this "irrational" conflict with the world is the proof of Bussy's essential nobility. Surely Chapman does not condemn Bussy for his idealistic crusade against policy. The crusade appears futile and therefore "irrational" only at the end of the play when we realize that the forces of policy are invincible.

12 Because Byron's fatuity is so obvious, it is difficult to believe that Chapman uncritically admired his hero's individualism. Even more difficult to believe is Janet Spens's theory that Chapman found a sanction for such individualism in Cicero's discussion of the individual natures of men in *De Officiis* ("Chapman's Ethical Thought," *Essays and Studies*, XI [1925], 145–69). In the first place Cicero's allowance of individuality is carefully circumscribed by an insistence that man must obey the universal rational law of his nature. In the second place Chapman's contemporaries correctly interpreted Cicero's discussion of the individual and universal natures of man as a piece of practical wisdom. In the *Governour*, for example, Elyot writes: "Wherfore Tulli sayeth we shulde so indevour our selfes that we strive nat with the universall nature of man, but that beynge conserved, lette us folowe our owne propre natures, that thoughe there be studies more grave and of more importaunce, yet ought we to regarde the studies whereto we be by our owne nature inclined" (Everyman edition, p. 63). In other words, if Chapman derived a philosophy of individualism from Cicero he was guilty of a unique and almost incredible misinterpretation.

13 It is of course difficult to criticize the dramatic construction of the *Conspiracy* because we do not have the play as it was originally conceived. But since the censor's deletions were apparently confined to the fourth act, they would not explain the abrupt denouement.

14 Una Ellis-Fermor, *The Jacobean Drama* (London, 1947; 1st ed. 1936), pp. 66–67.

15 It is quite true that Byron's treason initiates the chain of events which occur during the play. Still the dramatic action of the *Tragedy* is concerned almost exclusively with Henry's counterplot and not with Byron's conspiratorial negotiations.

16 Cf. the Judges' replies to Byron with Prince John's sanctimonious justification of his double dealings with the rebels at Gaultree Forest in the fourth act of *Henry IV Part II*. See also Charron's justification of political deceit in crises (*Of Wisdome*, Bk. III, Ch. 2).

17 Seneca, "Of Anger," *Workes*, pp. 538–39.

18 According to Mrs. Norman Dobie Solve's hypothesis (developed in "Stuart Politics in Chapman's *Tragedy of Chabot*," *Univ. of Michigan Publ. Lang. and Lit.*, IV [1928]), *Chabot* was probably written between 1621 and 1624, approximately ten years after the *Revenge*, which Mr. Rees assumes is Chapman's next to last tragedy (*Tragedies of Chapman*, p. 159).

19 *The Tragedies*, p. 637.

20 Discussing James's absolutist claims, J. W. Allen remarks: "What the King was claiming was not power to make law, but a right to break it. He claimed that neither statute nor common law bound him absolutely in all circumstances, and he claimed that whether, in a particular case, the circumstances were such as to free his hands, he alone could judge. He claimed, that is, a right to override and set aside law, temporarily, in particularly cases, when he judged it to be in the public interest that he should do so" (*English Political Thought 1603–1660* [London, 1938], I, 12).

21 See Bodin, *Commonweale*, p. 315; Charron, *Of Wisdome*, Bk. III, Ch. 17; Pierre de la Primaudaye, *The French Academie*, trans. T. B[owes] (London, 1594), p. 575. In the *Trew Law* James announces that the only action a subject can take when a monarch disobeys accepted law is to flee (*Works*, ed. C. H. McIlwain [Harvard, 1918], p. 61).

22 I am not convinced by Mr. Rees's argument that *Caesar and Pompey* is Chapman's earliest tragedy (*Tragedies of Chapman*, pp. 126–30). It rests upon a completely conjectural identification; and we need not move forward the date of Chapman's play to coincide with the apparent reference to a *Caesar and Pompey* in *Northward Ho*, because three anonymous plays of that name had appeared before 1606. It

seems to me, moreover, that all the internal "evidence" in the play supports the traditional dating of *Caesar and Pompey* as 1612 or 1613. The characterizations, the mood of resignation, the nature of its Stoicism, even the quietness and simplicity of its verse suggest that it is a late rather than an early play.

23 The authenticity of this scene is, of course, questionable, and one would scarcely build an interpretation of the play upon it. Its attitudes, however, do not contradict Chapman's implied comments on religious establishments in other tragedies. And although Chapman did not ordinarily leaven his tragedies with low "comic relief," there is a similar bit of graceless, irrelevant comedy near the close of the *Conspiracy*.

Chapter III

1 See the discussion of *Sejanus* in *Ben Jonson*, ed. C. H. Herford and Percy Simpson (Oxford, 1925–52; 11 vols.), II, 21 ff. All citations from Jonson are from this edition. *Sejanus* appears in Vol. IV, *Catiline* in Vol. V.

2 *The Complete Works of John Webster*, ed. F. L. Lucas (London, 1927), I, 19.

3 Cf. Herford and Simpson's discussion, *Jonson*, II, 4.

4 I refer, of course, to Jonson's extant tragedies.

5 Because Stuart absolutism claimed the precedent of Roman law, there may be a pregnant significance in Sabinus' statement that

> ... when the *Romanes* first did yeeld themselves
> To one mans power, they did not meane their lives,
> Their fortunes, and their liberties, should be
> His absolute spoile, as purchas'd by the sword. (IV. 167–70)

6 Herford and Simpson, *Jonson*, II, 21.

7 Cf. *Sejanus*, IV. 1–5, with *White Devil*, III. ii. 280 ff. (Lucas edition); *Sejanus*, I. 270 ff., with *White Devil*, II. i. 290 ff.

8 I find support for my reading of *Sejanus* in K. M. Burton's "The Political Tragedies of Chapman and Ben Jonson," *Essays in Criticism*, II (Oct. 1952), 397–412.

9 Herford and Simpson, *Jonson*, II, 25.

10 Burton, "The Political Tragedies of Chapman and Jonson," p. 404.

11 "*Catiline* and the Nature of Jonson's Tragic Fable," *PMLA*, LXIX (March 1954), 276.

12 *Discourses* (Modern Library edition), p. 200.

13 Bryant, "*Catiline* and the Nature of Jonson's Tragic Fable," p. 269.

14 Ibid., p. 270.

Chapter IV

1   The evidence, stylistic and otherwise, for Middleton's authorship of *The Revenger's Tragedy* is collected and summed by Samuel Schoenbaum in *Middleton's Tragedies: A Critical Study* (New York, 1955), pp. 153–82. Because Mr. Schoenbaum argues for Middleton, his discussion of the stylistic evidence for Tourneur's authorship is perhaps less than adequate.

2   *The Jacobean Drama*, (London, 1947; 1st ed. 1936), pp. 153 ff.; "Cyril Tourneur," *RES*, XVII (Jan. 1941), 29.

3   "*The Revenger's Tragedy* Reconsidered," *Essays in Criticism*, VI (April 1956), 131–43; *Middleton's Tragedies*, pp. 27 ff.

4   "The Influence of Calvinistic Thought in Tourneur's *Atheist's Tragedy*," *RES*, XIX (July 1943), 255–62.

5   "Cyril Tourneur," *Elizabethan Essays* (London, 1934), pp. 128–33.

6   All citations from Tourneur are from *The Works of Cyril Tourneur*, ed. Allardyce Nicoll (London, 1930).

7   Even as Vindice becomes more and more like the villain he once "put on," so Volpone, who complains of cramps and palsies and requires stimulants to bolster his sagging spirits, plays the part of the old man so well because he is rapidly becoming one.

8   Herford and Simpson, *Ben Jonson*, VIII, 597.

9   "*The Revenger's Tragedy* and the Morality Tradition," *Scrutiny*, VI (March 1938), 402–22.

10   "Tourneur," *Elizabethan Essays*, p. 128.

11   See "*The Atheist's Tragedy* and Renaissance Naturalism," *SP*, LI (April 1954), 194–207.

12   See Nicoll's discussion of Tourneur's imitations in his "Introduction," *Works of Tourneur*, pp. 6 ff.

13   See "*The Atheist's Tragedy* and Renaissance Naturalism," pp. 201–2.

14   *Lear*, I. ii. 146–50. See my discussion of Edmund's soliloquy in Chapter IX, pp. 262–64, below.

15   See my discussion of Tourneur and Beard in "*The Atheist's Tragedy*," *N&Q* (July 1955), 285–86.

16   See Robert Ornstein, "*The Comic Synthesis in Doctor Faustus*," *ELH*, XXII (Sept. 1955), 165–72.

17   *Sir Walter Ralegh: A Study in Elizabethan Skepticism* (New York, 1951), p. 90.

18   See Le Roy, *Of the Interchangeable Course, or variety of things in the Whole World*, trans. Robert Ashley (London, 1594), p. 126^v; Guillaume Du Vair, *A Treatise of Constancie*, trans. Andrew Court (London, 1622), p. 65.

19 Cf. Castabella's argument (*The Atheist's Tragedy*, IV. iii. 147 ff.) with Malheureux's revulsion against libertine animalism in Marston's *Dutch Courtezan* (see Ch. VI, p. 162, below). Castabella's thought is remarkably close to François Garasse's accusation that French libertines abuse the term *nature* to mean the animal part of man (*La Doctrine Curieuse* [Paris, 1623], pp. 685–86).

20 See Ch. VIII, pp. 203–7, below.

Chapter V

1 "Introduction," *Webster and Tourneur* (London, 1948; Mermaid edition), ed. J. A. Symonds, pp. xix–xx.

2 "General Introduction," *The Complete Works of John Webster*, ed. F. L. Lucas (London, 1927), I, 17.

3 *Ibid.*, I, 100.

4 See the detailed discussion of the contradictions and inconsistencies in the *Duchess* by Clifford Leech in *John Webster: A Critical Study* (London, 1951), pp. 66–68.

5 All citations from Webster are from Lucas' edition of the *Complete Works*, 4 vols. *The White Devil* is in Vol. I, the *Duchess* in Vol. II.

6 In the preface to *The White Devil* Webster precisely echoes the ideas, sentiments, and phraseology of the preface to *Sejanus* as if he were acknowledging some specific indebtedness obscured by the roll call of illustrious playwrights by whose "light" he would gladly be read.

7 There is no trace of irony in the use of the quotation in this particular context (IV. ii. 275–80). Hooker's axiom is included in a "legal" opinion as if it were a casual commonplace observation on the force of natural instinct. No doubt the axiom circulated as a copy book phrase and we cannot accuse Webster of reducing theology to natural history.

8 "General Introduction," *Complete Works*, I, 27.

9 *Webster*, p. 65.

10 See Leech's discussion of this particular "character" in the Overbury collection, which has been conjecturally attributed to Webster (*Webster*, pp. 69 ff.).

11 For Travis Bogard the *Duchess* expresses an utter despair of life: "It brings into focus on the stage all the terrors of a dying universe. Not sudden death, but dying by slow degrees, sinking into a morass of disease and rot—this is what the human integrity must now face" (*The Tragic Satire of John Webster* [Berkeley, 1955], p. 132). To share Mr. Bogard's impression, however, we must, like him, treat Webster's imagery as if it possesses an independent meaning of its own and can therefore be divorced from its dramatic context.

12   See Bogard, *Tragic Satire of Webster*, pp. 63–81.
13   Following E. E. Stoll, Mr. Lucas traces the inspiration for the character of Appius back to Marlowe (*Complete Works*, III, 226). But the conception of the whole play as well as of the hero-villain points directly to Jonson's Roman tragedies and particularly to *Sejanus*.
14   "The Play," *Complete Works*, III, 146.

Chapter VI

1   Although Marston was a relatively minor talent among the playwrights who wrote for the private companies, Alfred Harbage in *Shakespeare and the Rival Traditions* (New York, 1952) cites his plays more frequently than those of Middleton or Chapman in characterizing the repertory of the "select" theaters.
2   See "The Precarious Balance of John Marston," *PMLA*, LXVII (Dec. 1952), 1069–78.
3   For the extent of Marston's borrowing from Montaigne in a single play, see the notes to *The Dutch Courtezan* in *The Plays of John Marston*, ed. H. Harvey Wood (London, 1938), II, 310–26.
4   See Schoenbaum, "Marston," pp. 1071–72; Harbage, *Rival Traditions*, pp. 171–72; Travis Bogard, *The Tragic Satire of John Webster* (Berkeley, 1955), pp. 90 ff.
5   All citations from Marston are from *The Works of John Marston*, ed. A. H. Bullen (London, 1887), 3 vols.
6   Cf. the rejection of philosophy in the *Revenge* with the attack on Stoicism and Seneca's "atheism" in the *Scourge of Villainy* (*Works of Marston*, III, 331).
7   *Jacobean Drama* (London, 1947; 1st ed. 1936), p. 206.
8   See Harbage's illuminating discussion of the development of the Jacobean theaters in Part One of the *Rival Traditions*.
9   See Harbage, *Rival Traditions*, p. 89.
10   If it is true that the private theaters earned appreciably less than did the public playhouses (see Harbage, *Rival Traditions*, Appendix A), then we must assume that Shakespeare's company did not willingly shift their performances to the Blackfriars. Indeed, Harbage does once suggest (p. 304) that they moved because of "the rising tide of sectarian opposition to the stage." We must then blame the rift between the stage and the people on the growing philistine moralism of the London citizenry, not on the coterie theaters or on the popular companies' "compromise" with coterie tastes.
11   See the repertory of the Red Bull listed by Harbage, *Rival Traditions*, p. 349. It is possible that Heywood's *Iron Age* plays (included in this

list) were as popular as Heywood claimed them to be, but they were successful exploitations of a tried formula, not the freshly original work that renews interest in the theater.

12 Although I greatly admire John F. Danby's criticism of Beaumont and Fletcher, I am somewhat skeptical of his "sociological" explanation of their art in *Poets on Fortune's Hill* (London, 1952), pp. 152 ff. It is hard to believe that the posturing and psychologically inconsistent heroes and heroines of their plays are reflections of a contemporary "Cavalier" mentality. See the discussion of *The Maid's Tragedy* in Ch. VII, below.

13 All citations from Fletcher are from *The Works of Francis Beaumont and John Fletcher*, ed. A. Glover and A. R. Waller (Cambridge, 1905–13; 10 vols.), Vols. I, V, and VII.

Chapter VII

1 According to Henslowe's Diary, in 1602 Middleton collaborated with four other playwrights in *Caesar's Fall* and wrote *Randal Earl of Chester*, which was possibly not a tragedy. R. H. Barker and Samuel Schoenbaum have recently argued that in addition to *The Revenger's Tragedy*, Middleton also wrote *The Second Maiden's Tragedy* (1611) in his early career (see Schoenbaum, *Middleton's Tragedies* [New York, 1955], pp. 36–38, 183 ff.; Barker, *Thomas Middleton* [New York, 1958] pp. 112–16). One can understand why the frequently preposterous *Second Maiden's Tragedy* did not receive the contemporary compliment of print. Because its ascription remains conjectural and because it contributes little or nothing to the sum of Jacobean tragedy or to our knowledge of Middleton's tragic art, I charitably omit it from discussion.

2 In *Middle-Class Culture in Elizabethan England* (Chapel Hill, 1935), Louis B. Wright reviews the popular controversy over women from the middle of the sixteenth century to the middle of the seventeenth century (pp. 465–507). He notes that the debate in print over the nature and status of women heightened in the second decade of the seventeenth century and particularly about 1620.

3 It is interesting to note that in *The Family of Love*, one of the earliest of Middleton's plays, he imitates the balcony scene from *Romeo and Juliet*. (See Barker, *Thomas Middleton*, p. 30). The echoes of Elizabethan romanticism in this play and in *The Phoenix* may suggest that through the irony of his great tragedies Middleton turns on his own youthful sensibility.

4 It is generally assumed that *The Maid's Tragedy* and *Philaster* were

primarily, if not wholly, the work of Beaumont. I use only Beaumont's name in connection with these plays because in all likelihood he was responsible for their ironic designs.

5 *Fortune's Hill*, (London, 1952), pp. 165 ff.

6 Since Mr. Danby is apparently committed to a theory of the decline of Western culture since the early Renaissance, we must assume that his discussion of Beaumont and Fletcher is in some measure polemical and not a completely detached study in literary criticism.

7 *Fortune's Hill*, pp. 169–71, 188 ff.

8 M. C. Bradbrook, *Themes and Conventions of Elizabethan Tragedy* (Cambridge, 1935), pp. 213–24. In his introduction to the new "Revels" edition of *The Changeling*, N. W. Bawcutt argues strongly for the artistic value of the subplot (*The Changeling*, ed. N. W. Bawcutt [Cambridge, Mass., 1958], pp. lxii–lxviii). Although Bawcutt's text is superior, my citations are from *The Works of Thomas Middleton*, ed. A. H. Bullen (London, 1885–86; 8 vols.), Vol. VI, for consistency of reference.

9 If we assume that Rowley wrote the first and last scenes of *The Changeling*, then we must also assume that his collaboration with Middleton was in this instance remarkably close and harmonious. In the subplot he may be pursuing his own bent, but in his contributions to the main plot he is faithfully executing the tragic design which Middleton expands in those scenes that are unmistakably his own.

10 "Thomas Middleton," *Elizabethan Essays*, (London, 1934), pp. 90–91.

11 The italics are mine. Beatrice's care for her reputation is even more deeply ironic in her references to her honor in the last scene.

12 Finding the evidence that *Women Beware Women* was written about 1621 unconvincing, R. H. Barker puts it closer to 1627 (*Thomas Middleton*, pp. 193–94).

13 See Isabella's aside, II. i. 217–25, and Guardiano's answer to Bianca, II. ii. 449–52.

14 *Jacobean Drama* (London, 1947; 1st ed. 1936) pp. 140–42.

15 In view of the ironic romanticism of *Women Beware Women*, it is interesting that Leantio's acceptance of Livia's sudden offer of love closely resembles Sebastian's response to Olivia's similar offer in *Twelfth Night*. Compare Leantio's "This can be but the flattery of some dream" with Sebastian's "Or I am mad, or else this is a dream" (IV. i. 65).

Chapter VIII

1 A clue to the freedom with which Ford imitates Shakespeare may lie in the fact that there are no recorded Jacobean revivals of *Romeo and*

Juliet and only one recorded performance of *Othello* (in 1629) between 1610 and the publication of *Love's Sacrifice*. There were, however, Jacobean quartos of both plays.

2   Because Ford's tragedies were apparently written within a very brief span of years, their unsettled chronology does not have a crucial bearing on the interpretation of his art. Traditionally it has been assumed that *'Tis Pity* was Ford's first tragedy; recently H. J. Oliver has argued that it is Ford's last and finest tragedy (*The Problem of John Ford* [Melbourne, 1955], pp. 47–49, 86 ff.). In the absence of conclusive external evidence, I assume only that the tragedies were written fairly closely together some time between 1627 and 1633.

3   Citations from *'Tis Pity* and *The Broken Heart* are from *John Ford's Dramatic Works*, ed. H. De Vocht in W. Bang's *Materialien*, n.s. 1 (Louvain, 1927). Citations from *Love's Sacrifice* are from *John Fordes Dramatische Werke*, ed. W. Bang in *Materialien*, XXIII (Louvain, 1908). For ease of reference I have included the traditional scene divisions found in the Mermaid text. I have also preferred to use *Bianca* rather than the less familiar *Biancha* as the name of the heroine of *Love's Sacrifice*.

4   *La Doctrine Curieuse* (Paris, 1623), p. 964.

5   *Of Wisdome*, trans. Samson Lennard (London, 1608), Bk. II, Ch. 8, p. 310.

6   *Of the Law of Warre and Peace*, trans. C. Barksdale (London, 1655; first Latin ed. 1625), p. 365.

7   In *The Tragic Muse of John Ford* (Stanford, 1944), G. F. Sensabaugh argues that Ford "so absorbed the idea of [psychological] determinism that his plays are exemplifications of the formula of cause and effect" (p. 35). The only objective evidence that would support this theory, however, is the imitations of *The Anatomy of Melancholy* in *The Lover's Melancholy*. Moreover, Mr. Sensabaugh would have us believe that Ford viewed love as a "melancholic disease" (pp. 46 ff.) and idealized it as "all-important" (pp. 164 ff.) at one and the same time. One suspects that here the inconsistency is in the interpretation, not in the plays.

8   Even Joan Sargeaunt, one of Ford's most judicious critics, comments: "There might be some excuse for identifying Ford's point of view with Giovanni's in *'Tis Pity*, because Giovanni justifies his passion on the very same grounds that Ford justifies the four positions in *The Peers' Challenge*. The similarity of the arguments extends to the use of the same Aristotelian text 'that the temperature of the mind follows that of the body'" (*John Ford* [Oxford, 1935], pp. 133–34). It is true that Ford's romantic idealism, like most of the popular Neoplatonism of the Renaissance, involves a somewhat vague and un-

philosophical identification of beauty and goodness. But Giovanni, like Orgilus in *The Broken Heart,* betrays this romantic idealism in thought as well as act (see n. 10 of this chapter). Moreover, we may agree that Annabella's beauty mirrors her original goodness and still condemn Giovanni for corrupting her beauty and despoiling her goodness.

9 For a discussion of *The Broken Heart* as a "problem play," see S. P. Sherman, "Forde's Contribution to the Decadence of the Drama," Bang's *Materialien* (Louvain, 1908), XXIII, pp. xi ff.

10 Although I agree with Mr. Oliver (*The Problem of John Ford,* pp. 11–12) that we cannot take all the casuistry of *The Peers' Challenge* seriously, nevertheless it does seem to express Ford's ideal of love. Perhaps the finest comment on Giovanni and Orgilus is the following passage from the *Challenge:* "For this, in the rules of affection, is text: whosoever truely love, and are truly of their ladies beloved, ought in their service to employ their endevours; more for the honour and deserving the continuance of their ladies good-will, than any way to respect the free-will of their owne heedlesse dispositions; else are they degenerate bastards, and apostates, revolting from the principals, and principall rules of sincere devotion. It is not ynough for any man, that hath by long suit, tedious imprecations, jeopardous hazard, toyle of bodie, griefe of mind, pitifull laments, obsequious fawnings, desperate passions, and passionate despaire, at length, for a meed or requitall to his unrest, gained the favourable acceptance of his most, and best desired ladie: . . . Perfect service, and serviceable loyaltie, is seene more cleerely in deserving love and maintaining it, than in attempting or laboring for it. How can any one be sayd truely to serve, when he more respects the libertie of his owne affections, than the imposition of ladies' command?" (*Shakespeare Society Reprints* [London, 1843], pp. 10–11.

11 See Sargeaunt, *John Ford,* Ch. II; Harbage, *Annals of English Drama* (Philadelphia, 1940), p. 100; Bentley, *Jacobean and Caroline Stage* (Oxford, 1956), III, 451–53; Oliver, *The Problem of John Ford,* p. 48.

Chapter IX

1 *A History of Political Thought in the Sixteenth Century* (London, 1957; 1st ed. 1928), p. 478.

2 See n. 25, Ch. I.

3 Citations from Shakespeare are from *The Complete Works of Shakespeare,* ed. G. L. Kittredge (Boston, 1936).

4 *This Great Stage: Image and Structure in King Lear* (Baton Rouge, 1948), p. 26.

5 See Part I, "The Two Natures," *Shakespeare's Doctrine of Nature* (London, 1949).

6 See *The Counter-Renaissance* (New York, 1950), pp. 636–51.

7 This interpretation is developed most fully by Danby, *Shakespeare's Doctrine*, pp. 32 ff., and is supported both by Heilman, *This Great Stage*, pp. 225 ff., and by Haydn, *Counter-Renaissance*, pp. 638–42, 659 ff.

8 *Donne's Sermons, Selected Passages*, ed. L. P. Smith (Oxford, 1920), Sermon 107, p. 175.

9 It is possible, of course, that Edmund speaks much more wisely than he knows, because the circle was a familiar symbol of perfection (cf. Donne's "Valediction Forbidding Mourning"). That is to say, the fact that Edmund's journey ends where it began may suggest that in his case Fortune was very precisely just.

10 *The Enchanted Glass* (Oxford, 1950; first printed New York, 1936), pp. 202, 199.

11 Although the extensive borrowings of words and phrases from Montaigne in *Lear* have long been noted, critics have yet to assess how much of Montaigne's thought on primitivism and civilization, custom, reason, and nature is dramatically subsumed in the last three acts of the play. Shakespeare's view of life was, in important respects, different from Montaigne's, but in *Lear* he assimilated Montaigne's awareness of the many social and psychological forces which determine man's nature. For example, Lear's glorification of the disguised Edgar makes the same ironic comment on the ideal of man's primitive natural virtue as does Montaigne's apotheosis of cannibalism. While the action of *Lear* confirms Montaigne's opinion that one cannot define human nature apart from the "unnatural" customs which society breeds, Shakespeare does offer at last some positive definition of what man needs to become human. That need is for love.

Index

Aeschylus: and revenge ethic, 23; *Agamemnon*, 201

Allen, J. W., on Machiavelli, 230

Aquinas, Thomas: view of passions, 41; mentioned *passim*

Archer, William, on Webster, 128

Aristotle: *Nicomachean Ethics*, 35; view of passions, 40, 41

Ascham, Roger, 107

Bacon, Francis: and epistemological change, 4–6, 33; *The Advancement of Learning*, 11; view of history, 14, 87; and Machiavelli, 28, 33; mentioned *passim*

Beard, Thomas: and Elizabethan moralism, 17; *The Theatre of Gods Judgements*, 18; and Tourneur, 18, 123

Beaumont, Francis: and Fletcher, 151–52, 163; distinguished from Fletcher, 169; decadence of, 173–74; Petrarchanism in, 173–76
—*Knight of the Burning Pestle, The*, 178; *Philaster*, 178–79
—*Maid's Tragedy, The*: 45, 151, 171, 173–79, 223; and *The Changeling*, 169, 171, 173, 179–84 *passim;* and *Hamlet*, 171, 174, 177; compared to *Troilus and Cressida*, 223

Beaumont and Fletcher. *See* Beaumont

Bentley, G. E., 216

Bodin, Jean, 33

Bowers, F. T., on revenge tragedy, 23

Bradbrook, Muriel, on *The Changeling*, 180

Bruno, Giordano, 14

Bryant, J. A. Jr., on *Catiline*, 100

Burckhardt, Jacob, 15

Camus, Albert, 6

Cardan, Jerome, *Comforte*, 41–42

Chapman, George: political thought of, 16, 28–31 *passim*, 53, 73, 77–79; translations of Homer, 47; psychological determinism in, 48, 56; and Marlovian ideas, 47, 48, 51, 53, 60, 62, 64, 70; obliquity in, 56–58, 60, 61–63; Stoicism of, 48–49, 53; 56–58, 62–63, 70, 72–75, 80–83; and Seneca, 53, 72; and Plutarch, 80; and Epictetus, 82; influence on tragedy, 82–83; and Jonson, 6, 85–